THE MANDATE OF HEAVEN

John F. MELBY THE MANDATE

University of Toronto Press

photographs by **HENRI CARTIER-BRESSON**

OF HEAVEN

Record of a civil war   CHINA 1945-49

© University of Toronto Press 1968

Printed in USA / LC 68 9736 / SBN 8020 1520 4

Published in Great Britain by
Chatto and Windus Ltd
40 William IV Street, London, W.C. 2
SBN 7011 1458 4

For Lillian Hellman

PREFACE

As the defeat of Germany loomed and that of Japan lay
just over the horizon, Averell Harriman, the American
Ambassador to Moscow, looked at the signs and concluded
that the dream and hope of President Roosevelt that the
wartime alliance against the Axis would extend into peacetime could not long survive the first exhilaration of victory.
Whatever may have been the causes of the Cold War and
regardless of the validity of Harriman's reasons in fore-
seeing it, the estimate was correct – and in it he was far
ahead of almost every other American.

One of his precautionary recommendations to Washington was that foreign service officers who had had first-hand
experience in the Soviet Union be assigned to certain
obvious posts throughout the world. Although my Russian
experience consisted only of two years in Moscow, it was
my good fortune to draw Chungking for a ringside seat and
some small participation in one of the major episodes of the
twentieth century.

In part my selection was due to the fact that very few
people, apart from the China "hands," had any idea that
much of anything of consequence would happen in China
once Japan was defeated. In part it was due to the rather
mandarin attitude of the superb China Service of the US
Department of State, which had long viewed with amused
detachment and a certain amount of disdain the notion that
anyone outside the circle might have anything to offer.
They may have been more right than wrong.

My primary job was to keep track of what the Russians
were up to in China. The assignment was socially pleasant
since the Soviet Ambassador was an educated, charming,
and shy man whom I had known rather well in Moscow,
and several members of his staff were equally congenial.
But it was professionally rather nominal since it developed
that they really were not up to much of anything beyond
the usual diplomatic routine and formalities.

This for some time was puzzling. I suppose it was my
curiosity as to why this was so that led to my Chinese

initiation. Never having known anything about China or even been particularly interested in it, I began to wonder if as much of the answer to the riddle might be found in China as in the Kremlin. Indeed it was; and I acquired a fascination before long with all things Chinese and with the enormity of China's problems that is still with me. Awareness of my ignorance led me to jot down in personal letters and in notes for my own use observations and reactions as time went along. The diary part of this book has been extracted from these sources. The historical narrative has been largely based on the so-called *China White Paper* and my own experience. Although a monumental amount has been written about the People's Republic of China, it is extraordinary how little has been produced on the critical four years of transition from the defeat of Japan to the formal establishment of the People's Republic. Some of this is doubtless attributable to the vast confusion of the period and to the speed of developments which left most people who were in a position to know what had happened baffled and unsure of what it all had meant and how and why it had happened. Then came the McCarthy period, which effectively stifled all public discussion of China beyond the official line of John Foster Dulles. Now that discussion is somewhat freer it is understandable that the main preoccupation should be with the present, but it is unfortunate that the past, with its relevance for what could happen elsewhere, should be neglected.

I am indebted to Mr. Jan Schreiber of the University of Toronto Press for the impressive imagination and labor he devoted to the manuscript. I am most appreciative of the skill Miss Joan Robertson of the Department of Geography at the University of Guelph has applied to the cartographic work. Anyone interested in China is grateful to Dr. Lyman Van Slyke and Stanford University Press for the recent reissue of the *China White Paper*, which contains most of the basic material on the period and had become impossible to acquire and accessible almost solely in libraries.

I will eschew the customary practice of assuming responsibility for all errors of fact and opinion. In our times, China has been so controversial that any statement about it will be challenged. I learned about China from a great many people – far too many to list – and I invite them all to share responsibility for everything I have said.

CONTENTS

When the sun reaches its northernmost point the markets of west China are filled with the color of tangerines. The very young and the very old buy them to discard all but the white filaments found between the skin and the meat sections. They sell these strands to Chinese medicine men for a price greater than the original cost of the fruit.

Sir Horace Seymour, wartime British Ambassador to Chungking, once told a story about a tangerine. He was reading one night by candlelight in his bedroom. One of the legendary rats of Chungking crept toward a tangerine on a side table, stripped the peel from it, extricated the pips, skinned them, ate the meat, and then vanished.

Meanwhile, Imperial Japanese bombs were systematically destroying the shacks on the steep hillsides of the Yangtze; and the people who lived in them were just as systematically rebuilding. American military power was creeping up the island ladder of the Pacific to the preview of Armageddon at Hiroshima and Nagasaki. In Chungking Chinese and American political negotiators squabbled endlessly while the people of China, about to be defrauded of victory and peace, moved inexorably into civil war.

The news headlines still record what important persons say and do. None notice that despite the rats, tangerines still come on the market, and the very young and the very old buy and sell them.

THE MANDATE OF HEAVEN

INTRODUCTION
The background of 1945

China is the oldest continuous civilization in the world and can be traced back some four thousand years. It is quite possible that archeological work now going on will push its origins back even earlier. Roughly the first two thousand years were a formative period which reached a high point in the Han Dynasty (206 B.C.–A.D. 220). The Chinese still refer to themselves as the Han.

Han was the period which consolidated the hard core of the Chinese Empire geographically, even though the actual boundaries would ebb and flow greatly during ensuing dynasties. Much more importantly, it set the social structure and values and the political forms for the next two thousand years. There would be temporary aberrations and lapses, but the basis would generally remain constant until the twentieth century. This basis was the Confucian system. It was not a religion in the usual sense; rather, it was a system of ethics which prescribed in great detail the relationship of any one human being to any other, from the Emperor down to the lowliest coolie. Chinese civilization was built on acceptance of these relationships and was able to function effectively for an extraordinarily long period of time. Apart from the obvious applicability of the system to a stable agrarian society, there were several other reasons why this could be so.

There is a great monotony about Chinese history. In long-range terms it has been a succession of great dynasties of which the most prominent were Chou, Han, T'ang, Ming, and Ch'ing, or Manchu as we know it. Each lasted roughly three hundred years from rise to fall. In between there were shorter and lesser dynasties or periods of chaos. Each effective dynasty reaffirmed and refined the values and social system of Han. There are those who would argue that the process of refinement has actually been a long, slow, sometimes almost imperceptible downward spiral, and that Han was the high point. Be that as it may, the contemporary argument is whether China today is merely going through another periodic upheaval or whether for the first time a fundamental change is taking place which will obliterate the past. Only history will know.

One of the most important factors in this continuity was the relative isolation of China from outside influences. At no time was the body of China in close contact with any other culture even remotely equal to its own. The occasional invasions were by nomads from the north and west whose strength was military and who were invariably absorbed by the superior Chinese culture and vanished with little trace. To the Chinese this was proof of their innate superiority to all other peoples, a belief as strong and ingrained today as it has ever been. In fact, the only significant import was Buddhism, which by its gentle nature posed no threat and could retain its identity alongside traditional ways.

We now know, however, that the isolation was not quite as complete as had been supposed. The monumental work of Joseph Needham in *Science and Civilisation in China* has shown that for centuries China had very extensive contacts with India, the Middle East, and the Mediterranean across Central Asia; and that many, perhaps most, of the basic concepts of science originated in China and were exported westward, even though China for some reason developed very little applied science from them. But this was largely an outward movement which involved very few Chinese and in no way disturbed their sense of superiority. The internal contacts were largely with occasional travelers such as Marco Polo, and for a period Catholic missionaries who were tolerated until they came to seem a menace and were expelled, leaving no trace beyond the remnants of a few church buildings. The Chinese name for China is still Chung Kuo, the Middle Kingdom.

The administrative system played a vital role in preserving the Empire and holding it together. The key point in the system was the extraordinary nature and difficulty of the Chinese language itself. Obviously communication is essential in holding any organization together, and the larger the organization is the more important communication becomes. China still has many dialects which are as mutually unintelligible as Russian and English when spoken, but they all use the same written form. And this written form still uses the old characters – persistent efforts to convert it to some kind of alphabet still have not been successful – which are so difficult they require years of study to master them. (Drastic simplifications have been introduced since 1949 by the Peking government, but the difficulty still remains.) Add to this the requirement of the Imperial examination system for government employees that the Confucian books be memorized and it becomes apparent that only men with many years of education possessed the skills needed to administer an empire. The scholar-bureaucrats became the elite corps. Few cultures have thus elevated the intelligentsia to the top rank in society.

The system was technically non-hereditary and open to anyone who could qualify. In practice of course most civil servants came from the landed gentry class which could afford education, but this was not always so by any means. Sometimes a village or several villages would pool their resources to educate the brightest local boy. The system went even farther and anticipated possible abuses. In order to avoid the pressure of local vested interests no bureaucrat could serve in his home province or for more than a certain number of years in any other province, and he had to retire to a place specified by the Emperor. When corruption in the system began to appear it was an infallible sign the dynasty was beginning to decline to its end. When it worked well it was an unbeatable method of control, and the elite as well as the Emperor had every reason to resist any change. By the same token, when it worked well and served the people, they had no interest in change.

There was a rather unique corollary and steam valve in the system. The Emperor was never considered divine; rather, he ruled by the Mandate of Heaven. This simply meant, in accordance with the Confucian ethic, that he had certain well defined rights and responsibilities. Each citizen also had well defined complementary rights and responsibilities. As long as each performed properly the Emperor retained the Mandate. When he began to fail, for whatever reason, he lost it and it passed to whatever new man gave evidence of being able to perform. Naturally the transition tended to be chaotic and sometimes long drawn out, since few emperors anywhere have been known to admit they were not up to their job any longer. Of course this reluctance is no monopoly of monarchs. The unique feature was the principle built into the whole tradition of the right of revolution when the ruler failed. Legitimacy was accepted as transferable and definable without too much trouble.

One geographical fact about China provided another tool of control which is, if anything, even more important today than ever before. China has been called a hydraulic society. It is dominated by two of the greatest rivers of the world, the Yangtze and the Yellow, sometimes called China's Sorrow. These river basins contain most of the people and most of the food. Alternately they are subject to terrible drought and catastrophic floods. No locality, no province ever had the resources to tame these rivers. Only the Emperor could do it and with this tool he held the life and death of uncounted millions in his hands. This tool was used with appalling results as recently as the Second World War. The breaching of the dikes of the Yellow River, incidentally, did not stop the Japanese, but it did drown uncounted Chinese. Late in the civil war in 1947 the Nationalists seriously considered its use again, but in the end this time they backed away from responsibility for the consequences.

The Manchus were the last of the great dynasties. Unlike others of comparable stature, they were invaders from Manchuria who had learned the lesson of other intruders who had disappeared in the Chinese stream. The Manchus kept their identity by remaining aloof from the Chinese, but they utilized the Chinese system they found to govern. By allowing the Chinese to run their own affairs, they inherited the Mandate. For two centuries this was strength; and then it became weakness as their isolation kept them from becoming aware of the stresses and strains which were developing. The great Moslem Uprising and the T'ai-p'ing

Rebellion in the nineteenth century which devastated large areas of the country only gave evidence of their growing inability to fulfil the needs and desires of the people. They might have weathered these storms for some time to come except for one other major blow.

Unquestionably no outside influence has ever had the impact on or the consequences for China that the arrival of the Europeans did on East Asia. Japan responded quickly and with astounding effectiveness in assimilating and adapting those elements of strength from the West which it found lacking in its own society, and in relatively few years not only regained its full sovereignty but also became a major power in its own right as the world would find to its sorrow. The Manchus stubbornly resisted, from their humiliating defeat at the hands of the British in the First Opium War (1839–42) until their final collapse in 1911; but it was resistance that was accompanied by concession after concession in the face of superior force until Chinese sovereignty was more fiction than fact, even though China never suffered the total subjugation that India did. Not until final Communist victory in 1949 did China again become its own master. Given the Chinese sense of superiority, this accomplishment cannot be overestimated in calculating the attitude of all Chinese toward the People's Republic of China, even those who intensely dislike everything else about the regime.

Despite the official policy of the Manchus, there were many intelligent and educated Chinese who recognized that the industrial revolution had irrevocably changed the world, and for the better; and that China could not forever stand aside. For that matter, these men and women saw no reason why China could not retain its own values and still benefit from the new advances. It was a thankless position and it would be many years before the Manchus collapsed of their own dead weight in 1911.

The symbol of the new day became Dr. Sun Yat-sen and his revolutionary political party, the Kuomintang. A physician by profession, he was educated in Honolulu where he read a good deal of political science and became fired with a vision of a democratic China in the modern world. Dr. Sun's career was fortunate in that he died in 1925 before he ever had the opportunity to wield effective political power anywhere except in narrow areas, even though he was the self-proclaimed President of the Republic of China. He was certainly one of the world's worst administrators and probably one of its poorer politicians. His legacy was a series of almost unreadable lectures called the *San Min Chu I*, the *Three Principles of the People*. The impact of *San Min Chu I* has been such that no successor to Dr. Sun has done anything politically without appealing to his authority. Even the People's Republic of China retains Madame Sun Yat-sen (Soong Ching-ling), however ceremonial her role may be, as a Vice Chairman for her symbolic value. The reasons for his prestige are not hard to find.

San Min Chu I responded and still responds to the aspirations of China. Dr. Sun's first Principle was People's Nationalism, by which he meant simply the full and complete restoration of Chinese sovereignty. Any Chinese, whatever his ideological persuasion, would almost automatically sacrifice anything for this.

The second Principle was People's Livelihood. What he had seen of modern technology convinced Dr. Sun there was no reason China could not have the decencies and amenities of economic life the West had. He also believed that a country as poor as China could have them only through some form of socialism. Only a rich country like the United States could afford the luxury of free enterprise. No Chinese official or knowledgeable private citizen since Dr. Sun has believed there was any hope of solving Chinese economic problems by any approach other than something to the left of the British Labour Party. Even Ch'en Li-fu, head of the most reactionary wing of the Kuomintang, once insisted to me that this was the case unless there could be an immediate and massive use of atomic energy for industrial purposes at economic cost. In 1947 he quite correctly did not foresee this as likely.

Two developments of prime importance reinforced the socialist conviction. The geometrical increase of population imposes impossible burdens around the world on traditional agricultural food supplies. China was no exception, and Dr. Sun thought he had the answer in socialism. It is still far from demonstrated that collective agriculture is the answer. It is fairly certain that any social organization which cannot feed the people has only a limited future. It is probably just as certain that any country like the United States where available resources still far exceed population has little relevance for countries where population far exceeds presently developed resources. Nuclear advances get the headlines; but it is likely that the race between population growth and starvation is the greatest danger the human race has ever confronted, and there is little evidence anyone yet has a convincing practical answer. China with a quarter of the human race is a fearsome example because hungry men will do anything. What do they have to lose?

Albeit slowly, even limited industrialization has introduced a social problem wholly new to Asia. This is urbanization. Not many people in the West remember that an agrarian culture has no need or use for cities beyond marketing places which are not exactly cities. The West is still far from solving its long-standing urban problems. Some of the greatest cities of the world, such as Tokyo, Shanghai, and Calcutta have grown within living memory. Dr. Sun saw the answer to their formidable problems in central planning not only for the industry which provoked the problems in the first place, but also over many of the human activities which inevitably grow out of industrial production.

The third Principle was People's Democracy. Dr. Sun had no illusions about the ability of China to move directly into democratic practices as he had observed them in the West. He was quite aware there had never been any democratic tradition in China and that the customary attitude toward political life was a permissive one: the average Chinese had no interest in participation and not much in civil liberties as long as the ruler performed satisfactorily within the Confucian ethic. China was seeking a new political stability. Dr. Sun saw the evolution toward democracy in three stages. First, a military dictatorship until the Kuomintang had consolidated its power; second, political tutelage, the one-party dictatorship of the Kuomintang under which China would be educated in democratic forms and practices; third, the movement into full democracy which might take a long time. (Theoretically, political tutelage ended with the promulgation of the new Constitution in 1947, but for practical purposes it is still in effect on Taiwan.)

Dr. Sun had more than his share of problems in trying to implement his program, especially since the fall of the Manchus had precipitated the warlord period in which local military leaders liked their autonomy and had no desire for the establishment of any central authority. Not the least of his problems was recognition by and help from the western powers – which he never got. This failure forced him into a fateful decision. He sought and received aid from the new Soviet Union. The Russians sent him two missions. One was military to organize his army; the other was civilian to organize his Government and Party. Both were conducted along Soviet lines. Part of the agreement was that the new Chinese Communist Party which had been founded in Shanghai in 1921 was to cooperate with the Kuomintang and its members were free to join the Kuomintang as individuals. In fact they managed to place themselves in key positions throughout the Kuomintang and the Government. Probably no one knows whether Dr. Sun knew this and was aware of the risk he was taking, or what he thought of it – except perhaps his widow, who has never said.

After Dr. Sun died in 1925, the chaos continued. It was only now that his protégé and the first commander of the Whampoa Academy, the West Point of China, began quite unexpectedly to emerge as the new leader. Generalissimo

Chiang Kai-shek came to power through an undetermined mixture of support from the modern Chinese and foreign banks in Shanghai and its underworld, the missionaries (he had become a devout Christian when he married Madame Sun Yat-sen's sister), recognition from the western powers, and his own consummate political skill. This is the least known period of twentieth-century China, and probably many of its mysteries will never be unravelled, although some answers may well be locked in vaults around the world. Whatever the hows and whys, with the so-called Northern Expedition in 1926–27 he had made himself the master, and China embarked on its most hopeful decade. After Japan struck in north China in 1937 nothing would ever be the same again.

Following the Northern Expedition, the Generalissimo decided to tackle one of his most urgent problems, which in the end would prove his undoing because he never solved it. After the death of Dr. Sun the Communists came out increasingly into the open and it became more and more apparent that their eventual goal was full power. The Party at this time followed the orthodox Stalinist line that the industrial proletariat must be the hard core and source of strength. After several unsuccessful uprisings in the major cities in 1926, which only proved that there simply was not a large enough proletariat to win, the Generalissimo decided to liquidate the Communists. In a series of bloody massacres in 1927 he did decimate their ranks. It was also a convenient opportunity to eliminate other dissident elements in the confusion. The Russian missions were shipped off to Moscow and the current Party head, Li Li-san, eventually followed them. The problem was announced as solved.

But it was not solved. A nucleus of the Communists managed to survive, break out of the cities, and regroup in a desolate and forbidding part of the province of Kiangsi south of the Yangtze. Here Mao Tse-tung began to demonstate his heretical thesis that the Communists could come to power on an agrarian base. The Russians would not forgive him for his deviation until 1949; presumably the Generalissimo never has.

The Generalissimo did attempt to eliminate the Kiangsi Soviet with a series of what were called "bandit suppression campaigns" to impress their unimportance on foreign and domestic opinion. Although not successful, they did finally persuade the Communists that drastic action had to be taken or they would face annihilation. The result was the Long March, surely one of the great epics of this century. In 1934 some fifty thousand Communists broke out of Kiangsi and walked thousands of miles westward to the foothills of the Himalayas and northward over the mountains to the far northwest of China where they dug themselves into caves in the loess bluffs at an obscure village called Yenan in the big bend of the Yellow River not far from the Gobi and Outer Mongolia. Perhaps ten thousand men, women, and children had survived more than a year of marching under steady harassment. Until the Cultural Revolution destroyed some of the old loyalties and associations, having been on the Long March was all the credentials you needed in Communist China.

The problems, however, were not all internal. Over the horizon the spectre of Japan began to rise. In 1931, using a trumped-up incident, the Imperial forces occupied the vast and wealthy area of Manchuria. The great Manchurian warlord, Marshal Chang Tso-lin, who had never given more than lip service to Nationalist China and had been assassinated in 1928 for his lack of gratitude to his Japanese liberators, was succeeded as leader by his son, the "Young Marshal" Chang Hsueh-liang, who fled to north China, and organized resistance disappeared. Now Japanese pressure for concessions in north China began to intensify.

In December 1936 a group of Chinese leaders, at the instigation of the Young Marshal and including Chou En-lai for the Communists, kidnapped the Generalissimo while he was on an inspection trip to Sian. They charged he was spending too much effort on containing the Communists and not enough on the Japanese. Most of them wanted to kill him; ironically, his life was saved by Chou En-lai, who insisted that there was no other leader of comparable stature. The compromise was his agreement to concentrate all efforts against Japan, relax his pressure against the Communists, and seek a solution of internal difficulties through political negotiation.

For some years the agreement worked fairly well, undoubtedly due in no small measure to Japan itself, which was growingly fearful that events in China might block its ambitions. A minor clash at the Marco Polo Bridge outside Peiping* in July 1937 – there is still an argument as to whether it was planned or incidental – set off a chain of events which led to full Japanese occupation of the nine northern provinces within the Great Wall. Then in rapid succession came the attacks on and occupation of Shanghai, Nanking, Hankow, and Canton; and the Government fled to Chungking in the far west. What remained of Chinese armies either were pushed against the foothills of the Himalayas in the provinces of Szechuan and Yunnan (though Japanese forces never really occupied all the rural areas), or were Communist forces in the northwest. The Generalissimo was

*Peiping ("northern peace") was the name from 1928 to 1949 while the Nationalist capital was at Nanking ("southern capital") or Chungking. After 1949, when the capital returned to its former location, the historic name Peking ("northern capital") was re-applied.

obviously in no position to do much about the Communists. The Japanese had seized the urban and industrial centers and the lines of communication; they had not pacified the countryside and they never would. It was stalemate, but a stalemate in which continuing Chinese guerrilla operations tied down huge Japanese forces on the mainland of China which might very well have made the difference between victory and defeat after Pearl Harbor. Almost literally alone and unaided for five long years except for pious words from the capitals of the West, China was proving to be as indigestible for Japan as it had been for every other invader.

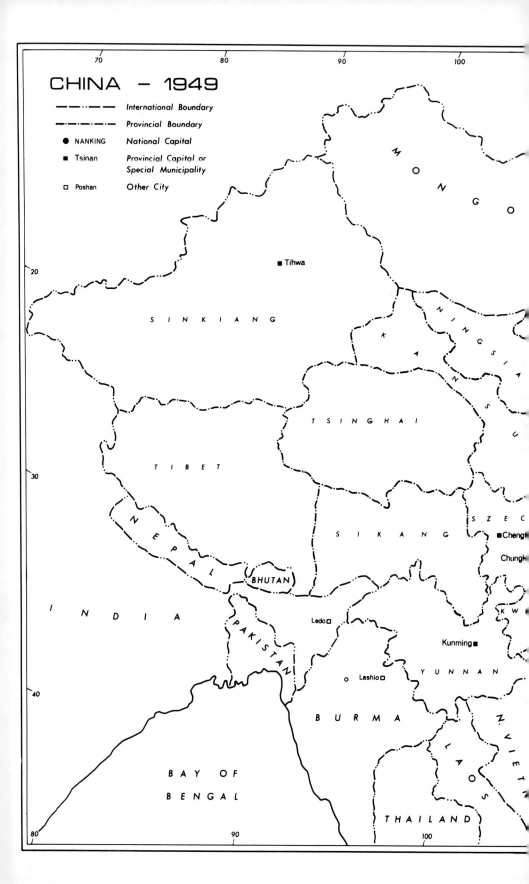

The new diplomacy

In 1941 the shaky foundations of Generalissimo Chiang Kai-shek's arrangement with the Communists began to collapse when Nationalist troops surprised and destroyed the Communist New Fourth Army north of Shanghai. Although the reasons for this incident are still somewhat obscure, the prospect of American entry into the war may well have played an important role. More accurately estimating American power than did Japan, the Generalissimo was convinced that the entry of the United States would assure a favorable outcome for the war in the Pacific, regardless of how many years it might take. And initially he could view with some satisfaction the prospect that as American forces landed on the coast of China and moved northward for the final kill, he could consolidate his position and complete behind the shield of American military power the task he had set for himself in 1927.

It must, therefore, have been a bitter disappointment to him when the success of the campaigns in the Pacific caused the United States to change its strategy from a landing on the China mainland to a plan of working up the island ladder of the Pacific for the assault on the Japanese home islands. In effect, this change relegated the China-Burma-India theatre of operations to the periphery of the war and made available to China supplies sufficient only to sustain what had become little more than a holding operation. Both the Generalissimo and the American Commander in the area, General Joseph W. Stilwell, were equally and understandably frustrated by this turn of events, and it showed in the growing acrimony of their relationship. The atmosphere was not improved when Stilwell, greatly impressed by their military performance, recommended that part of the available supplies be turned over to the Communists. The Generalissimo reacted violently and in the end the proposal was never implemented, but the seeds of discord and distrust continued to flower at an alarming rate, and even the indicated removal of Stilwell did little more than slow down their growth.

The seriousness of the situation was compounded by persistent rumors that the Generalissimo in his annoyance might make some kind of separate peace with Japan.[1] In retrospect, it is highly doubtful that he ever really considered such action, but it was also true that Japan was still far from defeated, and a spreading civil war could conceivably release Japanese troops for action elsewhere. The response of President Roosevelt was to send Major General Patrick J. Hurley to Chungking in August 1944 as his Special Representative and to name him Ambassador to China the following January. His instructions were to keep China in the war and by reducing the tension between the Nationalists and the Communists to keep their primary effort directed at fighting the Japanese instead of each other.

As matters turned out, Hurley carried out his instructions rather more successfully than he or anyone else probably had any right to expect in the circumstances; unfortunately for himself, he chose to interpret his mandate more broadly than had been intended. His objective became nothing less than the negotiation of a permanent and immediate political agreement between the two main factions.[2] The intent was certainly worthy, but there were plenty of people with impressive understanding of Chinese affairs who could and did tell him that what he sought just could not be, at least not for a long time or without a great deal more patience than he customarily employed. His own lack of understanding was an important factor in causing the troubles which arose after the surrender of Japan.

During his first few months in China, Ambassador Hurley had made no secret

1 See US Department of State, *Foreign Relations of the United States: 1943, China*, pp. 51, 86–87, 89, 167, 252–53; and *1944, China*, pp. 149–51, 213–14, 418–19, 610, 613, 726, 740, 753.
2 US Department of State, *United States Relations with China, with Special Reference to the Period 1944–1949*, Department of State Publication 3573, Far Eastern Series 30, reissued by Stanford University Press, 1967, as *The China White Paper* and so cited throughout this book; pp. 73 *et seq.*

of his fondness for the Communists. Their dedication and high competence deeply impressed him, as they did practically everyone else who came in contact with them, especially those who had become disillusioned with the Nationalists because of their growing cynicism and corruption. He in effect became their principal drafting officer for proposed terms of settlement, and he even went so far, to his later regret, as to announce that they were really nothing more than Oklahoma Republicans with guns. This rather exasperated the Communists, who had never heard of Oklahoma and had no interest in being Republicans. They, in fact, always strongly rejected the label of "agrarian reformers" – which of course they were – and insisted they were a lot more than that.[3]

These views did little to endear Hurley to the Generalissimo, who for once kept

3 To the best of my knowledge, the term had first been used in the 1930s by Stanley K. Hornbeck, then Director of the Office of Far Eastern Affairs, who was about as far removed from any Communist sympathies as Adam Smith would have been, and would later be one of the oracles of the China Lobby.

his opinions to himself and was rewarded for his restraint when Hurley began to sense that his affair with the Communists was not producing the results he wanted. He suddenly and violently turned against them, but the new devotion to Chiang Kai-shek proved to be no more fruitful. The wariness of the Generalissimo toward Hurley was not eased when the latter quarreled violently, mostly over trivia of a personal nature, with General Albert C. Wedemeyer, the Commander of the American forces in China, in whom he did have confidence.[4]

Wedemeyer, in October 1944, had succeeded the irascible and outspoken General Stilwell, who probably knew as much about Chinese troops and how to make good soldiers out of them as any Westerner who has ever lived. Stilwell, however, had made not the slightest effort to conceal his contempt for Chiang Kai-shek, to whom he referred publicly as well as in his diary as "the Peanut." In the end, General George C. Marshall, Chief of Staff of the American Army, who had long protected Stilwell because of his unique qualifications, had been forced to recognize that the liabilities had come to outweigh the assets, and had sent out Wedemeyer with strict instructions to get along with the Generalissimo. Wedemeyer did this very well indeed and would continue to do so in the bitter years ahead.

Shortly after the end of the war in the Pacific, it began to dawn on Hurley not only that the peace he sought for China was not to be achieved in any immediate future, but also that the prospects for it were growing dimmer at a disturbing rate. He returned to Washington on September 22, 1945, in a fury of frustration.

4 *Foreign Relations of the United States: 1944, China*, p. 177.

May 9, 1945 / San Francisco Conference on International Organization / Yesterday morning Harriman asked me to see him in his hotel room. Chip Bohlen was there, quizzically and listlessly scrutinizing the sunlight over the Bay through the amber of a glass of sherry. It was the first real conversation I have had with either of them since arriving for the Conference.

Bohlen, wartime Russian interpreter for President Roosevelt, would later serve, like Harriman, as Ambassador to the Soviet Union.

Harriman got right to the point by saying that an officer with Russian experience is badly needed in Chungking and he wants me to take the job. I know that for some time he has believed that officers with Moscow background should be stationed at strategic spots around the world. According to him, almost everybody in Chungking is misbehaving by doubting that the Kuomintang is necessarily the answer to the sorry China situation. He believes that we must realize what Communists really are wherever they are; that we must know how to protect future American interests; and that we must reinforce the case against the Soviets as the only possible defense. Since all I know about current developments in China comes from sketchy press reports, I am puzzled as to what he is driving at, but willing to learn—and I have been in Moscow. So I guess Chungking is the next stop for me.

June 1 / Last night I had dinner with the Communist members of the Chinese delegation at the Conference. They mix very little with anyone, including the other Chinese, and actually are here against the wishes of the Generalissimo only because of American insistence. They seemed unaware of a world beyond their own experience which because of years of Nationalist pressure has meant the countryside of China and not much else. The principal one, Tung Pi-wu, is an elder of the Communist Party and has a crinkled face with a wispy mustache, almost the prototype of an old philosopher. His main comment was that the recent personnel changes in the Nationalist Government made him think of the old proverb about keeping the same medicine and changing the water: the root of all evil is Chiang Kai-shek and as long as he controls there can be no real expectation of rapprochement between the Communists and the Kuomintang; coalition to be accepted must be genuine and not just a trick to destroy the Communists. Otherwise he was noncommittal.

This noon I had lunch with one of our China language officers and the Chinese who has the Russian desk in the Foreign Office in Chungking. It was quite a session since the American speaks English and Chinese, the Chinese speaks Chinese and Russian, and I English and what passes for Russian. The Chinese was plausible enough and believes understanding can be reached, but the concessions must be made by the Communists, the Russians, and the United States. Then all will be fine. He added, however, that T. V. Soong (brother-in-law of the Generalissimo and a prominent Shanghai financial power) was recently promoted to Prime Minister for foreign policy reasons to soothe the United States since he is supposed to be the businessman's friend. He claims a member of the Russian delegation here told him Sino-Russian relations could be improved by clarification of the Sinkiang situation, the dropping of Chinese claims to Outer Mongolia, and cessation of persecution of the Chinese Communists. He believes the Russians will probably want Korea, but have no interest in Manchuria. This last piece of nonsense can only mean someone has not yet told him about the agreements reached at Yalta last February that restore Russian rights in Manchuria as the price for Soviet entry into the war against Japan. All I have heard here so far about contemporary China makes me suspect I will get little illumination on this side of the Pacific, and that I might more profitably spend my time boning up on the past and leave the present for arrival in Chungking.

August 20 / Long Island / I have been feeling guilty about the weeks of leave on this lovely beach and in Texas while waiting for the bureaucratic mills of transportation to grind in Washington. But maybe it is just as well.

First came the atomic explosion in New Mexico in mid-July which spread confusion and uncertainty in all directions. Right after that came a subatomic explosion in the Department of State in the form of one of the seemingly endless reorganizations which caught the young lady who was typing my orders halfway through them. She simply stopped there for a couple of weeks until she was finally told to resume. Then came the Japanese collapse following the atomic attacks on Hiroshima and Nagasaki, and the Russian invasion of Manchuria. Had I been moving through the middle of some place when that happened, instead of being between trains in the Chicago Loop—the Windy City welcomed V-J Day with unaccustomed dignity and restraint—I could have still been sitting almost anywhere.

And now come the extraordinary agreements between Chungking and Moscow. Although it would be folly to have any opinion sitting here, it could be that Chungking has simply formalized its expectation of what would happen anyway and thus hopes to set legal limits to Russian ambitions. In any event, I am just as happy to arrive in Chungking innocent and uninvolved.

September 23 / Washington / More delays. I was to have joined the special plane going to Shanghai. In the confusion someone forgot to tell me when it was leaving. This has its advantages since I can now start to make my own way in the other direction by way of Rome to see my brother, India, and the Hump.

November 1 / Kunming / This trip is taking an incredible length of time to finish, although it is all interesting. Rome was chaos; Cairo not much less so. India was the most extraordinary, with a horde of Americans moving from east to west by any means available to the troop ships at Karachi —which, incidentally, have gone on strike. Our armies in China must simply have disintegrated.

Yesterday we flew to Chungking and, once over the airport, could not land because of soupy weather. So we came back here. Almost every time we have taken off, from Washington on, we have had to go back at least once because of some trouble. The Air Transport Command is beginning to fold up and those left on maintenance jobs are disgruntled and don't give a damn what happens.

Kunming is intriguing as an introduction to Chinese cities, and the broad valley in which it lies is very beautiful with sharp mountains in the distance, lush vegetation, a lake, and lots of sunshine. It is reputed to have the best climate in China. The setting makes the town, which by itself is undistinguished and rather surprisingly gray in color.

I went into town to see the Consul, who is an old friend. He was mostly gloomy. He says American Marines have already been killed in the north while riding trains as armed guards. We have fifty-three thousand men there. He also says that even the Kuomintang Chinese are laughing at us for a bunch of saps, and he feels it is too late for us to prevent catastrophe here: the civil war has irrevocably lined us up on the eventually losing side.

The Marines were there to maintain order until Nationalist troops could arrive.

After he had finished with some official drill given by the Governor, we went to a local restaurant where my first encounter with chopsticks left me humble and frustrated. The place was down a darkish alley where we stumbled over cobblestones with the help of occasional flickering carbide lights which competed only partly successfully with low-hanging stars above. There was much the same darkness in the restaurant, but there was nothing gloomy about it. Rather, there was a comfortable sort of gaiety, with staccato conversation and soft laughter coming from unexpected corners and directions. Most of the big, round tables were occupied by what were obviously family groups, all oblivious to anything but the pleasures of hot food and close companionship.

There were many small children, solemn-faced with shiny black thatches of hair and shoe-button eyes which intently took in the world around without missing a thing. Bundled up in quilted blue suits, complete with split pants, against the chill night, they looked like wise and sophisticated little butter balls: I know what people mean when they say that Chinese children are irresistible.

These people are terribly poor, but they have not let this corrupt their dignity, their gaiety, or their joy in living. I remember an Office of Strategic Services major I ran across in Calcutta who, when he learned I was on my way to China, insisted we get an open car and a bottle of gin, and tour the slums of the city. Under the influence of gin straight from the bottle, he revealed that he was just out of northern Indochina and an assignment with the Viet Minh guerrillas. This led to the confession that before this he had been with Communist guerrillas in the mountains of Greece. He had a compulsion to talk about this and about a girl he had finally left behind him in the hills—all punctuated with full-voiced rendition of wild Greek mountain songs.

The Viet Minh would eventually become the Government of North Vietnam. It was supported with military advisors and materiel by the United States in the war against Japan.

As we parked, he announced: "You have seen misery you never dreamed of before, dead eyes, sullenness, resentment, hatred, hopelessness, and all this in some of the most beautiful bodies in the world. It is the perfect introduction to

China." And then he weaved down the street through the
crowd, with another nostalgic song, not Greek this time,
sounding over the heads of the inattentive Indians.

Our group which is still waiting for the plane to Chungking is a good illustration of the unlikely people thrown
together by war: an unidentified Frenchman, several strong
German accents, Jacqueline Cochran inspecting air bases,
a Japanese general, a Swiss banker, an American Shanghai
businessman who talks vaguely of his connections, a Baptist
missionary openly smuggling blackmarket dollars, and
several very nervous Chinese. There is also of course a
Foreign Economic Administration man who spends his time
spitting in a corner, and three Red Cross girls who have
seen more of the hideousness of combat than the rest of us
put together.

November 2/ Chungking / We took off from Kunming in
a blinding fog, flew all the way in it, and landed in same.
By the time we arrived I felt made of fog myself. The airport, a good and hard twenty miles from the city, was over
a ridge of spectacularly beautiful mountains. The city is set
in a gloomy gorge of the Yangtze, clinging to its hillsides.
The streets are a deep brown mud, the houses are painted
black, it gets dark early, and the electricity is too feeble for
reading.

The Embassy is quartered in a series of buildings on top
of a hill, all gray. My room, which is not untypical, has in
it one bed, one chair, one chest of drawers, and an over-
head light. And the air is a damp chill from the fog in the
valley which I am told is mostly the winter fate of Chungking.

All this makes an appropriate backdrop for the poisonous
atmosphere around the Embassy which at first seems unreal.
Every officer here has already taken me aside to give his
version of what I can say to whom and who should be
trusted and who spies for whom. The principal occupation
seems to be eavesdropping and ducking around corners.
Those who hew the line with Ambassador Hurley swagger.

Others are mostly evasive. The evasive ones and the Hurley followers both, for different reasons, want me to pump the Soviet Embassy here to find out what devious schemes they are pushing. I could already tell them everything the Russians would tell me—which is nothing.

Puppets, collaborators, & civil war

Despite the brutal effects of eight years of war, the prospects for China were surprisingly good after the surrender of Japan. By virtue of his political skill and the long years of dogged opposition to the Japanese with only minimal outside help, Chiang Kai-shek had emerged as the undisputed leader in the eyes of all his countrymen. His reputation internationally was equally charismatic and for the same reasons. Furthermore, it appeared that the problem which bothered him most had passed some kind of watershed that gave hope for internal peace.

On August 15, 1945, the Republic of China and the Soviet Union signed a treaty which was the direct outgrowth of agreements which had been reached by the Big Three at Yalta early that same year[1] – in which China had not participated and of which it would have no knowledge for some months because repeated experience had demonstrated that if one person in Chungking knew a secret it became public knowledge as soon as the next editions of the newspapers appeared on the streets. The immediate purpose of the Yalta Agreements on the Far East was to assure Russian entry into the war against Japan once Germany had been defeated. Stalin had demanded and received a pledge of complete secrecy on this agreement to protect himself from a surprise attack on his Siberian front. In addition, President Roosevelt had long believed that the Russians were entitled to recover what they had lost in the Russo-Japanese War of 1905. In essence, these rights consisted of preferential commercial and railroad rights in Manchuria, a naval base at Port Arthur (the old Russian drive for an ice-free port), and renunciation by China of any claims over Outer Mongolia. It is true that China could claim that these same rights had historically been Chinese; and just as true that they had not been effectively exercised for generations.[2] More pragmatically, there was nothing in them that Russian armies could not easily have

1 *China White Paper*, chapter 4.
2 Until the Manchu Dynasty, China looked on Manchuria largely as an outer march of defense. Chinese were discouraged from going there, and few did. Hence, the population was negligible and consisted largely of nomadic tribes. To the Manchus it was the original homeland and was to be kept as such. Not until the latter part of the nineteenth century did the Chinese in substantial numbers begin to migrate there, and by then Russian infiltration denied them much influence in the northern half. Chinese defeat in the Sino-Japanese War of 1895 and Russian defeat in the Russo-Japanese War of 1905 assured Japanese supremacy until the surrender at Tokyo Bay in 1945. See Owen Lattimore, *Inner Asian Frontiers of China* (New York: American Geographical Society, 1940), pp. 133–51.

seized and held. Stalin saw no reason to disagree. The problem was to secure
Chinese acquiescence.

The Sino-Soviet Treaty[3] was the answer which ratified the Yalta Agreements.
For China, the victory in it was recognition by the Soviet Union of the Nationalist
Government as the *sole* government of China, and of Chiang Kai-shek as its
leader. This seemed to put the Communists exactly where the Generalissimo
wanted them, and the bitterness of their reactions to the Treaty, as expressed to
members of the American Embassy, suggested that they feared the same result. And
there was much in the circumstances to support the view that the treaty was only
the recognition of the facts – as Lenin once oberved, "Facts are stubborn things."

From a military standpoint, the ratio of men and rifles between the Nationalists
and the Communists was about five to one. By December the United States had
completed the equipping of the previously promised thirty-nine divisions with
heavy materiel and transport. Many of those divisions which had been American
trained were considered to be, in vindication of General Stilwell's faith in Chinese
soldiers properly handled, as good as any in the world. The Communists, on the
other hand, were organized as guerrilla units, equipped only with what they could
capture or manufacture in their backyards, but also recognized as having morale,
discipline, purpose, and, for the only kind of warfare they could then afford, skills
which few armies in history have ever possessed to the same degree.[4] The
Nationalists also had a complete monopoly of naval and air power, and they were
in the process of taking over most of the lines of communication, with the help of
an American airlift, which the Japanese had held in China proper. The Russians
had already occupied Manchuria and were showing little disposition to admit
Chinese troops of either political persuasion.

Economically – and this would be one of the most critical points in the future –
matters could have been much worse. Agricultural production had been maintained at pre-war levels because the Japanese had never succeeded in conquering
the countryside, and China is a rural country. American bombing had done
some industrial damage in areas such as Formosa and Hankow, and elsewhere
along the Yangtze, but the industrial complex which the Japanese had built in
Manchuria and north China was larger than the rest of China put together and
was still intact. Foreign exchange reserves, so important for imports to rebuild the
damage which had been done, were at an all-time high, due largely to American
aid.[5]

In the enthusiasm of victory, there appeared to be good reason for hoping that
the kind of determination which had enabled China to survive the desperate years
of one apparent defeat after another would be more than adequate for the tasks
of peace. Perhaps the most hopeful factor was that most Chinese could remember

3 *China White Paper*, pp. 105, 120.
4 Lionel Max Chassin, *The Communist Conquest of China* (Cambridge: Harvard University Press, 1965), pp. 247–61.
5 *China White Paper*, p. 129. Accurate figures have never been available, but conservative
estimates have placed the assets at several hundred million dollars.

only war and violence, and the only thing they wanted was peace – any kind of peace as long as it meant an end of killing and destruction. And then with dismaying speed the clouds of trouble began to pile up.

General Douglas MacArthur, as Supreme Commander for the Allies in the Pacific, had authorized the Generalissimo to accept the surrender of Japanese and Chinese puppet troops in China and on Formosa, which is exactly what the latter had intended to do anyway. Since Chiang lacked effective transport of his own, the American Air Force lifted several divisions for him to the north, and some thirty thousand American Marines landed in the Peiping-Tientsin area to help in maintaining order.[6] At the same time, General Wedemeyer urged the Generalissimo in the strongest terms not to include Manchuria in his field of operations until he had consolidated his position south of the Great Wall, lest he become dangerously overextended. At the moment the problem was largely academic since the Russians were already in full occupation, but when they withdrew the following spring Chiang ignored the advice and eventually paid the price Wedemeyer foresaw.

The Generalissimo instructed the Communists not to accept any surrender and to remain wherever they were. They ignored the order, having no intention of giving up anything they already held or of not seizing as much more as they could. In fact, they quickly brought much of rural north and central China under their control.[7]

Manchuria was an especially sore point for the Communists. More than one member of their delegation in Chungking on several occasions referred privately and bitterly to Russian activities. The Communists had quite obviously expected to be welcome in Manchuria, and they were dismayed when the Russians not only denied them military help, but excluded them as far as possible. The familiar pattern was repeating itself. Though the Communists were gaining and keeping control of the countryside, they could not take the urban areas and the lines of communication. But there was more to the bitterness than just this.

Rumors began to come out of Manchuria with increasing frequency that the Russians were systematically dismantling the great industrial complex in the area and shipping it to Siberia – hardly an indication that they were anticipating much of a future for the Communists as rulers of China or that they thought of Japanese property as other than the legitimate booty of war. Furthermore, it was said, the organized sacking was being compounded by disorganized and seemingly uncontrollable looting. Russian intelligence had just as grossly overestimated the likely Japanese opposition to the Manchurian occupation as American intelligence had, but since he had believed what he had been told, Stalin had made the not unreasonable calculation that if he had to lose large numbers of troops they might

6 *China White Paper*, pp. 311 *et seq.*

7 *Ibid.*, pp. 311–13. By the end of 1945 the Nationalists had occupied the urban centers and most of the lines of communication, but they had not taken control of any north-south railroads, nor had they made any appreciable advance in the rural areas between the Yangtze and the Great Wall. In these areas, the Communists took the surrender of most Japanese units.

just as well be those who would be the least desirable citizens in peace time. Hence, he assigned the job to Marshal Malinovsky, in whose makeup there was not a drop of gentleness or mercy, and gave him divisions, some of them Central Asian, which had been continuously in combat action for at least three years. When there proved to be no Japanese opposition the results were clearly predictable, and not even Malinovsky could control the brutalized men under his command.

Developments in China proper should also have been just as clearly predictable. The Generalissimo, who, whatever else he may have been, was not lacking in determination and stubbornness once he had made up his mind, had decided that every last inch of China belonged to him – he had the Sino-Soviet Treaty to prove it – and he was going to take it, regardless of the cost or of what else he had to neglect. At the same time there was no evidence in the record to suggest that Communist will and determination were any less than his. Inevitably the two forces clashed whenever and wherever they came face to face. The fighting spread like a brush fire and became even more alarming as Communist guerrilla units came to the surface in areas where they had not previously been known to operate at all. We shall probably never know whether they had been there clandestinely all along or had simply infiltrated with great speed and skill.

Ambassador Hurley returned to Washington on September 22. From then until the arrival of General Marshall late in December there was not even his uneven coordination or unpredictable leadership of the many-sided activities of the American Embassy in Chungking. Nor was there much guidance from Washington for the subordinates who found themselves temporarily in charge. Every shade of opinion in the Embassy tended to pull in a different direction, and animosity between these shades became very bitter. Largely, the controversies had begun during World War II from the frustration of limited American military activity while primary attention was given to Europe, and from the inability of the Chinese, Nationalist and Communist alike, to make any major offensive contribution against the Japanese.[8] The frustration had been best symbolized by the savage disagreements between General Stilwell and the Generalissimo about the prosecution of the war. By the time Hurley left for consultation in Washington, the conversations between the Government and the Communists, in which he had participated and in fact played a leading role since 1944, had come to a virtual standstill. It was apparent to everyone except himself that his erratic behavior and intemperate outbursts had cost him the confidence of all participants, despite the customary official courtesies.[9]

8 One should not, however, underestimate the contribution made by the existence of substantial Chinese armies which compelled Japan to keep over a million men on the mainland at a time when they were desperately needed against the American juggernaut. On the few occasions when the Nationalists and Communists stopped watching each other, when local warlords thought of China first and their own fortunes second, or when the Generalissimo allowed his troops to fight, the Chinese soldiers on both sides acquitted themselves most creditably.

9 See *Time*, December 3, 1945, p. 30; Arthur Krock in *New York Times*, November 29, 1945, p. 22, c. 5.

As fall blended into winter, the spreading of hostilities, the continuing lack of progress in political negotiations, the neglect by the Government of problems desperately needing attention, the concentration exclusively on the occupation of more and more territory, and the pervasive infiltration of a sense of terror induced by the insidious and prowling activities of the secret police – all contributed to a growing apathy and resignation. The peace which had been bought at such terrible cost was not, after all, in sight – not, that is, unless the United States could do something.

The puppet troops were Chinese troops of the "Reformed Government of China" which Japan set up in March 1938 and reorganized in March 1940 as the "Reformed National Government" under the leadership of Wang Ching-wei, an old-line Kuomintang revolutionary and rival of Chiang Kai-shek. To this day it is not hard to find Chinese who still think the Wang policy of cooperation with Japan was the right one.

November 3 / Chungking / All agree here that the fighting in the north is more serious than the papers have it, and that Chungking is using puppet and Japanese troops. One newsman recently back from Peiping insists that we have done nothing to disarm the Japanese there, but that the Communists are confident they can hold their own indefinitely. Chungking, others claim, has a blank check from us and the future is not pretty.

I had dinner last night with several American newsmen. Apparently like most people here they are violently anti-Kuomintang, speechless about the lack of direction or purpose in American policy, and disgusted with the way their news stories are cut or altered at home. What they did add specifically to my information is what the Sino-American Cooperative Organization (SACO) is. I had never heard of it, but it seems to be the Chinese gestapo, which behaves in a way and with methods which have become all too familiar in recent years. No one knows for sure when and where it will strike or who belongs to it. It is known to have headquarters at a place called Happy Valley, and to have a good deal of American cooperation.

The dinner was my second introduction to Chinese food, which is wonderful. Hot rice wine is both heady and intriguing. Generally this is the most liquorless place I have seen in many a long year. At the moment it is also cigaretteless.

This afternoon the fog cleared off and it is now warm and pleasant, but the warmth brings out a pervasive smell of urine. The vistas up and down the river in the sunlight are really breathtaking.

I am finding that Chungking is famous for the quality of its beds. They consist of a wooden frame with a rattan cover and on top of that a sort of padding which invariably wads. I may yet take to the floor.

This afternoon I made my official call on the Russian Ambassador, an occasion held with all the usual pomp and tea. He was most cordial and we limited conversation to Moscow days without referring to our squabbles when he was head of the Foreign Office Press Bureau and I was the Acting Director of our Office of War Information.

November 6 / There is a Chinese-American Vice Consul in the Embassy with the wonderful name of Fong Chuck.

This morning for the first time since I arrived we had water that was not only running but hot. Perched as we are on top of a hill, the local power supply is usually insufficient to bring water to the top. So we have cold water hauled up in buckets by coolies from the river far below.

Otherwise, it has been a dreary day, confined to more ugly war news of fighting in the north, an uninspiring talk on principles by a visiting deputy director of UNRRA, and corned beef for lunch.

November 7 / This noon the Russians really celebrated the Revolution. It is reported as being the biggest party ever given in Chungking. As usual at official Russian affairs, Ambassador Petrov received the important guests in a separate room. At one point I was standing outside with some of the younger Russians. One of them again proposed the usual toasts about peace and friendship. At this moment, unbeknownst to me, Madame Chiang decided to make her regal entry and a flying NKVD wedge led her through the crowd to the private room. Just as she passed me I raised my glass and clipped her sharply under the chin with my elbow. As she recovered her balance it was, doubtless understandably, not a pleasant look she gave me.

From up here on our hill the city looks very picturesque at night. Each of the innumerable street stalls displays a carbide light which looks like a candle burning steadily. It is very different from the daylight appearance, with the outer sheath of darkness somehow having an embracing, protective quality about it. Outlines are blurred, voices lower and more intimate, with the harsh edges of poverty lost in companionship and a sense of the dignity of life itself. Even in the lowliest coolie I find no sense of servility; rather, an innate gaiety and a quick feel for the comic.

United China Relief was a federation of the principal volunteer organizations to collect relief supplies for refugees and war victims. It did a yeoman job.

November 8 / The head of United China Relief here is a lifelong friend of my parents. This noon he took me to the weekly luncheon of the Chungking Rotary Club. It consisted of some twenty foreigners and Chinese who slapped each other on the back, heartily called each other by their first names, sang "Hail, Hail, the Gang's All Here" and "Smiles," ate nondescript western food, and drank something unidentifiable. We listened to a portly gentleman just back from Mongolia tell us he could not speak of what he saw there because of Chinese censorship, but instead would tell us about Chinese refugees. He then did not do so in a half hour of broken English. All this was to the accompaniment of rain soaking through a thatched roof and a Chinese band playing for a wedding somewhere on the other side of the fence. As Mark Twain said to his wife when she was trying to demonstrate to him how his famous swearing sounded: "You have the words, my dear, but not the tune."

November 9 / Each day the news from the north becomes more sombre. There have already been small incidents involving American troops, and I would guess that unless they get out, only a miracle can sooner or later prevent one which will touch off God only knows what ugliness. Actually the incidents are all being handled by our military, which tells the Embassy absolutely nothing beyond what we read in the papers. And even there we see little, only enough to know that things are bad and hostilities are cropping out in every direction. We don't know the coverage in the States or the reaction. Practically everyone now says there is little or no hope for bringing unity to China, that unity means suicide for whichever side compromises the most. The issues and the bitterness are too deep for peace. As far as we are concerned, we have by now jockeyed ourselves into a position where there is no longer any good answer. No matter what we do, we are in the wrong.

In a somewhat lighter vein, nothing in this country has the remotest chance of popular appeal which does not call for agrarian reform. In Canton there is even an organization known as the South Seas Basketball Association for Agrarian Reform! Actually, this is not as frivolous as it sounds. It represents a deeply felt need in this country which the Government will ignore at its mortal peril. It has ignored it so far, despite lip service.

Chou En-lai, who heads the Communist delegation here, has a nice sense of humor. He and K. C. Wu, Vice Minister for Foreign Affairs and Press Liaison, were schoolmates at Nankai Middle School. Of that period Chou says, "I organized the students and Wu organized the Boy Scouts."

November 10 / Last night I had a talk with Tillman Durdin of the *New York Times* who has just come back from a visit to Kalgan in the north. According to him the Communists are behaving very well here, being quiet and unobtrusive, and are trying to conciliate the people who are still suspicious and at the same time fearful the Kuomintang will come and wreak vengeance on them if they cooperate in any way with the Communists. It is the first time the Communists have had to administer a city and they are finding that urban and rural skills are very different. In the meantime a lot of racketeering groups are taking advantage of them. It is apparently the old story of the country boy who came to the big city. One pathetic note is the women in their country padded jackets and pants, gawking in amazement at the painted ladies of the town.

As far as Durdin could tell, all Communist troop movement was in the direction of Manchuria, something worth keeping in mind. They looked good. Many, however, are very bitter and charge they have been abandoned by everyone, some even including the Russians in this category.

They claim that in Jehol, Inner Mongolia, the Russians disarmed them along with the Japanese. And they are tired and weary at the prospect of having to continue fighting. But they are determined to go on if necessary.

We have received some fragments here of a speech Secretary of State Byrnes made at the *New York Herald Tribune* Forum in which he apparently announced American recognition of a Soviet right to establish its own Monroe Doctrine around its borders. This is somewhat different from our hard insistence on literal compliance with the "no interference in eastern Europe" provisions of Yalta. I remember that Ed Flynn, who had accompanied Roosevelt to Yalta, was talking this same line when I last saw him just before I left the States. He said then he had called Byrnes to tell him so.

November 11 / Today we are celebrating Armistice Day and the Chinese are celebrating the birthday of Dr. Sun Yat-sen. I spent part of the morning in town revelling in the pure joy of some Chinese usage of the English language.

One sign read: "Sing Sing High Class Tailor—Ladies May Have Fits Upstairs." There is another: "Dental Plumbing Inserted by New Methodists."

At noon I had lunch with Chou En-lai, an intelligent, perceptive, and handsome man who talked quite freely without adding much to what we already know. He asked the usual question as to why we proclaim non-intervention and then intervene without disarming the Japanese. Since he obviously knew the answer there was no point in repeating it. He seemed to have very little faith that any settlement would be forthcoming, though he thought there was a chance that popular pressure from beneath might force the Generalissimo to alter his determination to occupy the entire country. I could not see that he was terribly upset by the continuing erosion of negotiations and the ebbing prospects of peace. He is confident who wins in the end.

The town is spending its time speculating about what comes next. This weekend all the Kuomintang generals are in town for a war council, presumably to decide whether it will be civil war. I suppose they are faced with a hell of a choice, for they must wonder whether anything they do can be right. The American master minds around here argue and argue and twist and turn and then always come out where they went in. They are pretty unanimous about who loses, and then suddenly reticent as to who wins. And all are hurt that they should have been so betrayed. It would be interesting to know real press reaction at home. The Office of War Information sampling shows great anger at our intervention. The State Department one shows indifference.

Domestic press coverage and reaction were extremely limited and for the most part uninterested. Americans were preoccupied with getting the troops back home and resuming peacetime activities. Where there was resentment of American activities in China it was largely from concern that they would slow down the liquidation of the war, rather than from worry that the United States was becoming involved in an ugly situation. The cold war was still in the future.

November 13 / A friend has just come back from a trip to Chengtu in west China. The town has just recently held its first election in its 2500 years. At first, the people did not know what to do about it or how. A couple of weeks before the election, the film *Wilson* showed up and created a furor. So that was the way Americans held elections! What was good enough for Wilson was good enough for Chengtu. So the entire town assiduously studied the picture and then went out enthusiastically to put on Wilson's campaign of speeches, rallies, posters, parades, etc. It was apparently the most excitement and fun Chengtu has had since the birth of Confucius.

November 14 / Last night I decided to investigate what is known locally as the Chinese modern experimental theatre. It was the story of a man and his wife who didn't get along. He falls in love with a girl who is still in school in Kweilin where they all live. Japanese planes raid the town and shellack it. The man and his wife mournfully go off to Chengtu, while the girl gaily joins a bucket brigade. End of story.

Today I have been trying to trace down the flood of rumors on Russian behavior—or rather misbehavior—in Manchuria, which has certain people terribly exercised. Rumors in abundance I find, but no one who has really been in and seen anything. There is so far only one gripe for which there are witnesses and that comes from recently released American prisoners: the Russians preempted all the best whorehouses in Mukden for their own exclusive use.

At that point I was taken across our garden wall to meet the Vice Ministers of Foreign Affairs—all suave, correct, and very interested in the man from Moscow. Somehow, having been in Moscow seems to confer on me an aura of mystery and authority which I strongly suspect is not destined to last.

November 16 / The time having arrived when the matter could no longer be postponed, I took the plunge and had my first local haircut. Well . . . at least that part of me now looks like everyone else here.

Last night I had dinner with our Chargé d'Affaires, Walter Robertson, a Virginia gentleman and a banker conscious of eight generations behind him; he has nice manners and a sensitive mouth. In his spare time he does parlor tricks and does them well. He chose to do them last night. Also present was Kan Nai-kwan, a Vice Minister of Foreign Affairs, who is a remarkably well educated man

Robertson would become Assistant Secretary of State for Far Eastern Affairs in the Eisenhower Administration.

with gentle eyes and uneasy hands. The parlor tricks baffled
him; all his basic superstitions rose up and made him so
jittery he had to go home, convinced the devil was at work.

After dinner I stood on the street looking at the moon. A
lone beggar came by singing—something you seldom hear.
Despite the falsetto, it was the most extraordinary tune.
Although unlike anything I have ever heard, it also had a
curious resemblance to "Clair de Lune."

November 17 / Last night the Embassy political officers had
dinner with representatives of the Democratic League, the
so-called Third Force in China that stands between the
Kuomintang and the Communists. It was organized in
1941 to coordinate all the tag-end democratic and liberal
groups who had no voice in the Kuomintang and thought
they should. They were almost all educated abroad, call
themselves the intellectuals of China, make a precarious
sort of living writing ambiguous editorials for Kuomintang
papers, and discuss the situation in their spare time. They
believe the civil war will be continued—the Military Council has finished, results unknown, but fairly predictable for
war—and advocate discussion groups as the way out of all
troubles, possibly because they do not have an army and are
most unlikely to get one. Despite the tremulous and ineffectual air about them, I have to admire their guts. They never
stop their criticism of the Government, even though they
know they are under continual secret police surveillance.
Every so often one of them disappears, and his death is
seldom quick or gentle; they also know it could happen to
them all at any time. Probably the only thing that saves
most of them is Kuomintang awareness that too big a purge
would look bad in the American press.

We have a new report on Shanghai conditions. Nothing
is being done by the Government. The Japanese are still
armed. Racketeering of the most shameless kind goes on.
Puppets and collaborators hold many public jobs. Foreigners
are respectfully handled, but behind this the Kuomintang
is laying the groundwork to make life difficult for foreign

business. This is going to be a very ticklish affair. I have
only sympathy for Chinese desire to repossess what the West
has grabbed over the decades, but the way they are going
about it will do no one any good. Certain well placed and
well connected Chinese have been very apt pupils in the
school of exploitation. They are known as the running
dogs of the imperialists among those who have not been
permitted to share in the exploiting.

One thing I will get out of this place is a pair of reinforced legs. From the Embassy to the street is exactly 106
steps—I counted them—and the only way up or down is
to walk. The whole city is like that.

Down the street from the Embassy there is a park with
a high concrete tower for parachute jumping. On its opening yesterday all the local bigshots came with tables and
chairs and cups of tea, and with substitutes to do their
jumping for them. Came the time for the jumping event
and all the substitutes disappeared. For a while the afternoon looked like a failure until a couple of very drunk
American newsmen wandered by and volunteered to jump
to the acclaim of the crowd and the sipping of much tea.
It was a huge success.

November 18 / This is a sad still Sunday afternoon with
the fog very thick and a flock of buzzards hovering over
something that died or is about to die on the next hill.
Beyond the buzzards and across the river there is a lime-
stone cave which has allegedly never been explored because
a dragon lives inside. He is the dragon of rain. During a
drought last summer the Ministry of Agriculture sent some
Buddhist monks over there to pacify the old bugger. It
rained.

November 19 / With a full-blown civil war going on
(though battles are fairly short since both sides tend to
run out of ammunition at the end of a half hour) the
Communist press operates at full blast in Chungking, calling
the Government and its officials all sorts of names. I have
discovered, incidentally, that Chinese capacity for and

imaginativeness in invective are impressive. It is in fact the only uncensored press here, not that its version of the news is necessarily any more reliable than that which is censored. But it can and does publish what it wants to. Of course, it indulges in the turgid prose typical of Communist papers everywhere and, as elsewhere, after an initial period of amazement and almost disbelief over the "miserification of the masses" approach to communication in writing, one finds it pretty soporific. The same freedom is permitted the members of the Communist delegation who talk about and with whom they please. There is growing reason to believe this is not true elsewhere in China. I suppose it is done to impress Americans; sometimes it works.

November 21 / A lot of Chinese, especially intellectuals and businessmen, are becoming uneasy over our help. They are caught in the dilemma of wanting this help to suppress the Communists while fearing that we will become so entrenched we cannot be thrown out when we are no longer wanted. Communist propaganda is not calculated to assuage or lessen the fears. Wang Bing-nan said recently: "It is all right for the United States to arm the Kuomintang because as fast as they get it we take it away from them." The three Kuomintang divisions recently captured were American-armed.

A press officer of the Communist delegation in Chungking, Wang Bing-nan would subsequently for a number of years be Ambassador to Poland and the only official point of regular contact with the United States.

November 23 / Yesterday was Thanksgiving. A few of us went off on a trip down the river with a Chinese professor to visit the Government school which trains administrators for the Kuomintang. The school is located in one of the lateral gorges of the Yangtze, a spectacular location surrounded by lovely countryside. There was one sinister note over the area which is just to the north of the route of the great Communist "Long March" of the early 1930s. All along the crest of the mountains at half-mile intervals there are blockhouses. They were originally erected as anti-Communist defenses and now look like deserted fingers against the sky, an ominous portent. In the school itself the students who were not being put through military exercises either slept or gambled. As far as I could make out, the training they receive is more political indoctrination and discipline than administration.

The professor took us to lunch where we got half stewed on the hot rice wine which goes so well with Chinese food. One gowned gentleman kept after me to find just what I thought of the Communists. After lunch we were invited to a public bathhouse for a soaking in the local hot springs. The tubs were enormous, carved out of single blocks of stone and set into the ground. The water was boiling hot and sobering. Since we came by sampan on the Yangtze, we returned the same way, poled against the stream by sweating coolies. Gradually, the cobbled embankment, the swarming life on the shore, even the gorge itself melted together; and then there was nothing but water, land, and sky—and the empty silhouetted blockhouses.

November 26 / I am both intrigued and uneasy that within the last two weeks there have been the following press reports about Hurley, who is home for consultation, for which we have no explanation whatsoever from any official sources and which do not fall into any pattern: his belligerent interview in New Mexico against the Communists, the *Life* editorial and his comment thereon, the *New York Times* announcement of its support for the Kuomintang, the Scripps-Howard articles by Parker LaMoore (one-time Naval aide and press officer to General Hurley), the report by China Central News (the official Government news agency) that Hurley has been in Washington for a week and has not even been to the State Department or the White House, Wedemeyer's statement that if and when Hurley does come back to China the decision will be based solely on grounds of health. With all this there have been the usual news reports of spreading hostilities in the north for background. But the Communists have launched the most ferocious attack on the United States in many a long year. And the Kuomintang is indulging in an orgy of I Told You So The Yanks Are Coming To Help Us.

The subtle reign of terror

On November 26 Ambassador Hurley submitted his resignation with explosive charges: his efforts had been sabotaged by the career Foreign Service Officers who, he said, favored the Communists and the "colonial imperialists" who wanted China divided.[1] Not even a subsequent investigation by the Senate Foreign Relations Committee[2] managed to explain this implied contradiction, and little came of the matter beyond an uneasy presentiment which would later become grim reality when Senator McCarthy and the China Lobby succeeded in destroying the highly competent and respected China Service and in reducing the Department of State virtually to impotence.[3]

Thinking he had persuaded Hurley to return to China, Secretary of State Byrnes at first refused to transmit the resignation to the President. It was therefore with no little surprise that President Truman received the bombastic announcement which finally arrived just at the end of a cabinet meeting. Momentarily baffled as to what to do next, he asked for suggestions. It was Clinton P. Anderson, then Secretary of Agriculture, also appalled at the implications of this development, who proposed General George C. Marshall as the only person with sufficient stature to salvage anything from the impending calamity. The President readily agreed. Although Marshall had only recently retired in exhaustion, his concept of selfless devotion to public duty made it impossible for him to refuse the request.

1 *China White Paper*, pp. 581–84.
2 These hearings were never made public, nor was there any report from the Committee. Herbert Feis subsequently had access to them and used information from them in chapter 36 of his volume *The China Tangle*, which is concerned with Hurley's resignation and the circumstances surrounding it. Feis also had access to Hurley's private papers and still could find no satisfactory explanation. His speculative conclusion was that the China Lobby, which feared successful negotiations, put pressure on Hurley not to return, and that, in any event, Hurley no longer really believed he could accomplish his original mission. Hurley only increased the confusion further by his testimony in 1951 before the Joint Committee on the Military Situation in the Far East, which investigated the dismissal of General MacArthur.
3 Little more would be heard of General Hurley beyond an occasional expression of approval for the views of the China Lobby, and an unsuccessful bid for a Senate seat from New Mexico some ten years later.

November 28 / Chungking / The news from Washington has had this place in an uproar for two days now, with all barriers down and all tongues wagging with what they have wanted to say for a long time. All animosities are in the open now. Hurley in his resignation letter, of course, has made a damned fool of himself. There is much in his statement that is true and pertinent, but his vanity and personal rage got the better of him. The Foreign Service has been called a lot of things, but this is the first time anyone thought of labelling it Communist. And it seems we are imperialists at the same time. Among other things, his statement brings into the open the internal controversy over what we should do here and the deep bitterness between opposing points of view.

Byrnes's statement also is curious. He expresses surprise, says that he thought he had persuaded Hurley to return, and that he so notified the White House. Byrnes was not only surprised, he was piqued. Did he know nothing of this? Was it a surprise to the White House too? If so, how did it manage to appoint a new man so soon and get his consent? General Marshall is a natural for it, not just someone drawn from a hat. His prestige and apolitical background should help in finding some kind of solution here— if this is still possible.

November 29 / The air seems to be getting heavier and thicker. One gathers from the Chinese press that there is a real storm at home. Just what it consists of is a little hard to tell because Central News always twists news to suit its own end, but it is definitely gleeful about something now. Byrnes's second statement is a disgrace. He had a chance to ignore Hurley or to use the statement to build Foreign Service prestige. Instead, he quibbles, equivocates, hedges, and names names to the point where no one will know what to think of us.

In addition to the inconclusive hearings of the Senate Foreign Relations Committee, Byrnes had instructed the legal advisor of the Department of State to investigate Hurley's charges. His report in March 1946 produced no substantiation.

November 30 / The confusion continues to mount here. Fuller press accounts now indicate that Hurley may not be getting the complete public approval the Chinese have led us to believe he has. And it looks as though we would get a Congressional investigation out of it and the results of that, depending on what happens and who does it, are unpredictable from here.

It is just five-thirty and as usual the house boys start

cleaning fireplaces and mopping floors with a peculiarly fragrant water that I think they got from a drain.

December 2 / Most street peddlers here carry a small drum attached to a long handle, with the hammer attached by a string to the head. It works from the wrist and makes a wondrous, penetrating, musical staccato note you can hear for miles. I bought one and when depressed use it, which immediately brings down a storm of protest on my head from everyone in the house, but it makes me feel better.

Recently I acquired a jeep for transportation. It is about the only kind of vehicle that always works around here, even if you are continuously splashed with mud. I also now have a pillow. I even have a rug in my room which has a sort of history. When Henry Wallace was here in 1944 a delegation from Chengtu waited on him to wish him well. They presented him with two rugs done in a monstrous combination of bright reds and greens. He had to leave one behind. Sometimes it gives an illusion of growing vegetation and even is rather beautiful in a horrible sort of way. Anyway it helps keep my feet warm.

December 3 / We are just beginning to get fairly full details of student activities in Kunming during the last ten days. A mass meeting was scheduled for the twenty-fifth in the Central Hall of Yunnan University, but it was barricaded and surrounded by troops. The students then marched to the campus of Lienta for an open air meeting which was addressed by four distinguished professors. The troops fired over their heads and continued doing so for the hour and a half of the meeting. Other efforts to break them up also failed and they ended with a resolution demanding the end of the war, withdrawal of American troops, and the right to hold meetings. The next morning they went out on strike and were joined by the middle (high) schools. Efforts by the teachers to convince them they had won a moral victory and should return to classes failed. The garrison commander reportedly announced that the students were free to meet and he was free to fire.

Lienta was a consolidation of several Peiping universities in exile during the war.

Small disorders continued throughout the week and several students were either killed or wounded in police raids on Lienta. Tension has increased steadily. It seems the students are determined to keep up their agitation and the authorities are equally determined to put it down. In the meantime American prestige keeps on dropping since we are blamed by both sides.

December 4 / I have started taking Chinese lessons, not with any idea that I will ever really know much, but because I think it helps to know something of the way other people express themselves in their own language. All the words seem to have meaning as abstractions and seldom can you be precise or definite in meaning. Pronunciation is built around vowels and the consonants are not clear and definite. To me they sound like echoes of sounds. All this is amazingly representative of Chinese ways of thinking and methods of doing business. Even in something like the present Kuomintang-Communist negotiations they talk about arrangements, principles, understandings, points of view. Never does it get to the stage of a formulated proposal and then you take it or you don't. This has been going on for years and seems to bother no one, even while heavy fighting is going on. It is like walking in fog.

The Chinese have been complaining about Russian looting in Manchuria and the failure to reach any agreement about their departure. And now Malinovsky comes out with an announcement that on the request of the Chinese they will stay there a little longer because the Chinese do not yet feel competent to take over. The Chinese never told us they were holding these conversations, and when we ask what gives, they say oh yes there is some sort of agreement, but of course it was the Russians who brought up the subject. But it has stopped the yapping about looting; in fact no one wants to mention Manchuria any more. Now all the talk is that General Marshall will fix everything when he arrives.

It is fun to wander the streets here and watch the endless stream of life. Stores along the streets are one-room affairs with all phases of life going on in that room. Some streets sell pottery, others peanuts, porcelain, cloth, scrap iron. Each street has its own specialties. One thing stands out about the people—they are always amiable. Time means nothing and they like people. You may never get anywhere, but you do it pleasantly and easily.

Students and intellectuals as individuals played a central role in the Chinese revolution from its inception. They became an organized movement, known as the Chinese Renaissance because ostensibly its purpose was the modernization of Chinese culture, especially language. In addition, it had two political purposes: the restoration of Chinese sovereignty through the abrogation of unequal treaties, and internal political democratization. Although closely allied with the Kuomintang, the movement is still celebrated in Communist China as one of the most significant developments in twentieth-century China. Certainly it foreshadowed the high premium the Communists have always placed on student allegiance.

December 6 / I had lunch today with a man named Chun who is a statistician and population expert from a school in Kunming. We got to talking about student activities, since during the last couple of days there has been another bad and bloody student strike in Kunming which the Kuomintang is putting down with machine guns. The facts are a little obscure from this vantage point, but the general outline is fairly clear. The Kuomintang is alleging that the Communists instigated it, and furthermore that they hired thugs to shoot down their own people. I asked Chun why the really great upsurge of student activity during the twenties had died down, he having been one of them. He said that Chinese students and intellectuals, for the most part, have come to the conclusion that there is no point to it anymore since it will only lose. It is better to contribute something by working in a non-political field. It also saves your hide—or so you think.

There is a wonderful story going around about Madame Chiang. She entertained a few of the newly arrived ladies at tea the other day and was telling them about her aches, boils, blisters, and rashes. As she finished, the wife of the British Ambassador chimed in with a "Hong Kong foot, eh!" They say the Madame was peeved.

Last night the Office of War Information (owi) sponsored a dance troupe that put on Tibetan and north China folk dances. They were fascinating, especially the north China ones, filled with charm and simple artistry. The director of the group is a Chinese who was born and raised in Trinidad, studied ballet in London, and is now married here to one of the leading cartoonists. She is also highly decorative.

The music is full of strange half monotones, very haunt-

ing and reminiscent of music in the Ecuadoran highlands.
As I have travelled around the world I have realized
increasingly how much you can tell about people from their
folk music and how much they—and their music—are
formed by their surroundings. Tibet and the barren
stretches of north China may seem a long way off from the
high plateaus of the Andes. And yet both have this in
common: cold, aridity, a harshness of life, detachment from
the teeming world, and over it all a transparency of sunlight and blueness of sky that make all edges sharp. It
somehow adds up to a kind of ingrained sadness, even
melancholy. Most of the Communist leaders, who come
from warmer and more responsive climates, must find the
bleakness of Yenan hard to take. I will always vividly remember Indian villages in the uplands of Latin America.
The peons were wretchedly poor, illiterate, beaten down,
drugged or drunk, and yet from snatches of conversation
you got from them an atavistic, if unformed and incoherent,
sense of Inca and Aztec glories past and still to be reborn.

When I watch the line of coolies hauling up buckets of water hundreds upon hundreds of stone steps from the river below to our superior eminence it looks like the yoke of slavery. And so it is physically. But take the trouble to look into the eyes, to listen to their chants. Defeat? No. Resentment? Yes. Alone? No. Man? Yes.

December 8 / Last night we had some of the Communist delegates in to dinner. We had heard from pretty good sources that the Kuomintang was going to raid them today and figured that if we had them here everyone in Chungking would know it and the Government would hesitate to take action. We will probably never know if such action was intended or whether we stopped anything.

I have been very naive in my amazement at the freedom of movement they are allowed here. As they pointed out, they get hell kicked out of them everywhere except Chungking where their freedom is designed to impress foreigners with Kuomintang tolerance. The Kunming student strike is an example. The murder and brutality going on there are shocking. A lot of Kuomintang people are genuinely horrified by it, but it still goes on.

One of the great mysteries to me is why one group of people retains faith, whereas another from much the same origins and experience loses it. Over the years the Communists have absorbed an incredible amount of punishment, have been guilty of their own share of atrocities, and yet still have retained a kind of integrity, faith in their destiny, and will to prevail. By contrast, the Kuomintang has also gone through astonishing tribulations, has committed its excesses, has survived a major war with unbelievable prestige, and is now throwing everything away at a frightening rate because the revolutionary faith is gone and has been replaced by the smell of corruption and decay. It is too simple to attribute the difference to ideology. In the context of a generation ago both were equally revolutionary. There has to be another explanation, but I don't know what it is.

December 13 / I had a long talk the other day with a man
named Liu, a member of the Chinese commission which
observed the independence plebiscite held in Outer Mongolia as provided in the Sino-Soviet Treaty of last August.
It is the first time I have talked with anyone who has
actually witnessed the operation of a plebiscite under Soviet
auspices. In this one only those between the ages of 18 and
45 were permitted to vote, which eliminated all who had
grown up under the control and tutelage of the corrupt old
lamas (before Soviet intervention in the twenties), most of
whom are still illiterate and beyond the period of possible
understanding of the new order. It was an open ballot, the
first vote ever taken in the country, and staged as a holiday.
Every vote was for independence. For some reason, Liu
believes it was a useful exercise in political participation,
not a farce as many claim. Be that as it may, the Russians
are most unlikely to be disturbed by what half a dozen
Chinese observers think; and it is the mournful contemporary fate of the Mongols that no one else really cares
what happens to them.

According to Liu, each voter came up to the polling place
where he filled in a questionnaire giving his name, residence,
age, sex, his vote on the question—and his reasons for the
way he voted! Surely, it must have been the first time this
ever happened anywhere. Those who seemed to have
trouble making up their minds were helped by a representative of the Mongol People's Independence Party. Many
voters had obviously been coached since as they approached
the booths they shouted one of three slogans, "Long live
independent Mongolia," "Long live the Soviet Union," or
"Long live Stalin." Liu's party was under constant supervision with almost no opportunity for independent contacts.
Each senior member had one Mongol officer assigned to
him who never let him out of sight. This resulted in considerable loss of sleep and much physical activity for one
Mongol when one of the Chinese came down with a bad
case of dysentery at night.

They saw very few Chinese, although they estimated there might be thirty to fifty thousand there. Nor did they see many of the stores usually found around Chinese colonies. The Russians were conspicuously unnoticeable, and even at official functions there were Mongols and Chinese present, but only an occasional Russian. Liu thinks Marshal Choibalsan, dictator of Outer Mongolia, was once associated with Dr. Sun Yat-sen.

It would be nice to be clean again. What with the absence of dry cleaning, omnipresent mud, stoves that fill the place with fumes and coal dust, and plaster walls that continually shed chalk dust, you no sooner get sponged off than you are dirty again, to say nothing of what happens to clothes. Hands are the worst.

Right now the fog is so thick you can't see fifty feet. Often it is like this by day, and at night it clears off, crisp, clean, and bright-skyed. I suppose the nights are about as beautiful as any I have ever seen anywhere. When I went walking last night, there was a wonderful deep yellow, heavy-lidded moon.

December 14 / I had hoped to go on some kind of trip this weekend, having in mind a little junket to Chengtu, and then persuading the pilot to fly into Tibet and circle the Minya Konka, the fourth highest mountain in the world. It is generally considered out of bounds, I gather because the weather can turn foul in almost no time. But now we all have orders to prepare our own drafts of recommendations for General Marshall, and do it now.

Last night I was reading some new short stories by Mao Tun, a leading literary figure. Marvelous stuff as pictures of Chinese peasant life with its circumscribed outlook and complete inability to understand anything outside the family circle. Along the sides of the narrow paths that we walk all we see is change and upheaval. Yet, repeatedly I hear stories that the vast countryside where most Chinese live is largely untouched; and it is true that on the few forays I have been able to make off the usual trails I get a sense of

stepping over a line into another world. Equally frequent is
the story that the Communists, perhaps as much through
necessity as wisdom, are penetrating the villages and finding
a response where for a long time no one has cared what
happened or who thought what.

December 16 / Last night I played a little poker, which I
usually regret. Afterwards one man got a little tight and
added some details to a story whose echoes I had heard
before. Shortly before the Stilwell crisis, Roosevelt sent the
Generalissimo a very stiff note saying he was about to name
Stilwell commander in chief of all forces in China, including the Communists, which is what the latter had been
seeking in order to eliminate internal frictions. (Actually,
the Generalissimo had agreed to this most reluctantly more
than once, but always managed to find some excuse for not
implementing it.) Meanwhile Harry Hopkins had been
interesting himself in China, had come to the conclusion
the Communists did not have any direct tie to Moscow, and
therefore were no great force. So through H. H. Kung, a
brother-in-law of the Generalissimo and a powerful financial figure, he sent word to Chiang not to pay any attention
to the President. He (Harry) could be counted on to do the
right thing. The Generalissimo stiffened his position, Stilwell
was fired on his insistence, and Hurley was sent out. The
source was good, but the bit about Hopkins sounds strange.
In any event, it is typical of the local rumor factory.

It is a clear day for Chungking and the other side of the
river stands out sharply in contrast to the usual hazy outline.
In the middle of the river far below there is an island large
enough for an airport, usable at this time of year but under
water at floodtime. To land on it now, planes must snake
down through the crowding walls of the winding gorge. It
is considered desirable to make it the first time. Sampans
abound in the surrounding water and the hills on the other
bank look like mounds covered with rubble, which is what
they are. The tinkling of bells on pack mules makes a
pleasant background sound. Right now, however, the bells

are drowned out by six Kuomintang soldiers in faded yellow uniforms who are standing in a circle below here, facing each other, and for all they are worth practicing four notes on six bugles.

Tonight we are dining with some of the Communists, despite a visit a few days ago from representatives of the secret police who in their politest Chinese advised us it was considered "indiscreet" for us to see certain "nonconformist and dissident" elements. The Communists in Chungking may still walk freely here, but it is a subtle reign of terror to which they are subjected. And they never know when events may decide the Kuomintang to crack down on them.

General Marshall

General Marshall wrote his own instructions as Special Representative of the President to China, with the personal rank of Ambassador. He preferred not to be the regularly accredited Ambassador in order to avoid dissipating his time and energy with the usual routine activities which would inevitably be involved. That position remained vacant until the following summer. In a public statement on December 15, the President summarized Marshall's instructions as being American policy. He was to make available his good offices – mediation was ruled out – in helping to bring about a cessation of hostilities as the only condition in which the Chinese could work out their own political problems. The end was a "strong, united and democratic China" achieved by "peaceful, democratic methods" as soon as possible. General Marshall would not be concerned with politics, but he was authorized to tell the Generalissimo with complete frankness that "a China disunited and torn by civil strife" was not a proper place for American assistance of any kind, economic or military. To continue such assistance in the circumstances would simply be wastage. American troops were in North China for the sole purpose of disarming and evacuating Japanese troops still on Chinese soil.

Doubtless Washington and General Marshall at the time really believed that the statement of December 15 represented the limit of American intentions in China. Certainly it coincided with what public opinion would have tolerated, assuming that actions and reactions meant what they seemed to mean, since with the end of the Second World War, the American people wanted only to get the boys back home and the consumer goods again flowing from the production lines. The boys themselves fully shared these views, especially in the Pacific as they indicated when they rioted in Manila, Shanghai, and reportedly even in Tokyo. In West China the troops, including some officers, did not bother to riot; they simply left by any transportation available over the Hump and westward across

India to the troop ships at Karachi. Despite the fervent pleas of those who knew better, the Congress found the pressures for immediate demobilization irresistible. The most imposing structure of military power in history was dissipated almost overnight.

Yet, though it attempted to limit American involvement, the President's statement contained a proposal which, in retrospect at least, could have been interpreted as veiled and preliminary intervention in the internal political affairs of China. He urged the convening of a national conference of the major political groups to seek a solution for peace and unification which would give all principal political elements fair and effective representation in the Government, although he disavowed any American intention of participating in any way in the working out and implementation of the general proposition. General Marshall, who had not yet even left Washington, would within the month discover that this self-denying ordinance had contained more purity of purpose than practicality – a lesson which to this day seems to have been inadequately understood even in those high quarters where it has most needed to be understood. By implication, the political proposal contained two other relevant points.

It was quite clear, in the first place, that the United States was supporting a Nationalist Chinese coalition with the Communist Party. (To make this pill easier to swallow, President Truman had promised that as China moved toward peace and unity it could count on economic and military generosity from the United States. Even diehard elements in the Kuomintang which made little secret of their irreconcilable opposition to coalition initially found the lure irresistible.) When, after the Communist coup d'état in Czechoslovakia in 1948 had overthrown a similar coalition government, China later joined the Communist bloc, the whole course of events in China became a subject of bitter dispute in American domestic politics. It made no difference that such a coalition in China never actually materialized even though the Generalissimo, whatever his private thoughts and intentions, did not openly oppose the idea as long as Marshall was in China; it was enough that the American career men, with but very few exceptions, believed that this idea, any idea, was worth trying in the hope of avoiding civil war – and very few of them had many illusions about the prospects. Support for coalition was all the evidence needed to persuade the American people that the State Department had "sold China down the river," was "soft on Communism." This was one mistake no official would make again. Senator McCarthy and the China Lobby wrought more effectively than they knew.

The second point sprang from the first, but was more directly related to internal Chinese affairs. The United States said, in effect, that by the end of 1945 the time had come to end the political tutelage which, in the threefold program of Dr. Sun and the Kuomintang, represented the second stage preceding full democracy. Many Chinese felt this was unwarranted interference in their internal affairs – especially since the United States had disclaimed any such right or intent. For a proud people, fully aware of its great and long history and cultural tradition, and innately convinced of its superiority over all other peoples, the admission, even privately and unconsciously, that the final hope lay in foreign intervention was probably the crowning humiliation. A principal casualty was the charisma of the Generalissimo himself. As a result of his dogged insistence on improving his military posture to the exclusion of everything else, and his failure to solve the problem he had openly set for himself, his prestige plummeted at a frightful rate. He would never regain it. Typically in Chinese history, once the Mandate of Heaven begins to slip away there is no turning back.

December 17 / Chungking / The President has now at last stated American policy toward China. All Government circles rejoice in generalities over the wisdom and understanding about China which the statement shows. It is a great beginning, they say. Me, I don't know. It states a position, for what that is worth, and states it so broadly it can be stretched to cover any eventuality. It is no doubt the mark of desperation that people here, all people, simply expect too much from Marshall.

Tonight there is an almost full moon and it is clear and bright across the river. The only difficulty is that the river is giving up a delicate odor of sewage which seems to seep into every corner. When you live with the smell all the time you tend to get used to it, which is fortunate literally, and unfortunate figuratively.

In contrast to the Government, the Communists are more specific. They think Truman's statement is fine as a set of principles, but what do they mean? I suggested that granted the principle of self-rule in the provinces under their control, there is only one crucial point: the separate army. They say they will give that up if they can have adequate guarantees that once they do so the Generalissimo will not turn his army on them. What constitutes an adequate guarantee? They shrugged their shoulders. Further, they added, his mentality cannot see beyond his own appetite for power, but he does know that under unarmed conditions he lacks the offering power to keep what he has; their superior offering power and technique would win under such conditions. Again, they shrugged.

They have a new line on Manchuria to the effect that

they do not want it. All they want or have a right to are
the areas in which they fought the Japanese. Something
about that sounds phony to me and something has happened
I don't know about. At its face value, that line is straight
out of Sunday School. These characters are too tough and
have suffered too much to give up a great area.

In this house we have a wild cat, gray with yellow eyes.
It really is wild. It has to be wild to hold its own with the
rats of Chungking. Suddenly and without warning it will
start a crazy yowling, dash up through the transom, around
the room, up one wall and down another screaming, and
out the transom again. About the time I arrived here she
gave birth to kittens. One was wild too. This noon at lunch,
the kitten let out a shriek, dashed into the blazing fireplace
in the dining room, up the chimney, and that is the last we
saw of it.

December 19 / Everybody scurries around here doing not
much of anything, but with the impression of great accomplishment, and all scared to death over the impending
arrival of the great man himself. Since Washington has told
us nothing, no one knows what he is going to do, what his
instructions are, or how long he will be here. He is bringing
with him a military aide, already named "Side-Street," a
photographer, a publicity man from *Time*, an unidentified
civilian, his valet, and his cook. It begins to have the ear-
marks of anticlimax, and I have a growing feeling that the
whole thing was dreamed up under pressure and panic.
Many here now regret it, but don't know what can be done,
except to go through with it. Most are agreed that it cannot
help but impair the great reputation.

Last night the Chargé d'Affaires gave a little dinner for
all officers, presumably a sort of social briefing. Mostly it
was a continuation of the endless policy fight which this
time reached a unanimous, if uninspired, agreement by all
that for the United States there is no longer any good
answer. It is a choice now of evils only. One colleague who
knows all the big words and few of their meanings set some
kind of high-water mark when he asked me if I did not

think the poor quality of Russian propaganda was due to
"the lack of rational specificity arising from failure of
conscious mentation."

December 20 / It was a rarefied company that forgathered
last night for one of those exclusive little dinners which are
supposed to be among the glamor reasons men become
diplomats. The Russian Ambassador was there, as was the
Agent General for India whose Oxford polish and elegantly
gowned wife were deceptive. When I asked him what he
thought of Indian troops being used to kill Indonesians and
restore the Dutch he said "Quaint, eh!" For a moment I
thought he was joking, but he wasn't. The Chinese included
a Vice Minister of Foreign Affairs who tried to act as
though he were at a fraternity meeting, and the Secretary
General of the Kuomintang, who was simply noisy without
reference to anything.

The Chinese interested me the most. These men, and
others of their rank today, were at one time the flaming
revolutionaries of Asia who cut their way right and left,
passionately devoted to Dr. Sun Yat-sen and what he stood
for. Their Northern Expedition which consolidated Kuomintang control was one of the sagas of our times. Now
they are sleek, polished, well fed, worldly, cynical, reactionary, interested only in maintaining their own positions and
prerogatives. The same is true of their women, some of
whom once marched barefoot out of Canton to the north.
Now their hands are soft, and so are their heads and their
morals. To see what has happened to them is the saddest
and most depressing part of Chungking. This does not
apply to the Generalissimo. Whatever may be wrong with
him, he is not soft.

Two strange announcements have come from the White
House. One is that Wedemeyer may in his discretion move
Kuomintang troops to the north; the other is that we are
going to build a Chinese navy. This does not parse with the
policy statement, but maybe there are wheels within wheels.

Marshall stops first in Shanghai to pick up Wedemeyer.
Then he goes to Nanking to meet the Generalissimo and

Madame, where he can be shown in mass fashion how the people love their leader and revere the tomb of Dr. Sun who is buried there. Then, in the great shadow, they start their talks before coming to Chungking.

December 21 / The highlight of an OWI party last night was a phalanx of Communists who decided to have a good time. Also present was K. C. Wu, Minister of Information, and certainly among the best of the Kuomintang. The Communists decided it would be fun to get him drunk. When he refused, a couple of their burly generals pinned him down in a corner, another held his nose, and a fourth poured straight gin into him. He got drunk.

December 23 / This morning I went down to Communist headquarters to arrange for them to see Marshall this afternoon. It had been raining all night and the streets were a sea of slimy mud. Off one street, there is a long alley flanked with little restaurants, shops selling food, clothes, junk, nails, anything you can think of, and lined with thundermugs containing the night's accumulation. At the end of the alley there is a damp hall. When a knock on the door opens the peephole, you try to convince the eye to let you in. For an American there is less trouble than for a Chinese and you are ushered into a forbidding room and served hot tea to counteract the chill. Then you get down to business with a minimum of amenities.

At noon all shades and grades of brass turned up at the airport for the arrival of the American and Chinese Generalissimos. There was almost an incident when the Government police started to chase the Communist representatives off the field until we intervened. At that there was a lot of shoving around and the mood was anything but joyous. Even the weather joined in, for it was windy, cold, and raw. The clouds toiled over the hills, all shades of black and gray, lovely and ominous. People huddled in small groups, saying nothing. Marshall looked grim, unsmiling, tired; the Generalissimo was grim and unsmiling, but if he was tired it did not show. There was the usual troop review and the arrival was over. Still nothing had been said.

Marshall went at once into retirement, though his press officer answered one and all: he wanted to see everyone and had come with an open mind.

The leaders of the Kuomintang assembled make quite a study in contrasts. T. V. Soong, elegantly dressed and as hard faced as they come, a few other civilians equally hard faced and not elegantly dressed, a few generals with whom one would obviously avoid an argument if possible, but mostly they are weak faced and sycophantic. The Generalissimo dominated the group completely, even the hard faces. His personal control over them is impressive, perhaps a little frightening.

A total of over 50,000 Marines were moved to the north to help the Nationalists hold certain key spots and to assist in the repatriation of Japanese troops.

Events have created a depressing weekend. Wedemeyer's statement that he was moving more troops to the north must have been made with prior knowledge and consent and must also make a lot of people wonder just what goes

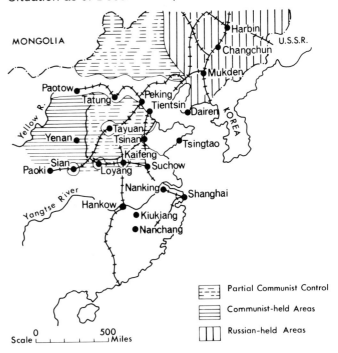

Situation as of December 25, 1945

Partial Communist Control	
Communist-held Areas	
Russian-held Areas	

on. It also gives the Generalissimo another weapon for bargaining. At the same time MacArthur announces there will be no further drastic social, economic, or political changes in Japan. I did not know they had even begun, but this is bound to alarm the Chinese. Statements from Washington are pious generalities which do not go beyond or clarify the President's directive of December 15. And from Manchuria there are press reports that the Chinese are still reluctant to take over from the Russians until conditions are more favorable to them. Presumably it is the Russians who are to provide the right conditions.

December 24 / I don't suppose any evening ever seemed less like Christmas eve than tonight. It is miserable and rainy and those who are not out drunk are just plain gloomy. And there are too many people just wandering around aimlessly. The social event of the day was an enormous cocktail party given by General Randall who commands American troops in Chungking. It was stiff and formal and full of eggnog.

All the Communists turned up at Randall's party, including Chou En-lai's wife, who has just arrived here. A political power in her own right, she is a real cutie, almost as broad as she is tall, features like a Navajo, and all the personality and intelligence in the world. The coarse blue woolen slacks she was wearing were, well, different; and she aroused Marshall's curiosity. He seems to handle the Communists well.

I had a brief conversation with Marshall this morning. He makes a good and direct impression and I got a feeling he is already a little sad about what he has got himself into. He is shorter than I thought. One thing was a shock. His hand is soft and the flesh gives; his eyes don't meet yours. I think he is a very tired and sad, perhaps sick, man. Some think he is sick because he brought his own cook and announced he would accept no public invitations while here. (Actually, he accepted a great many invitations and although somewhat formal was invariably gracious, even convivial. The cook was strictly a waste because whatever may have been the limitations of life in Chungking, food was most assuredly not among them.)

December 27 / For some reason I wake up early these days. The advantage is that the sunrises are magnificent. This morning it was an unusual shade of copper that filled all the sky and air, from a deep copper to a thin one. The whole river valley radiated it and the sampans on the river were made of copper too.

Marshall continues to make a good impression. Quiet, modest, unassuming, I suspect he is fooled by very little. So far he handles all factions with the same friendly ease, listens, and tells no one anything.

I still don't understand about the Japanese. Officially they are being disarmed, but the fact is they never seem to be. In Shanghai fifteen thousand still walk the streets with full equipment. In Nanking the high Japanese generals are bosom buddies of the Chinese. In the north tens of thousands of Japanese soldiers are used to guard railroads and warehouses and to fight Communists. If you ask what this is all about the answer is either a denial or in more candid moments a "Shhh, we don't talk about that."

December 28 / The road in front of the Embassy is getting some badly needed repairs. The paving blocks are stone boulders about ten feet by ten feet by two feet. The slope of the street up which the coolies pull them is so steep it takes twenty of them about an hour to pull one block a mile. And as they strain at it they chant something that sounds like *how bu-how, how bu-how, bu-how*—undoubtedly what it really is since it is Chinese for "how do you do," literally "good, not good." With each accent you hear their joints give. Three or four years of this labor usually kills them. And all day long the chant continues. . . . This morning the Government paper announced that the Communist army is the only obstacle now left standing between China and the fullest completion of democracy in its highest sense.

Quicksand

General Marshall was confronted with an insoluble dilemma almost immediately after his arrival in China. On the one hand, his role was limited to assistance in stopping the hostilities, and did not include involvement in political matters, beyond benevolent approval of motion toward peaceful settlement of political differences. On the other hand, he quickly discovered that there was no disposition on the part of Nationalists or Communists to separate the issues of war and politics. Both sides frequently made military action or inaction the levers for political concessions, and vice versa.[1] Either he could become involved in detailed political negotiation, or he could virtually abandon all hope of a military truce. Most reluctantly, he chose the former and step by step became further entangled, to the point where he was actually initiating political solutions and moves. Throughout, his decisions and actions had the unqualified support of the President and the Secretary of State. The diagram of ever deeper involvement in this kind of mire, without

---

1 *China White Paper*: the account of negotiations during the winter of 1946 (pp. 136 ff.) repeatedly shows the interlocking dependence of one upon the other. Marshall probably first became aware of this when he found that argument on various aspects of military reorganization was held up pending agreement on membership in the State Council, and vice versa. No one ever said this in so many words, but the conclusion was unavoidable from the actions. Considering the stakes involved and the long record of mutual distrust, the fear of taking any unnecessary risk was doubtless inevitable.

prior intent, would be repeated in numerous situations around the world as the United States felt itself compelled, for varying reasons, to become interested.

There is always, of course, a justification for the first steps, usually with the assumption that they are the terminal ones. That first steps more often than not require subsequent ones is a reflection more on judgment and perception (and in some cases, doubtless, skill at duplicity with the public) than it is on the inner logic of situations; but that is more properly the subject for a wider study than this one. China was no exception, except that here the past record possibly made the prospects look brighter. Yet many of the men with the widest and deepest experience in China felt that record to be essentially meaningless and misleading.

December 29 / Chungking / Marshall has this country in a stew by the simple expedient of not saying anything and of not reacting when he is asked a question. Even to our own people who are explaining something and who artlessly and tentatively inject an "Of course I don't yet know just what you have in mind or what your objective is and so . . . uh . . . " he graciously and unsmilingly refuses the proffered opportunity to explain by simply telling them to proceed with what they were saying. So they find themselves talking into a vacuum, which is unnerving to those who are experts in taking their cues from their superiors.

As for the Chinese, they are the unhappiest bunch yet seen; and even T. V. Soong, who has seldom been rattled, is rumored to be walking in a circle muttering to himself, "If there is any idea of threatening me. . . . " What apparently bothers Soong most is that Marshall, who was supposed to do all the initiating, is for the moment anyway just sitting quietly to see what the Chinese themselves have to offer and consequently negotiations on all subjects have stopped. Even the Chinese press, which for some time has specialized in blandly repeating that their friends were here only to help them with their enemies, the Japanese, is now boldly blustering that China is humiliated and that Marshall has come to intervene in their affairs; their advice to foreign friends, if they want to stay friends, is to stop meddling in China's internal business and get out *now.* Only the Communists seem to get a certain amount of amusement from the silence.

December 31 / Here it is the last day of the year and a sorry ending it is around this place. It is foggy, rainy, and cold, and half of the staff is down with some kind of ailment. The Navy doctor says that an assignment to Chung-king is as good as a postgraduate course in respiratory troubles. On top of that we have a number of people who went through Japanese internment, some of them women, who underwent varying degrees of rough handling. And now slowly and in strange ways the physical and psychological results of that treatment are beginning to show up. It is most noticeable in those who had a good three years of it, or in the women who had the rough rape treatment.

January 1, 1946 / For the past ten days the local foreign colony has been in a spasm of apprehension over the Government order that on the first day of the year all vehicular driving would change from right to left hand. As a topic of conversation it completely displaced the servant problem and served as a peg on which to hang all the hackneyed observations and attitudes about the utter incapacity of any Asian to manage anything more complicated than chopsticks. Faced in trepidation, the day has come and gone. One would never know that China had ever driven any other way, and the servant problem quite suddenly came back into its own this evening with renewed enthusiasm. When all else fails there are always the servants! The only casualty of the day was an American sergeant. It is expected he will survive to face a court martial. It is less certain that his jeep and the truck he ran into have much of a future, except to be cannibalized for spare parts.

Hence, it was something of a relief to have been invited to join some Chinese students and older intellectuals, who have neither servants nor the problems arising therefrom, in a sort of Chinese Beaux Arts. It was fun and different. They all had a good time and did it without liquor which they could not have afforded anyway. The entertainment included an elaborate array of parlor games of such subtle simplicity I would not begin to repeat them without elaborate coaching. Naturally much of the subtlety was political and rather merciless. Given the nature of the group I would have expected it to be directed largely against the Government. But, no, everyone got his share, including themselves. I am finding that the Chinese dearly love to make someone look ridiculous, and if you cannot laugh at yourself along with the others, you are considered to be very cloddish indeed. The Chinese have this kind of inner personal security and integrity more than any other people I have ever known.

A foreign official's first exposure to the Chinese sense of the ridiculous comes when he is given a Chinese name by the Foreign Office upon his arrival. The Chinese name comes as close in sound as possible to the foreign surname. Since there are usually several alternatives, the one which sounds the silliest is chosen for the unsuspecting victim. Mine translates back into English as Plum Blossom Your Jade, which is always good for a laugh. Marshall's name comes out as a horse, which is most appropriate for a warrior, but has the added twist of referring to the back end of the horse. The General, whose sense of humor is not among his most highly developed qualities, was not amused, and it took some argument to get him to be at least philosophical about it.

The group included the left wing of the local intellectual world, which means the Government sees to it they are half starved most of the time. One interesting man was Kuo Mo-jo, who has an international reputation as an archeologist, linguist, novelist, and revolutionary political leader, and has managed to escape with his life by the skin of his teeth on several occasions. I suppose his connection with the Hankow Government, the extreme left wing of the Kuomintang in the 1920s, represents about the most conservative thing he has ever done. He looked me in the eye, owlish deadpan, and said, "I am non-political," and put another cake in his mouth.

Kuo Mo-jo is now one of the top intellectual bosses of Communist China, unless the Cultural Revolution has been his undoing.

January 2 / The Chinese opera last night was an extraordinary performance and like nothing else I have ever seen. All parts are taken by men, and the costumes are unbelievably gorgeous and beautiful, always in the old style since all the operas are several hundred years old. The only scenery is a plain backdrop, one table and two chairs. All else is represented symbolically in the action—Pyramus and Thisbe and the peekhole. A couple of stagehands loitered around on the stage to move the chairs, meanwhile smoking cigarettes, talking, eating oranges, or picking their noses. To one side there was a group of noisy children; people wandered on and off the stage and no one paid any attention to it. The audience behaved as though it were at a county fair, eating, talking, walking around, watching for a while, going out, coming back. The lights were out at one point and the opera went on while electricians worked on the stage and competed with the actors in making noise. I suppose the Elizabethan stage was something like that—except the electric lights.

In the opera itself all acting, all gestures, everything is completely stylized and conventional—exactly what it has been for hundreds of years. The singing is weird in sing-song falsetto voices, all meaning something according to a pattern, and with the accompaniment of screaming Chinese violins, small wooden drums, and brass cymbals. Although I think it would get tiresome after a while to an unattuned western ear, it is fascinating in small doses. On first hearing, all the music sounds very much alike. Each performance lasts five to eight hours, so it does not seem to matter much when you come in or go out.

January 3 / Matters are in a quiet stage now. All relations and contacts and negotiations between us and the Chinese have been frozen and Marshall has the authority to start what he wants when he feels like it. It is giving some of the Chinese the creeps because he will not say anything about anything. He just sits and listens, letting them sweat it out. Proposals have been made on both sides for the cessation of hostilities as the prerequisite for anything else. This is Marshall's primary objective. After that I think he intends to let them fight out the political questions themselves. I

have some mental reservations about this, but maybe it will
work. I think there is also something to the idea that some
part of the answer may lie in Washington-Moscow understandings, not all in Chungking and Yenan. Chou En-lai
may have had some version of this idea in mind the other
day when he became impatient and said he wished people
in the United States would stop talking about the Party
members in Yenan as though they were agrarian democrats: "You must realize we are not that; we are Communists and Marxists with all that means now and for the
future." It rocked some people back on their heels, but
Chou is usually franker than most Chinese. Communist confidence is in interesting contrast to the real uneasiness of the
Kuomintang.

From the way the rats are operating through the walls of
this building tonight one could easily get the idea that all
military operations in the country were taking place here.

Shadow boxing

The distrust and distaste of the Generalissimo for the Communists went back to
his early days. From the beginning of his career he had been in an excellent
position to observe how they had used membership in the Kuomintang to insinuate
themselves into key positions with the intent of eventually taking full control. After
Chiang had assumed leadership of the Kuomintang and became determined to
eliminate all opposition, he initiated the massacres of 1927 which drove the remaining Communists into the wilderness of Kiangsi and the later "bandit suppression
campaigns" which sent them on the Long March to Yenan.

It was only to save his life when he was kidnapped at Sian in December 1936
that he agreed to halt the military effort against them and cooperate with all
factions in trying to turn back the Japanese. He kept the bargain more rather
than less, although from the standpoint of Western Machiavellian eyes there was
certainly nothing to have prevented him from renewing the assault once he was
released and was back at his own headquarters. It may have been nothing more
than expedience to keep the bargain once the full-scale Japanese invasion was
launched in July 1937 and later in 1943 when the United States made known its
support for coalition. His own words further compromised his previous stand.

A draft constitution had been announced by the National Government as far
back as May 5, 1936. The National Assembly, scheduled for late 1937, was

repeatedly postponed because of the war with Japan, but preparations for it continued.[1] At a meeting of the Kuomintang Central Executive Committee in September 1943, the Generalissimo had stated that when representative institutions
were established the Kuomintang would lose all exclusive privileges and all other
parties would be equal to it in rights and freedoms. He added, " . . . I am of the
opinion that first of all we should clearly recognize that the Chinese Communist
problem is a purely political problem and should be solved by political means."[2]

The Central Executive Committee then passed a resolution which announced
that the Government would convene a National Assembly to adopt and promul-
gate a constitution within one year after the end of the war. The Generalissimo
named a committee, which included Communist representatives, to lay the groundwork for constitutional government. Communist and Nationalist representatives
did, in fact, meet in Sian during May 1944, and the negotiations were later moved
to the capital at Chungking.

When Ambassador Hurley returned to Chungking from Yenan in July 1945 he
brought with him a new set of proposals from the Communists, most of which he
had drafted himself. Among them was one for a Political Consultative Conference,
to be composed of representatives of the Government, the Communists, and the
minor parties, most of which were grouped within the Democratic League that
came to be known as the middle or moderate force. Its purpose was the negotiation
of a new government – in other words, a coalition. The Government did not accept
this proposal until just after Hurley left for Washington.[3] Convening of the PCC
was repeatedly postponed as hostilities spread throughout the fall and early winter.

The discussions were summarized in a statement released in Chungking on
October 11, 1945. They showed agreement on general principles such as democracy, the equality of parties, and the need for a National Assembly and a new
constitution, and they set forth the views of both parties on these problems. But it
was also clear that there was little agreement on details or how the general was to
become specific; most particularly there was wide divergence as to control and
administration of areas then under Communist control.[4]

The important point was that questions which had not been settled by the conversations should be referred to the Political Consultative Conference. It was on
this basis that President Truman in his December 15 statement gave American
support for a national conference of all parties to solve the problems politically.
The announcement by the Generalissimo on December 31 that the PCC would
convene in Chungking on January 10, 1946, was probably decisive in convincing
General Marshall, who until then had done little except listen to what others had

1 *China White Paper*, pp. 52–54.
2 *Ibid.*, p. 54.
3 *Ibid.*, pp. 107–10.
4 *Ibid.*, pp. 110–12. The Nationalists had proposed that agreement be reached within one
month as to where Communist troops were to be stationed, especially with reference to
certain railroads. Later the Government merely informed the Embassy that Communist
counterproposals were unsatisfactory.

to say, to accept the public positions of both sides at face value, and hence the calculated risk of his own and American involvement in non-military matters.[5] The October 11 statement had showed how inextricably the Nationalists and the Communists both considered military and political matters to be intertwined. Although he probably did not realize it then, General Marshall had crossed his Chinese Rubicon, and both Nationalists and Communists now had a foreign devil on whom to blame any failures.

Shortly after the announcement of the convening of the PCC, the Generalissimo, on the insistence of Marshall that the PCC not meet until a ceasefire had been arranged, proposed a Committee of Three to discuss the cessation of hostilities and immediately related matters. It was composed of one representative each of the Government and the Communists, with General Marshall as chairman. Marshall realized that the agreements reached at Yalta between the United States, the Soviet Union, and Great Britain, and the subsequent Sino-Soviet Treaty, specifically recognized the Republic of China as the supreme authority in all China – and that this included Manchuria. Hence, on January 4 he informed Chou En-lai, who represented the Communists on the Committee of Three, that the United States was committed to the movement of Nationalist troops to Manchuria. Chou En-lai accepted this statement as being entirely in accord with the Sino-Soviet Treaty and other agreements.

Nevertheless, when the Committee held its first formal meeting on January 7, the basic distrust between the two protagonists immediately became apparent. The Government was convinced that the Soviet Union had obstructed its efforts to assume control over Manchuria, despite the Sino-Soviet Treaty, and that the Chinese Communists were only Soviet tools. The Communists believed the real Kuomintang objective was their destruction, since the Generalissimo was unwilling to permit their participation in the Government until they had disbanded their armed forces, whereas they were convinced that to do so without acceptable guarantees of their legal political status would only seal their doom.

5 The December 27, 1945 communiqué of the Foreign Ministers Meeting in Moscow – the United Kingdom, the United States, and the Soviet Union – insofar as it dealt with China was largely concerned with withdrawals of foreign troops, but it contains the following sentence: "They reaffirmed their adherence to the policy of noninterference in the internal affairs of China." Although we did not know it at the time, this sentence seems first to have been proposed by the Russians.

January 4 / Chungking / Somewhat to my surprise the Communists have accepted the proposals for a Committee of Three unconditionally, which is not unbright since it leaves the next move up to the Kuomintang. They even came and told us about it before they told the Kuomintang. I have a sneaking suspicion, which I cannot prove, that the offer was made with the expectation it would be turned down or at least so qualified as to prolong negotiations and in the end befog the issue. The Government seems confused as to what to do next except the obvious and unpalatable task of going through with it. Meanwhile I think we continue to be in an uncertain and precarious position. It may be a temporary expedient, but nonetheless worth something.

A man from the Office of Strategic Services has just come down from Kalgan in the north with tales of what has happened to the Japanese puppets. In some parts, the Communists permitted the local populace to stone them to death. In others, they have arrested them, given them heated quarters, private rooms, personal servants, and the best food around. Just what this is all about is obscure.

January 5 / It turned out to be quite a night after all. The rats did not give up their close-order drilling in the walls until near dawn. Prior to that one of our military colleagues wandered in stewed to the gills from a Chinese dinner. He was then sick in the urinal and passed out in a tub half full of water. He will live. Those who rescued him did not notice that the can was stopped up, but with the water valve broken and wide open. It must have been around three that the Chungking Water Works decided to give us the strongest water pressure we have had since I have been here. The household also failed to notice this until the water level in the house passed the six-inch level and the cat protested vociferously.

It is very much like spring today. Since I have had the weekend duty I have spent most of the time watching it from a distance. I did, however, get out for a couple of hours into the nearby terraces and rice paddies. The countryside here, and I guess most of the province, is like a huge piece of paper that had been crumpled in the hand of God, with alternating ridges, valleys, and pockets in no discernible pattern. As a road building problem it is staggering, which no doubt accounts for the absence of roads and the prevalence of paths suitable only for foot or sedan chair traffic. The paths which wander through the terraces and paddies are paved with enormous flagstones, worn and closely fitted by the endless and innumerable footsteps of peasants over the centuries.

The stones also tend to be slippery from the high moisture in this climate. The slipperiness would be of little more interest than as a warning to watch your step except that the peasants in this province collect their nightsoil in huge, wide-mouthed jars which are buried for convenience' sake next to the paths and with their mouths flush with the surface of the stones. Naturally, tales are legion of what happens after an errant footstep by a foreigner, and they are doubtless embroidered in the retelling. But it can happen, as I so well remember from a chance personal and careless boyhood encounter with a recently abandoned and insufficiently covered pit privy in a YMCA camp. Sometimes it is necessary to keep reminding oneself that as rich as the soil on the terraces is, it is fortunately made ever richer for the swarming millions of Szechuan by the return to it of some part of that which has been taken out. After all, no one ever heard of a Chinese being so out of tune with the rhythm of nature as to fall into a honey bucket.

January 6 / Someone named Wang Hsien, claiming to be the representative of CNNRA (Chinese counterpart of UNRRA) for the province of Shansi, called on me this morning. I am not quite sure what he was after except to sell me a bill of goods on old Marshal Yen Hsi-shan whose private secretary he had been for fifteen years. He sounded as though he still had the connection or was trying to get it back through delivering good works for the Marshal. Shansi adjoins the main Communist area.

Yen was one of the more powerful and colorful warlords before the war who was never really brought under Kuomintang control.

He said conditions in Shansi are bad. Before the war the Marshal had made it a model province (obviously a matter of opinion in view of his personal interest in poppy culture for opium at the expense of food crops), but the Communists had ruined it and the people now preferred the Japanese. Wang thought Communism had much to commend it, but in actual practice it just did not work. He referred to the wide range of the Marshal's activities and connections. A decade ago he had tried an arrangement with the Communists, but had been doublecrossed by them. He tried the same with the Japanese, but nothing came of it. Actually he had always maintained ties with the Kuomintang. None of this means he has any sympathy for any particular group; he is just looking out for himself. Right now he is in trouble because his troops, some one hundred thousand, are ill-equipped and poorly trained. Two-thirds of them have already deserted to the Communists.

The Committee of Three meets informally today in an effort to stop hostilities so the PCC can still meet on January 10, since this depends on a ceasefire after which the political problems can slowly be worked out. Negotiations last fall reached an impasse over the Communist demand that they be able to appoint the governors in provinces under their control, and their opposition to the Kuomintang insistence that all autonomous armies be merged into one national force. The Kuomintang was reluctant about the first and tentatively agreed to allow the Communists twenty separate divisions. It seems conceivable the Government will yet yield on the civil administrative point if the Communists will concede the army argument. The Communists might even accept on the theory they can take care of themselves politically if they can secure adequate guarantees against annihilation by Government troops. Will—or even can— the Kuomintang give such a guarantee? If the PCC is again deadlocked, then solution may only be possible on the Washington-Moscow level with appropriate pressures elsewhere. Chungking must realize that abandonment by Washington at best can only mean stalemate which would in effect mean partition and the eventual fall of the Generalissimo for failure to accomplish his basic objective, namely unification. And Yenan is quietly bitter at the absence of real Russian support, although I personally cannot conceive that Moscow would not do something if they were in real danger of annihilation—which at the moment they are not.

Manchuria is another tough problem. Until recently the indications were that the Russians would pull out on schedule, but only after having permitted the Communists to infiltrate and secure key positions before Government forces could do anything about it. Now there is a change. The Communists speak openly of having no objections to the occupation of Manchuria by the Government as long as civil administrators are chosen by free elections. I do not know what has caused this change. On top of this, there is continuing acrimony over Japanese disarmament or lack of it, the presence of American troops, student agitation, especially in Kunming which is alienating a serious amount of liberal sympathy to the Communists, and a tribal rebellion in Sinkiang.

January 7 / I still don't see any pattern shaping up or any reason for optimism. The report of a truce was premature. The parties did agree in principle, but the haggling on details continues. The Russians tossed in another problem by suddenly and for unknown reasons evacuating Jehol, which both sides are now scrambling to occupy. Marshall still operates on his own and the Embassy is largely in the dark as to what he is thinking or doing.

The only cheerful note of the day is that Mr. Fong Chuck, employed by this Embassy, has received a Christmas present from his cousin in the States, Mr. Dung Duck!

January 9 / Last night the Russian Ambassador gave a dinner for Marshall to which he invited only his own staff and Americans, instead of the usual row of brass. It got off to an embarrassing start when Marshall was an hour late because of another mediation meeting. But despite that, it was an informal and cordial affair with lots of Russian vodka and Caucasian wines. At such affairs Marshall is friendly and gossipy and anecdotal. Unfortunately some of his stories are colloquial, such as the one about union suits and red flannel underwear, which means something only to Americans. I get the growing impression of a man who is a

really great soldier and a great man in the sense of being
truly humble and unimpressed with himself, but whose
outlook and experience have the limitations of a professional soldier. He learns fast, but has little sense of history
as a starting point. His conversation never goes beyond the
scope of his experience; he sees a movie every night he is
home, and reads cheap fiction endlessly. I don't yet know
about his judgment of men. He reminisces well about his
early days in the Philippines; he is fascinating on the technical advances in teaching which came out of the war
experience. He is honest and open when he talks about the
atomic bomb, and even said we only had two at the time of
Hiroshima. He minimizes the importance of the bomb and
said that some scientists who have been talking publicly
about the need for controlling it have had to be silenced by
threat of arrest since they did not know what they were
talking about.

The ceasefire

On January 10, the Committee of Three completed a ceasefire arrangement.
Under this, the Generalissimo and Chairman Mao Tse-tung at once issued orders
to their armed forces to stop hostilities and to halt all troop movements. The agreement permitted two exceptions: Nationalist movements south of the Yangtze River
in connection with the reorganization of their armies – and Nationalist troop
movements into Manchuria. In addition, all destruction of and interference with
lines of communication were to stop at once. The orders became effective at midnight January 13.

The agreement also contained another and unique provision. It established
what was to be known as the Executive Headquarters at Peiping, which was to
supervise the implementation of the ceasefire. There were three Commissioners:
one Nationalist, one Communist, one American, and every supervisory team sent
to the field (and there were hundreds of them) was to be similarly composed.
Necessary instructions and orders were to be unanimous and to be issued in the
name of the President of the Republic of China. It was specifically stipulated
that the American role was exclusively to help the Chinese members implement
the ceasefire. As a field operation, the performance of the Executive Headquarters
was magnificently effective and uniformly harmonious. It is not too much to

speculate that this performance accurately reflected what the mass of Chinese wanted most and that it could have kept the peace – if only the captains and the kings had been similarly motivated. One cannot help but remember a comment by President Eisenhower, in one of his rare flashes of insight, to the effect that the people of the world so desperately want peace that it was high time the leaders stand aside and let them have it.

The ceasefire agreement coincided with the opening of the PCC which met in Chungking from January 10 to 31, 1946, and was composed of representatives of the Kuomintang, the Communist Party, the Democratic League (a loose federation of liberal and left-wing non-Communist groups – sometimes hopefully referred to as the "Third Force in China"), and the Youth Party, and distinguished non-party delegates. It was a consultative body only, since all its decisions were subject to approval by the central committees or governing bodies of the component parties; but there was, at least implicitly, a moral obligation by the parties to accept the decisions.

At the opening session, the Generalissimo announced that the Government would immediately grant certain fundamental democratic rights: freedom of speech, assembly, and association; equal legal status for all political parties; popular elections; and the release of political prisoners. The resolutions of the PCC were announced on January 31 and fell into five main categories: (1) Government Organization; (2) Program for Peaceful National Reconstruction; (3) Military Problems; (4) Agreement on the National Assembly; and (5) The 1936 Draft Constitution.[1]

As with almost all Kuomintang-Communist negotiations, the points of real interest in the PCC resolutions were limited in number, and agreement was fuzzy or left for future discussions. It was agreed that the National Assembly would meet on May 5, 1946, to adopt a constitution which was to be drafted by a new Constitution Draft Committee. The Committee would revise the 1936 Draft Constitution in accordance with the principles agreed upon by the PCC. Pending the National Assembly action, the Kuomintang would revise the organic law of the National Government to make the State Council the supreme organ of the Government until a new constitution had been adopted. The Council was to have forty members, chosen by the Generalissimo, half Kuomintang and half non-Kuomintang. The specific allotment, however, of non-Kuomintang seats was to be decided separately and after the adjournment of the PCC. The resolutions empowered the President to veto any decisions of the Council, and his veto could be overridden by a three-fifths vote of the Council. General resolutions on legislative principles and military and fiscal matters required only a majority vote, but administrative policy would require a two-thirds vote, although a majority vote would be sufficient to decide whether a proposed action did indeed involve administrative policy.[2] Superficially, the voting procedure seems unduly com-

1 *China White Paper*, p. 139.
2 *Ibid.*, p. 140.

plicated, quibbling, and obscure; in reality, it was all-important and the main source of trouble.

Under the Program for Peaceful National Reconstruction, the equality and legality of all political parties was recognized, and all were pledged to accept the national leadership of President Chiang Kai-shek. But the Program also stipulated the maintenance of the status quo in liberated areas where government was in dispute until the State Council had been reorganized, and then the Council would decide in which group control rested. Eventual control over an area in dispute would obviously be a matter of administrative policy. The Communists had already let it be known that they would insist on at least fourteen seats in the Council for themselves and their friendly nominees; the Generalissimo was just as determined that they would have fewer seats. The sticky point was that with fourteen seats the Communists could prevent a Kuomintang-dominated State Council from awarding an area in dispute to the Government. Actually, since all recognized the Republic of China as the legal government of the whole country, there was really no reason why the Kuomintang, at least theoretically, could not declare even an area clearly under de facto Communist control to be in dispute and call on the State Council for decision. With one vote less than they were demanding, the Communists would be lost. On the control of that one vote the whole political process would eventually founder.

Finally, the resolutions established a "Three-Man Military Commission" to work out practical means for the reorganization of the Communist armies as soon as possible. Once both Nationalist and Communist armies had been reorganized, they would then again be reorganized into a single army of 50 or 60 divisions, to be entirely apart from and free of political activities.

In his final remarks to the PCC the Generalissimo said: "I wish to declare first on behalf of the Government that they [the resolutions] will be fully respected and carried out as soon as the prescribed procedures have been completed. I pledge at the same time that I will uphold this program faithfully and will also see to it that all the military and civil subordinates follow it strictly. From now on, I will, whether in the Government or out of it, faithfully and resolutely observe, as a citizen should, all the decisions of this Conference."[3] All other participant parties also issued equally categorical statements of support. Actually, all was not quite as unanimous as this. There were powerful right wing cliques in the Kuomintang which made it just as clear, if somewhat more obliquely at the moment, that they in no sense felt bound by the pledges of their Party and Government leader.

General Marshall did not participate in any of the actual discussions of the PCC in any way beyond drafting a brief act, at the request of the Generalissimo, which the Government might wish to use in promulgating the decisions of the PCC.[4] He did agree to be the third member, as advisor, of the Three-Man Military Commission for the reorganization of the Nationalist and Communist armies.

3 *Ibid.*, p. 138.
4 *Ibid.*, p. 139.

January 10 / Chungking / The military truce has been
signed, to be effective at midnight January 13. In addition
to a general ceasefire order, it specifically recognizes the
right of Nationalist troops to move into Manchuria as well
as the American commitment to assist the movement. The
unique feature of the agreement is the establishment of an
Executive Headquarters in Peiping to implement it. There
are to be three commissioners representing the Government,
the Communists, and the United States, with the American
to be chairman. It is to have as many three-man teams,
of the same composition, as needed to supervise the ceasefire in the field.

The PCC has now been able to convene at once. If this does not mean anything else, at least it will halt the killing for a while. Now the ancient battle of words can start on the political questions, and possibly go on forever. There should be rejoicing and relief over this, but instead there is only an uneasy silence. If the people at large are aware of what has happened, they give no evidence of it or are unimpressed. Those who do know have little to say.

January 12 / Implementation of the truce is causing enormous confusion, and the long awaited PCC is already bogged down in a swamp of words. The Kuomintang is obviously worried because Marshall has been using a ballbat on them—that is the only way he got them to agree to the truce, the turning point having been their right to occupy Jehol which they were demanding and he was refusing. They know that if we pull out the props they are finished. The Communists prefer political to military war since they are quite confident they can win it in time. Hence they are cautiously pleased with the truce and prepared to sit down for a year of argument.

Yesterday the Communist newspaper *Hsin Hua Jih Pao* celebrated its eighth anniversary with a party out in the hills. It was an expansive affair with lunch served al fresco and washed down with baigar, a foul concoction made of gaoliang (a grain sorghum grown especially in Manchuria) which can blow off the top of your head and damn near did mine since I did not know what it was and was beguiled into a bottoms up toast of a tumblerful of it under the mistaken impression it was a light wine. After lunch there was a presentation of yangko dances, the native north China folk dances. They are marvelous, full of life and originality and little morals designed to appeal to the peasants. The original moral themes have been altered to give them a political content. The music was beaten out on huge hogsheads covered with skins and producing a kind of rhythm that was new to me and very infectious. The people are rough and untutored, but they do convey a

sense of men who know what they want and are unafraid of
anything. It is a striking contrast to the rest of Chungking.

Lao Shaw, whose latest novel was published in the States
as *Rickshaw Boy*, is much amazed at its success, particularly since he did not authorize the American version, which
has an opposite ending from the one he wrote, doesn't have
the faintest idea who translated it, knows nothing of who
sold it to a publisher, and has never gotten a nickel from
the proceeds. He is shortly going to the States as a cultural
relations guest of the State Department and will doubtless
be lionized for it. But these things don't seem to bother the
Chinese much. There is now an art exhibit here in which
all the pictures are signed by one man who everybody knows
never painted in his life and furthermore is blind.

January 13 / This has been quite a day, even if it is Sunday,
a day which around here bids fair to lose any special meaning. Overnight the military commission has stripped us
of personnel and until the new people arrive life will be
complicated. The PCC is going full blast using all the epithets
in everyone's vocabulary and for us the really hard work
is just beginning. From sketchy news reports the truce
announcement seems to have made big headlines at home,
and I will bet that shortly it will disappear as quickly as it
appeared, on the assumption that the troubles of China
have all been solved. [*It did.*]

January 14 / It has become very fashionable here to entertain Russians, and no party is complete without at least
two. Yesterday Marshall asked me who some of them are,
since he sees them wherever he goes. He said that every
time he talks with one he gets a little lecture on the true
meaning of democracy and he considers this impudent. The
way he said it left no doubt he is annoyed and more suspicious of them than I had previously gathered.

January 15 / I used to think that Latin Americans wrote
more letters than anyone else in the world. I was wrong.
The Chinese write more to generals and an impressive

amount of the time of us all is spent answering them. I suppose the volume is a pretty good indication of how desperately these people want peace. Some come from enchanting organizations. In today's batch there was one from the Anti-Mosquito Incense Burners Association and another from the Chungking Wharfside Orange Brokers Protective Guild.

Last night one of our jeeps was stolen; by noon today pieces of it were showing up in stores all over town. You think more than once before doing anything about such incidents. Shortly after I arrived here we found that the police who guard the Embassy were stealing our gasoline. Someone notified the Foreign Office. That night every one of them was shot. Some time ago one of our Chinese press monitors was arrested on unspecified charges. Despite all our efforts, he was not returned to us until two days ago. He was dead, and what had happened to him first was appalling. I guess we have to assume all our Chinese employees report to someone else or face the same fate.

January 18 / It has been a hectic week since it is my turn to do the political briefing of Marshall. This involved scrounging around in odd corners for information and eating too many Chinese meals which are hard on my guts that are still aching from a bout with the Yangtze Rapids. Chinese feast food is the most wonderful food in the world, but too rich for a steady diet. Naturally, even Chinese who can afford it have sense enough to eat it only on special occasions.

January 19 / The pcc still moves in a sea of verbiage. The open meetings are for the public benefit, the closed committee meetings are only slightly less vague, and the real business is done privately by a few. It does look now as though an at least superficial arrangement will be reached which may prevent new fighting for a while. This will give both sides time for breath and a chance to look around for what opportunities time will bring.

Meanwhile there are growing signs of violence. Each

Tai Li was head of the highly efficient and dreaded Kuomintang Bureau of Investigations and Statistics one of whose primary functions was suppression of political activities to which the Government objected.

night since the start of the PCC there have been big mass meetings to discuss the issues publicly. And at each one, groups of Tai Li police have heckled and thrown stones a little more than at the preceding one. The subject of political prisoners is getting particularly hot. Last Monday the Government promised to release them all in seven days, but there are repeated stories that many are being killed. Malaria, of which there is plenty here, is given as the cause of death. Now there are rumors of big trouble for Sunday night. The Russians are the only people here who are enjoying the troubles, and they are increasingly sarcastic about our difficulties.

I had dinner this evening with a Dr. Tao, a most interesting man. He is mild, cordial, well educated, and a professor in the People's University which exists God only knows how. He is also Director of the Yu Tsai School out in the countryside. The students are mainly in their late teens and study all sorts of things, but mainly folk art and politics. In their spare time they make the rounds of the villages in the province teaching the peasants reading, writing, music, dancing, hygiene, agriculture—and politics. It is a brave thing to do and no one quite understands how they get away with it. Tao is ostensibly connected with the Democratic League, but while I can't prove it I am almost certain he has connections far, far to the left of that.

January 21 / Marshall got back this afternoon from a short trip to Shanghai and will start asking questions in the morning. The nine public sessions of the PCC are finished and there is a subdued atmosphere around town. Now that the oratory has stopped the hard committee work is well under way over the five subjects on which the public talky-talk centered without producing any resolutions or doing much more than reveal how far apart all concerned really are, and without introducing anything not already known. So far there is no progress in the committees, as no one will budge, or is likely to, without a heavy hand from the outside.

There is great secrecy about the proceedings and any reports are to a degree speculative. Democratic League people are inclined to be the most pessimistic and to feel Government insistence on its own program is the great obstacle to compromise. The Communists are noncommittal beyond expressing their hope for agreement despite the distance between the respective positions. Government people, curiously enough, have nothing to say. Although the committees on the Assembly and the constitution have only started, reorganization looms as the big hurdle because the Government so far refuses to give the opposition any positions in the Yuan.

In accordance with Dr. Sun's plan, the Nationalist Government had and has five branches, a combination of traditional Chinese and western systems, called Yuan, the functions of which are indicated by their names: Executive, Legislative, Judicial, Examination (to admit persons to government service, traditionally very important under the old scholar-gentry control of public affairs), and Control (review of government activities). In practice, Examination and Control have played no role of significance, and in view of the radical depar - ture from imperial practice, the Generalissimo gets what he wants.

The Society for the Promotion of the Political Consultative Conference which was organized by local cultural and Democratic League people to stimulate public discussion of the issues has been attracting increasing attendance. The first meeting drew only some sixty people, the next one a thousand, then two thousand, and disturbances have increased with the crowd. The number of secret police has also increased, as has the throwing of cobblestones. Each time more people have been seriously injured, although there have been no deaths as yet.

The deadline on the promise of the Government to release all political prisoners except traitors (meaning collaborators with the Japanese) within seven days has passed with no demonstrations, no prisoners freed, no word from the Government, no nothing except a query from the Communists wanting to know what we proposed to do about it. The Communists continue to charge that the Government is killing off prisoners whom it does not want to release—an assertion that could very well be true but is not yet susceptible of proof. For a few days it was rumored that a large demonstration scheduled for yesterday would welcome back the prisoners or protest against Government violation of its word, as the situation might indicate. Nothing happened. Government and Communist papers also carry daily stories in great detail charging that the other side is violating the military truce and that hostilities still continue on all fronts. In private conversation yesterday, however, one of the Communists said that implementation of the truce is proceeding satisfactorily and that as far as he knew there was no fighting in any area thus far accessible. The American newsmen tell me they have instructions from home to cut their reporting to an absolute minimum.

January 23 / This afternoon the local labor leaders gave a tea for someone—all the unions being controlled by the Kuomintang. I have never seen a group that looked less like labor leaders and more like Chicago ward politicians; nor did their conversation indicate much concern for or knowledge about labor. Mostly they divided their time between eating pastries and reading newspapers. But I did learn what happened to all the money the International Labor Organization gave them. It was used to build a new clubhouse for officials.

As for local politics, the rumors are suddenly encouraging about a new agreement to solve everything. I wonder how long any agreement would survive Marshall's departure. Anyway, the first signs of spring are showing today and that is worth a lot.

My new domicile has two great advantages. One, the coffee is always hot and strong. Two, there is no continual coal gas in the air as in the place where I lived before because here we don't use that kind of stove. Instead we use what the Chinese use, something called a hopan, which is a wooden frame, and a circular iron pan on top of that in which charcoal burns. It heats a room in five minutes and since the charcoal is almost pure carbon, it gives off heat and light. Sitting in the middle of the room, it makes an inviting picture.

January 26 / Shortly after Marshall arrived the Generalissimo's son, Chiang Ching-kuo, made a sudden trip to Moscow. We have just learned what that was all about. He went to ask the Russians to mediate in China and was turned down. Before the trip he asked Marshall what he thought of it, though I do not know if at the time Marshall was told the real reason for it.

Chungking in a sense is a dying city. Not that the population is decreasing, for as fast as the people move east and north, others from the west move in. But the foreign group is drifting away day by day, as are the universities, the intellectuals, the Government, and those we know and work with. Slowly the city drops back into the provincialism and insularity of centuries past. It is like watching the recreation of an ancient order, but with an overtone of uneasiness and self-consciousness about it. It seems that in this world where there is not death there is confusion.

January 29 / Last night the press officer of the Soviet Embassy, who is a very bright guy, talked about Mongolia. He says an experiment is being tested there on the orthodox Marxist thesis that society moves from feudalism to capitalism to imperialism to socialism. The experiment is to see whether it is possible to move directly from feudalism into socialism. If successful, the implications are obvious, especially for China.

He has little more to say about China, beyond alleging a strong and growing anti-Soviet feeling among American troops here which he thinks is stimulated by directives from above. He added that if this continues the Russians might against their will be forced to make mistakes of their own. Just what he meant by this was not clear.

January 30 / There is little reliable evidence on progress in the PCC committee work, but it seems to be proceeding satisfactorily on military affairs, the draft constitution, and the National Assembly. Government reorganization is still the big problem, with innumerable proposals and counter proposals, none of which is uniformly acceptable, but step by step they are moving closer to some sort of balance between the Government and the Communists. On January

26 Chou En-lai told the Government he would have to
go to Yenan for further instructions. The Generalissimo
thought it inadvisable because it would delay the negotiations, but apparently he changed his mind since Chou
went and returned this morning.

The most recent demonstration was Government inspired.
Five thousand students were brought in from out of town
and received their instructions and slogans from the Ministry of Information. The slogans, a mixed bag, called for
the return of Hong Kong, Kowloon, and Macao, the recall
of the French Consul in Shanghai, and support for the
compromise work of the PCC. It quickly got out of hand
as the number of demonstrators increased to ten thousand
and other slogans appeared calling for the release of political prisoners, liberalization of the Government, assurance
of civil liberties, and elimination of corruption in the
Kuomintang. It remained orderly, however, and proceeded
to National Government Headquarters where it was addressed by leaders of all factions, who claimed to support
the objectives of the students. It then proceeded to the
British and French Embassies. The British were much
upset by the affair, feeling it a slight to British dignity,
and at least one Embassy officer asked the demonstrators
why they did not include Dairen (the Russian naval base
in Manchuria agreed upon at Yalta and in the Sino-Soviet
Treaty of 1945) in their demands.

The same day and during an afternoon session of the
PCC, ten policemen entered the house of a Democratic
League delegate and searched the place thoroughly, including his papers. They then went to another League house
and Communist headquarters to do the same. The League
subsequently made an impassioned plea to the PCC demanding guarantees of civil liberties and personal security for
all delegates. Later at night the League informed the
Government that unless these guarantees were given along
with some explanation of the failure to implement the
Generalissimo's January 10 assurances on civil liberties

the League would no longer participate in the PCC. The
following day they were, in fact, absent. That night the
Kuomintang sent a letter on behalf of the Generalissimo
which seemingly satisfied them because they were back
the next day. The Kuomintang explanation is that it was
all part of a routine annual search prior to Chinese New
Year in order to place undesirable citizens under arrest. It
claims the search was especially strict this year since
numerous suspicious looking people have been hanging
around and unauthorized ones including, they say, two
sons of General Sheng Shih-ts'ai, ex-warlord of Sinkiang,
have been found carrying weapons. The letter further said
that the National Defense Council will shortly reach a
decision on the relaxation of wartime civil liberties limitations to be announced at the next session of the PCC. And
of course there was a promise to investigate and punish.
Actually, there is some reason to think the searches were
instigated by the CC clique (the extreme right wing faction
of the Kuomintang, named for the two Ch'en brothers who
control it), which has never really wanted any settlement.
This view is supported by a manifesto published in the Central News and the Army paper signed by thirty-five Chungking organizations which stated that the Kuomintang had
no right to share power with any other group. In any event,
the incident has caused great embarrassment to the Government.

There is a report that several days ago the Kuomintang
official newspaper, *Chung Yang Jih Pao*, and the Communist
Hsin Hua Jih Pao agreed to stop charges of truce violations.
This is not confirmed, but since the 26th there have been
none in the Communist paper. The Kuomintang continued
until the 28th and then apologized.

January 31 / Lunch yesterday with the famous old warlord,
General Feng Yu-hsiang, was staggering. He had said it
would be just a peasant's lunch. Such peasants! Fourteen
courses that almost foundered me, but new because they

were New Year's dishes. Mostly heavy pastry and meats, very tasty and very filling and ending up with something called the seven precious fruits which is a sort of fruity rice pudding. Feng is a great bear of a man, with huge hands and a real Neanderthal face. They say he used to put down mutinies in his troops by strangling the men with his bare hands. He was exiled for a while in Russia with Madame Sun after the Shanghai massacre of the Communists in 1927; then became a Christian and got a good deal of publicity for baptising his troops with a firehose. After that he tried to be more than just a local warlord and played around with others of his ilk, but the national scene was a little beyond his capabilities and the Generalissimo succeeded in stripping him of his troops. Now he has prestige, some kind of title, and no power. I gather that what really broke him was his rule over Shansi and Kansu during the twenties, where for three years he bled the provinces white and, by forcing the farmers to grow poppies instead of food, was directly responsible for the appalling famine of that period.

A few years later Marshal Feng was burned to death in a fire on a Russian ship in the harbor of Odessa.

February 2 / Today is Chinese New Year. All last night and all today there has been a deafening racket of firecrackers and brass gongs. These holidays last for several days, for such occasions are the only time off the Chinese ever get and they make the most of them. They have no Sunday and no regular day of rest.

The PCC is over and no doubt all the press in America is now rejoicing that democracy has at last come to China. The Generalissimo's final speech was an impressive performance. He had all the words and all the sentiments and all in the right order. Even the agreements are impressive on paper. For what it is worth, it does have at least the advantages of putting all parties on record as favoring these things and of legalizing the opposition parties. Marshall is quite aware that so far it is only words, words, words. And when I suggested that one of its main secret objectives was to get him out of China, he agreed.

The cockpit of Asia

The fortnight between the end of the PCC and the first meeting of the Military Subcommittee was officially quiet, if tense, and almost anticlimactic. Beneath the surface, however, there were ominous rumblings that all was not well. Unless the nature of Chinese politics had changed radically, it had to be assumed that a vast amount of intricate maneuvering was going on, much of whose meaning would escape even the most sensitive western perceptions.

There could not, on the other hand, be much doubt about the basic significance of the public disorders which erupted with increasing frequency and violence. No one could prove with any legal nicety who started and organized them, but the pattern which slowly emerged could only mean that the groups which made little secret of their opposition to the PCC agreements were expressing their displeasure through the mobs in the streets. No one took seriously the occasional charges of Communist responsibility. No one really knew the attitude of the Generalissimo toward the rioting; if he disapproved of it, he certainly took no overt action to prevent its recurrence. The Communists were uneasy and wary. But what was most evident was that Marshall was becoming a very angry man – and perhaps a little discouraged.[1]

One point of confusion which emerged at this time would later be crucial. Published versions of the PCC agreements were either contradictory or obscure as to whether Manchuria was included in the ceasefire agreement. There is as yet no public evidence to clarify the matter; Marshall was always vague with us as to what he thought about it. In retrospect, it seems probable that the mistiness, however unfortunate its consequences would be, at the time suited the purposes of all concerned. Manchuria, after all, was still occupied by the Russians, and the cold war had not yet crystallized, though there were portents. Marshall may very well have been reluctant to ruffle Russian sensitivities by making future disposition of territory still under their control. The Nationalists and the Communists, both of whom intended to occupy it when the Russians left, could also have seen advantages in leaving the status unclear. It must of course remain speculative as to whether specific inclusion could have prevented what happened. Manchuria had long been too big a prize to be forsworn lightly. Hallett Abend, who wrote a book about it in the 1930s when Japan had invaded, called it "the cockpit of Asia." It would be that again in the Chinese Civil War.

1 *China White Paper*, pp. 143 ff. A series of public meetings to discuss the PCC resolutions had been organized by private groups supporting them and were being attended by increasing numbers of people. Each meeting was disrupted by officially unidentified elements. As the crowds grew larger, so did the amount of violence and the number of people injured. Minor Communist Party delegates were searched and harassed in various ways. Publicly Marshall maintained a stern silence; privately he made no secret of his displeasure not only to us, but also to the Generalissimo. In time the disorders subsided.

February 3 / Chungking / There is something I do not understand. The version of the ceasefire agreement as published in the press excluded Manchuria. When the Democratic League suggested to Marshall a few days ago that it be extended to include Manchuria, he said that it already did and the error in the press had not been publicly corrected because of a delicate situation and for reasons of international politics. He refused to elaborate.

The sun is shining today for the first time in weeks. So it is pleasant to sit alongside an empty swimming pool while Millicent, the house pooch, is busy giving lunch to a large and nondescript and cute litter of pups.

February 5 / Sunday afternoon being a nice day several of us went into the country. We drove along the Chialing River for a few miles, then walked several thousand steps down to the river, across it in a sampan, up more steps, and out across the fields and rice paddies to a place where we had heard there was a stone column dating back two thousand years to the Han Dynasty. There it was, with a carved strangling tiger hanging by a ring and an animistic human figure gesturing in the direction of the moon. There was another column, almost completely buried, which seemed to be in even better condition. Han is particularly interesting because it is pre-Buddhist, and hence all Chinese—the last great school that shows no Indian influence.

Then suddenly through the quiet of the place a line of soldiers came along the path dragging a half dozen youngsters, all protesting loudly, two badly beaten up, and one with his face heavily cut. I don't know whether it was an arrest of students for political activities, that being a university area, or a press gang conscripting for the Army. Whatever it was, the glint faded off the afternoon sunshine.

Last night I was talking with a woman from the Central University who had been teaching in Nanking and quit in disgust over a lot of things, but mostly over the tolerant attitude toward the Japanese. They seem to be living as though nothing had happened, no resentment of the people against them, Chinese and Japanese mingling together. The only resentment is against the Government, for the people say conditions were better under the Japanese.

The other day I happened on what looks like authentic secret instructions to the Kuomintang Youth Corps membership from its leaders. They compare the Corps to the Hitler Jugend, state that Fascism is the only government for China, and urge all members to prepare for the day when China will conquer the Orient which rightfully belongs to it.

This morning I saw Lao Shaw and Wan Chia-pao who are on the point of leaving for the States on State Department cultural relations grants. I am always amazed at Lao Shaw. One of the foremost living Chinese literary figures, he is unimpressive looking and badly groomed, and he has so deep a voice I always wonder how that body can hold it. But he has a truly imposing mind when you know him. He is a great organizer of writers in opposition to the Government, which means he has courage. He was thoroughly questioned by the local gestapo before he got his passport, and completely puzzled them by saying, in answer to all questions, he had never heard of the Kuomintang. So they let him go. He is terrified by the tales he has heard of the way American ladies' clubs lionize authors of best sellers, and he says he likes people who know how to keep quiet. Wan Chia-pao, who writes as Tsao Yu and is a leading dramatist, is looking forward to the literary teas.

February 6 / Life is quiet around here while we wait to see what happens next to the PCC agreements, just how and how far the main protagonists will implement them. Marshall sees the situation in terms of things and personalities, rather than as ideas and conceptions as well. My first reaction was that this is unfortunate, but I am no longer so sure. It may well be that since he has to do this thankless job, he is right in looking at it in terms of limited objectives, both in time and in space.

There is no evidence in his comments and speculation that he really relates his period here to what has gone

before, or that he tries to foresee how it will influence what
will come. In other words, he overlooks today as integrated
into the sweep of China. This, as much as anything, may
account for Chinese bafflement as to what he really thinks.
They are acutely conscious that "today" includes great
stretches before and after today. One can only hope he does
not try with them, as he did with us, to find parallels
between what is happening here and our own nineteenth-
century Indian wars.

February 8 / At the moment I feel downright gay. For the
first time in over two months my incoming box is completely
empty. This will have changed by tomorrow morning, but
for the moment it is progress. I even managed to get out a
report for Marshall on a great tribal rebellion in Sinkiang
which has been hounding me for weeks. Another cause for
rejoicing is that there is sunshine for the second day in a
row.

Last night I went into town to see another Chinese opera,
called *The Red-Maned Fierce Horse*. The costumes were
even more gorgeous than in the first one I saw. It was all
about a general who sadly leaves his wife to go off to the
wars, is captured by the Tatars, marries one of them,
becomes Tatar king, eighteen years later gets a letter from
his Chinese wife wondering what is keeping him away so
long, remorsefully goes home, becomes Chinese emperor,
and gets even with a brother-in-law who had been playing
games behind his back. I never did find out the rest of the
story since I left at the end of the first four hours. I still
do not understand Chinese music, but propose to keep on
trying. Maybe it would be well to listen to it as the Chinese
do, namely, listen for a while, go out, and then come back,
instead of staying glued to the seat until paralysis begins to
set in.

February 10 / Today is the rueful aftermath of a long and
sometimes rough night. This is the way it happened. The
owi dormitory in which I live has become Embassy property
because there is no longer an owi. It is known as Blake's

Place in honor of the new mess manager. It seemed a good idea to have a gala reopening under the new dispensation. It was also a good occasion to pay off a lot of unmet obligations. So we rounded up the Embassy, Army, diplomatic corps, Government, and all other Chinese whom we know. Two hundred people consumed forty gallons of liquor and proportionate amounts of food, as typified by one item of nine hundred and seventy oranges.

It would have been just another unremarkable party had it not been for the Chinese. Large numbers of intellectuals of all shades of opinion and occupations, and Government, Democratic League, and Communist officials were present. It was the first time many of them had ever met each other and they responded jubilantly. Just why so many had never met, I don't know; but they were full of curiosity about each other. And they made all sorts of discoveries. Right wing Kuomintang members who had always suspected the Communists were not really people found themselves face to face, others found they were related, some had been at the same school, and still others met who had not seen each other in twenty years. At no point did the Chinese sense of propriety and manners give way to political considerations. It was impressive.

This is the plum blossom season here. I think they may be the most beautiful flowers to look upon and smell I have ever known. I am developing a theory that three thousand years of Chinese culture have been built upon plum blossoms. The idea is so simple that people believe me and I expect to end up with a reputation for profound understanding of the inner China.

February 12 / This has been one of those screwball days. It started before dawn when the dying night was suddenly torn apart and made hideous with screaming and yelling. A strange dog had wandered into the compound and Millicent, magnificent mother that she is, came to a quick conclusion that the intruder was after her brood. She kicked him out all right and in so doing scared the living squeak out of the pups, who then joined the chorus. About this time she realized one of the pups had disappeared. It was a good hour before she decided to return her attention to the others.

The main business of the day was to find out something about some very serious riots yesterday in which too many prominent skulls were cracked. It was a put-up job by the right wing, which wants to wreck the PCC agreements. Marshall is furious about it and is playing with the idea of getting American newspapers to raise almighty hell because the Kuomintang is fantastically sensitive to American press reaction.

Kung P'eng, a Communist press officer in 1946, later became Minister of Information in Peking.

Part of the information came from Kung P'eng, who is one of the better sources, being very intelligent, well educated, from an old Mandarin family, and more relaxed than most of them. She was just back from a trip to Peiping. According to her what happens there to those with opposition views is too monotonously like Chungking to need repetition.

Just to prove that life even in Chungking has its lighter moments, the serious business of the day was punctuated by a maiden reporter from some local paper who has been bobbing in and out of my life. It started when Marshall sent over for action a letter W. H. Donald, for many years an Australian advisor to the Generalissimo, had written to Mai Yu (that being the maiden's name). It was about his internment during the war, his present illness, how much he missed her, etc., etc., and was signed "Your Papa." Then came a letter from her to Marshall saying that since Donald was ill in Honolulu she felt it her duty to be by his side and console him, and would the General get her there. This was followed by another letter asking for a scholarship to study journalism at Missouri. Finally, the lady herself appeared.

She was putting on the little girl act, with pigtails and bobby socks, but I remembered her from the party the other night when she was squired by an American naval lieutenant, and the couture that time was anything but little girl. Late in the afternoon I happened to see her dancing in a local pub with a young member of the secret police. I finally cornered the lieutenant to find out what goes on. The liquor treatment did not work because he does not drink, but he does eat chocolates and went through a one-pound tin. For my chocolates, I got a dreamy-eyed account of what a sweet, simple, innocent, dear little girl she is. After that I gave up, and I still do not know what it is all about.

Incidental information for today from a Japanese Communist: Mao Tse-tung has two sons by a first wife, who have been going to school in Moscow for the past fifteen years.

Incidental information for today from me: This morning I forgot to tell Marshall he had an appointment with General Feng Yu-hsiang. This did little to endear me to either general.

February 13 / Kuo Mo-jo and his wife came for dinner last night. He is one who had his skull cracked in last Sunday's riot. The skull-cracking can be taken quite literally. The police wore leather belts with heavy brass buckles. The usual method of breaking up demonstrations is to move into the crowd swinging the buckles. The effect is always painful and often murderous. He is still an irritant to many people with his bland contention he is non-partisan when he is most assuredly at least almost a Communist, and unlike many Chinese intellectuals takes a strenuous part in politics. As a result he is as poor as a churchmouse. Communication with him is slow because he professes no knowledge of English—I am certain he at least understands it well—and furthermore is quite deaf from another beating he received as a student.

What he had to say about the Sunday affair further confirmed the growingly ugly story: the cc clique met on Saturday and decided to show the men and the boys who had the real power. Then while the riot was going on, the Ch'en brothers went across the river to spend the day with the Generalissimo. Maybe he knew about the plans, maybe he did not. Certainly he knew as soon as it broke out and the police started throwing bricks. One policeman was unfortunate enough to be caught with written orders in his britches. It has caused a bad impression that the Generalissimo left town on Monday in the face of the howl and without settling it. He went to Nanking to open a meeting of the generals to decide on a plan for demobilization. "Now," said Kuo, "there are a lot of generals with power, prestige, money, and squeeze. Well might they join with cc to hang on to what they have, break the truce, mutiny against the Generalissimo, with or without his consent, and keep the Army big. All other signs are that cc is determined not to give in without a fight. What can they lose if they fight?"

February 14 / The rioting and disorders are beginning to get on Marshall's nerves, and he is sharp about it, as he begins to suspect that he has something by the tail that is bigger than any one person. Nothing he does or says to anyone stops the violence, and this exasperates him. He also begins to wonder if the Generalissimo may have something bigger than he can handle; if he can go into the council of generals in Nanking tomorrow and break them to his will, it will indeed be quite a feat. Sometimes Marshall reacts as though he were slowly coming to the reluctant and rather sickening conclusion there is only one answer left and that is to pull the props and turn the country over to civil war. As he put it once, "I don't see any other way of arousing a consciousness of political realities, of eliminating the reactionary groups, and of convincing these fine talking liberals around here that they will get just what is coming to them unless they are prepared to take to the barricades in defense of what they say they believe. There is the risk of what the Communists might do, but right now it does not seem they could or would do much militarily, and in any event as things are going now the Kuomintang will lose in the end. So perhaps it is not such a risk after all."

The Russian party for the Mongols marked the start of diplomatic relations between Mongolia and China.

Now to a reception for a delegation from the Mongolian People's Republic and after that to an exhibition of Argentine culture which here and now seems a little irrelevant.

The crowd as animal

The Military Subcommittee to reorganize the armies first met on February 14. On February 25 it announced an agreement entitled "Basis for Military Reorganization and for the Integration of the Communist Forces into the National Army."[1] The intent of the agreement was stated to be to facilitate the economic rehabilitation of China, and to provide for the national security, while at the same time safeguarding the rights of the people from military interference. This last point was especially important in China where the military had traditionally been considered the scum of society and hence, not surprisingly, had behaved accordingly. This low status had never prevented political forces from using armies for their own purposes, even though they frequently tended to get out of control and behave oppressively or, on occasion, even assume political jurisdiction. In any event, they were usually involved in politics one way or another.[2]

General Marshall never tired of emphasizing the extreme importance for China that the armies become technical and professional bodies completely separated from politics, as in the western tradition. He was quite aware that the Communist Army was perhaps the first one in Chinese history to be assigned a respected role in society and that it, in response, behaved responsibly. The Chinese people with whom the Communists came in contact were also quite aware of the fact and, wholly oblivious of ideological considerations, came to regard them as defenders rather than oppressors of the people.[3] If the Nationalists knew this, they most certainly never acted upon it; if they had, it might conceivably have made the difference between defeat and victory for them.

In brief, the reorganization was to be completed within eighteen months. The ratio of armed forces between the Nationalist and Communist forces was to be maintained at five to one; thus when the integration had been completed the National Army would have fifty Government and ten Communist divisions. All other forces were to be demobilized and the men absorbed into civilian life. The country was divided into five military zones with the divisions deployed throughout them, but with a significantly higher concentration in north China and Manchuria. All Communist divisions, although outnumbered, would remain in

1 *China White Paper*, p. 142.
2 The Generalissimo was a soldier by profession, as were all the provincial governors since the overthrow of the Manchus. It should be remembered that the ending of their autonomy did not for the most part end their power; rather, they retained it locally, while submitting to central Government control in national matters. It is true that during the period of the civil war civilians were a majority in the cabinet, but the generals were the influential members. Mao Tse-tung's famous dictum that "power comes out of the barrel of a gun" applied with equal force to the Kuomintang.
3 See the reports from members of the Yenan Observer Mission (Operation Dixie) in the *China White Paper*, pp. 564–76.

the three areas where they were already operating, namely, central and north China and Manchuria. They would have no forces in south China, Formosa, or the far northwest. The agreement also required both parties to submit within three weeks lists of forces in being, divisions to be retained, and units to be demobilized.[4] The Government gave its lists on March 26; the Communists never did comply. The Executive Headquarters in Peiping was charged with implementing and supervising the agreement.

At the time of signature on February 25, General Marshall said, warningly and a little prophetically: "This agreement, I think, represents the great hope of China. I can only trust that its pages will not be soiled by a small group of irreconcilables who for a selfish purpose would defeat the Chinese people in their overwhelming desire for peace and prosperity."

4 *Ibid.*, pp. 140–43.

February 18 / Chungking / Yesterday I joined the French Counsellor, a Chinese archeologist, and several of our people for a foray into the hills to look over some Han tombs. It was fun just to wander around the rice paddies and the hillside terraces. The area was almost all graveyard, with tombs of many periods, some running back two thousand years, and present life going on all around them. I don't suppose a great deal has changed in the country way of life since the first tomb was put in.

The quiet reign of terror gets a little worse each day with innumerable small instances of individual coercion and intimidation. It is still uncertain whether the Generalissimo can prevent the threatened revolt of his generals, and in the uncertainty everything grows proportionately sloppy and uneasy. Marshall is daily more angry and stubborn in his insistence that the Government will behave his way—or else.

February 21 / All day long yesterday groups of people, large and small, milled and eddied around the streets, gathering and dispersing. Talk was alternately excited and quiet. There was no leadership, no organization, just emotion spilling over in all directions, as though building for a concerted explosion of unpredictable dimensions. All innate Chinese gaiety and friendliness were submerged in irritation and hostility. With nightfall all quieted down, but the darkness was sullen with unseen eyes watching and waiting. By this time my mind seemed to be the consistency of birds' nest soup.

Some of the Yenan people came for dinner. Jubilation over the PCC is beginning to wear off and they are increasingly worried. They don't have much to say, but it is apparent they have little hope.

February 22 / In the middle of the morning I heard a roaring noise and sallied forth to find out what was going on. It was a huge parade of some fifteen thousand students staging an anti-Russian demonstration and demanding the return of Manchuria. Some nosing around produced the fact that it had been organized by the CC clique, with a large part of the crowd participating only under the threat of having their food rations cut off for two weeks. The howling was frightening.

A Russian officer I ran into told me the Russians would not get out of Manchuria until they had a firm control over at least fifty per cent of the economy. This, he said, is necessary to prevent us from taking over the province, since that is obviously what we are trying to do. I did not get any sense, however, that he knows any more of what is really going on there than we do.

The demonstration went on hour after hour, so peacefully for such affairs, apart from the noise, that we all proceeded to forget it. Then late in the afternoon, when it seemed to be petering out, the CC police moved into action and suddenly the whole city ran wild, or seemed to. The mob broke into Communist headquarters and messed things up a bit. Then it went to the Communist newspaper office and sacked the place. This developed into a pitched battle, with the fighting working its way up floor by floor as police reinforcements showed up. People were hurt, some badly. Then the liberal newspapers were attacked, and then the violence ebbed away.

That night the atmosphere at Communist headquarters

was grim, only candles for light, the gates barred, and armed guards mounted on the wall. They were an angry group of people, declaring their readiness again to take to the caves and ditches if necessary, and fully aware that for the moment they must take what happens here without striking back openly. Their anger was laced with frustration. They resent the growing signs of Russian reluctance to get out of Manchuria, especially since they are so far not allowed to get in any more than is anyone else. Chou En-lai was bitter: "After all these years this is too much!"

February 24 / Yesterday being Red Army Day there was the customary celebration, but the atmosphere this time was tense. Many, many people did not show up, and many of those who did came in for a few minutes and left quietly. Government secret police officials swaggered openly, the other guests were wary and evasive, and the Russians, half hysterical, were buttonholing passers-by to take them into corners and tell them the Russians had no intention of getting out of Manchuria until they had a firm grip and until the Americans left north China. T. V. Soong and the Ch'en brothers elbowed their way around, talking noisily. Another Manchurian demonstration started just after the noon reception; but only a few hundred turned out for it, and they were dispirited and uneasy, soon drifting away. This morning all was quiet on the surface.

The last three weeks since the end of the PCC have been mostly a series of incidents, demonstrations, and riots, not only here but all over the country. It is frightening to walk in and around them, talk with people, and know what will come next. Sooner or later the police turn the crowd into an animal that destroys and kills, leaving it drugged and drained and wondering just what had happened and why and how. But it did happen. That is the point. It will again.

February 26 / Yesterday the Military Subcommittee finally agreed on a plan for the reorganization and integration of all Chinese armed forces into a single national army. We will help in the training and equipping of this force once it exists. Marshall is convinced that unless this one works the rest is pure illusion; the ceasefire will be meaningless and the PCC only a dull debating society. The two-sentence speech he gave at the signing was a real shock to all present. The threat is not just idle chatter either, for he is a rather angry man and Chinese time is beginning to run very short in his mind.

Nothing more was heard at this time about disaffection among the generals. The primary source of the Generalissimo's power was his genius at manipulating and exploiting the rival factions around him, even when the odds seemed all against him.

In the confusion of the last weeks, incidentally, everyone has forgotten that the generals were supposed to rebel and complicate life even more. Either they never tried or tried and were brought back into line by the Generalissimo, as has happened before.

February 27 / The riots continue and the whole atmosphere is so hysterical it is hard to make sense of anything. Yesterday's Manchurian outburst was composed of students from the Central Political Institute (the official Kuomintang training school) and related groups located on the South Bank of the Yangtze. There were perhaps five thousand participants who were better organized and disciplined than previously. It was initially enthusiastic and at the end a little aimless. Interestingly enough the slogans and cartoons were more in English than in Russian this time.

In a new twist during the last few days the CC clique people have been seeking out Soviet Embassy officers to apologize for the anti-Soviet character of the demonstrations. Their line is that the trouble was instigated by Americans who want the PCC to fail in order to secure their control over Manchuria, and that Americans are annoyed with the peaceful nature of the disorders. Most people believe that the CC hopes to create a situation in which the Kuomintang can with some show of justice void the PCC and let the clique take over. Right or wrong, this interpretation is in fact spreading rapidly.

February 28 / Chungking this morning made me think of Quito with bright patches of light spotted here and there in the mountains and contrasting black and heavily rolling clouds that continually changed the focus of the light and sun.

There is a nice dopey lull today because Marshall took off early for Peiping. It is interesting to watch him in his dealings with people. Yesterday he came in spluttering because some Chinese had parked in his reserved spot which he felt he was entitled to have without interference. When he motioned him to move out of the way, the Chinese thumbed his nose at him. Finally he decided it was funny. But he can be ruthless with people. No one ever makes a second mistake around him.

Tomorrow or shortly thereafter the Central Executive Committee (CEC) of the Kuomintang meets. All signs are that the CC is going to raise a rumpus and crush all opposition. I think many people overlook one factor in all the talk about the sincerity of the Generalissimo and his desire for reform. Assume for argument's sake that this is true, we don't give enough weight to the fact that for years the Kuomintang has been oriented and built away from reform and that all posts with any power have been given to the reactionaries. You don't change their attitude by fiat and really to reform means the greatest political purge in the history of the Party. That isn't easy; probably it isn't even possible.

March 2 / The current lull continues. The CEC has gone into session and I suppose almost anything can happen, though it will not if the right wing is smart. The really serious problem is Manchuria, which has so many unpredictable elements in it that it is hard to figure out what the solution can be. Russian statements are ambiguous and I think unnecessary, though the meaning is fairly clear to anyone who wishes to look for it—they will get out when it suits their purposes. Washington makes hard statements that the Russians must get out, but everybody knows it is in no position to back them up. The most triumphant— and pathetically frustrated—boast came from the Chinese

Catholic newspaper which warned the Russians to be careful because Russia is no stronger than was Japan before the war and everyone knows what a beating China gave Japan.

The prize opinion of the week is the Central News announcement that MacArthur really means what he says and the proof is that he has reduced the Japanese toilet paper ration to twenty-four sheets a month.

March 4 / Yesterday being Sunday and pleasant, several of us ate Peking duck, got mildly tight, walked along the remnants of the old city wall, bought some pewter, priced Chinese coffins—very ornate and expensive—and let the day go at that. The most filial and prized gift a son can give his father is a coffin in the tradition of ancestor worship.

Today we are getting the first rumors of reports written by the newsmen who have been allowed to go to Manchuria, and the first of the American reaction. If what we get is true, there isn't much left that is movable and the American press is beating the wardrums.

March 5 / We now have the correspondents' stories about Russian looting in Manchuria. Their version is bad enough, although not as bad as rumor had had it. Sometimes I get the feeling here of looking out at the world through a small window, but without knowing whether it is plain glass or a trick carnival model.

There is one interesting development during the last week in the Communist line. In the past they always spoke of reactionary elements or destroyers of Chinese unity or some such thing. Now they have blossomed out with the word "fascist" and are using it in the Moscow sense and context.

"Fascist" had been used by the Soviets specifically to describe the Nazis.

March 7 / There is an ominous lull due to the heavy secrecy around the CEC. I assume all factions are circling each other and sparring for position. No one seems to dare take any overt step just now since they know Marshall is returning to Washington next week to report to the President, though not before the end of the CEC. They would rather move in his absence. He says he is coming back, but they may be gambling that something will happen and he won't. Soong made the remark openly the other day that China should not worry about Washington: "I can handle those boobs."

March 8 / This is a strange day. The clouds are heavy, black, and thick high above. There is a haze on the ground, but in between the two layers there is bright and glaring light and the mountains stand out more clearly than I have ever seen them; and the Yangtze winding down the gorge and away into the distance looks like something out of a storybook. If the town itself were cleaned up and painted and had some new buildings, with this location it would be one of the dream cities of the world.

March 9 / We had a rough session on Manchuria with Marshall this morning. He is furious about the Russian looting; and he is irritated that the Communists, although not defending the Russian actions, remain silent about them. He has insisted all along that the Communists are just that ideologically, but that they are without ties to Moscow. Now he is not so sure they are not playing the Russian game, and he is in a mood to demand categorical assurances that no ties exist (he says he believes the American Communists have such ties) or he will wash his hands of them. He seems to feel that the Communists here and the strikes at home are making life very difficult for him. Just what the strikes have to do with it is not quite clear, but the rising bitterness here is increasingly telling on everyone.

American labor's demands that wages be pushed to levels which would maintain purchasing power at V-J Day levels were finding expression in one strike after another, culminating in the railroad strike, President Truman's seizure of the railroads, and the Supreme Court declaration that his action was unconstitutional.

The end of optimism

General Marshall now decided that the time had come for a brief visit to Washington to report personally to the President on what he had been doing. He was also anxious to initiate steps for rapid and massive economic help because he realized that during the six months since the end of the war, nothing had been done about an economic situation which, although hopeful in the beginning, was deteriorating at a frightening rate.[1] Unless something was done and done quickly, the prospects for any military and political agreement would at best be poor.

When he left for Washington on March 11, General Marshall could feel with much justification that the accomplishments of two and a half months were impressive. The ceasefire of January 10 had stopped the fighting and was working smoothly. As to the PCC resolutions of January 31, the Central Executive Committee of the Kuomintang on March 17 announced that it had accepted them without reservations. The Central Committee of the Communist Party was scheduled to meet on March 31. Finally, the military reorganization plan of February 25 had been concurred in by all participants. Nonetheless, Marshall planned to make his trip brief because he knew that inevitably there would be difficulties of implementation with all the agreements.

If ever there was a case to demonstrate that life operates on more than one level, it was China in the spring of 1946. On the level of formal agreements, there were grounds for optimism, and the Chinese public reacted with enthusiastic approval; but there was another and ominous level. There were disquieting incidents such as disruption by Kuomintang plainclothesmen of mass meetings in support of the PCC resolutions, continual interference by the police with the movements of minority party delegates to the PCC, and the looting of the Communist Party newspaper headquarters in Chungking by "unidentified elements." Even more serious were the indications that the right wing cliques in the Kuomintang had succeeded in attaching a series of unpublished reservations to the Central Executive Committee approval of the PCC which would, in effect, have sabotaged the whole program.[2] The Communists and the Democratic League then announced that pending clarification of this matter they would not nominate their members to the State Council, and the Communist Central Committee postponed indefinitely its March 31 meeting. In the circumstances, the Constitutional Review Committee suspended its work. At the same time, it was becoming apparent that a powerful group of Nationalist generals were opposed to military reorganization because it would damage their personal positions.

None of this was calculated to be reassuring. Many Americans in China who knew China and Chinese ways best were alarmed when General Marshall decided to go home, even briefly. He had not participated openly in any of the political activities, but the mere fact of his presence was a restraining influence. The fear was that in his absence, disaffected groups would feel freer to pursue their disrupting objectives. Whether he could have prevented the troubles can of course never be known; what did happen is a matter of record.

1 *China White Paper*, p. 145.
2 *Ibid.*, p. 142. Reportedly there had been reservations about the principles approved by the PCC as the basis for changing the Draft Constitution in order to bring it closer to the May 1936 Draft Constitution which the Kuomintang had originally supported in the PCC.

There was one other element in the situation of which perhaps only Marshall was fully aware, and it limited what he could do. The United States obviously had tremendous economic power which it could use to influence events; but it no longer had military power of enough consequence to be used as a final instrument. Marshall had warned the Congress strongly about the dangers of precipitate demobilization. He made little reference otherwise to this handicap, but as the architect of the most powerful army in history he could hardly have been unaware of the limits this weakness placed on the range of his alternatives.

The reaction of others to the withdrawal of American forces was incredulity and confusion. The Communists, who must have feared that an imposing American military presence could only hamper their activities, slowly came to realize that the only thing they had to fear was the Nationalist Army, and they had reason to believe they could cope with it, even if it took a long time. The Nationalists, on the other hand, regretted the absence of the American shield; but the Generalissimo had unlimited confidence in his own military genius. In addition, this absence left him freer than he would otherwise have been to pursue the desperate military course he had chosen.

The Russians were the most baffled. They could see the facts, but Stalin apparently could not bring himself to believe that such formidable military power would be deliberately dissolved. There had to be a trick somewhere. It took him several years to realize that there was none; he would then proceed, in Korea, to make his second major mistake by not understanding that in some circumstances the Americans can and will pull themselves back together again with extraordinary speed and determination. In China, in an already chaotic situation, the missing component certainly changed earlier calculations as to how events might be expected to develop.

Later on, in fact, groups in the United States which were seeking a scapegoat for the Communist victory in China would make precisely this charge, namely, that the failure of Marshall to use American military power for an acceptable solution was the cause of the disaster.[3] The charge of course completely ignored American domestic political realities of the time; but it might be tempting, if unprovable, to think that it had some validity, except for the sobering example of Vietnam, where the application of massive American military power in an infinitely more limited situation has thus far failed to accomplish its objective, and never will unless the internal conditions become favorable. Those conditions are strikingly parallel with the ones in China in 1946. It may well be that the American popular political instinct of the time, even if for the wrong reasons, spared both the United States and China many additional years of trouble and misery. I have no reason to think that Marshall then or later would have disagreed with this conclusion, although on occasion he might have wished he had

3 Ross Y. Koen, *The China Lobby in American Politics* (New York: Macmillan, 1960), pp. 84–89. Shortly after publication this book was withdrawn by the publisher, allegedly to correct a statement which could not be substantiated. A revised version has not yet appeared. See also *New York Times*, April 6, 1960, p. 20.

more military power as a lever, especially in persuading the Generalissimo to do certain things whose importance Chiang consistently seemed incapable of understanding.

March 11 / Chungking / Marshall left this morning for Washington and maybe I can get to Peiping for a few days now. General Gillem, who replaced him in his absence, is a very nice guy and from all reports an exceedingly competent military man, but politically he is limited and is the first to say it. This morning he asked what is "this Kuomintang thing."

The best of the correspondents has returned from Manchuria and we now have a firsthand account of what he saw. He says it is quite true that the Russians have stripped the area of its industrial plant and done a lot of other needless damage to property. But as for the rest of the stories, he says the tales of shooting, terror, rape, etc. are plain fabrication. The so-called rape of Charlotte Ebener is the best. The man who wrote the story for *Time* was not even present at the party where it is supposed to have happened. What did happen is that an affectionate Russian colonel put his arm around her waist and when she told him to stop it, he did. The man who went into Dairen did so knowing he would be arrested, but he did it to get his name in the headlines and to beat out an AP story. As for the rest of the correspondents, he says that they behaved outrageously, drunk and raising hell much of the time, and building up in their own mind the idea that they were on a dangerous mission designed to save a suffering world from a fate worse than Charlotte's.

March 15 / A surprising amount of effort here goes into trying to build up a modern Chinese theatre. The writers must know it cannot be particularly good—and it isn't—in this revolutionary atmosphere, but I find it very moving that they keep on trying so hard to create some of the attributes of civilization. Any performance at all is crowded, which can only mean there are a lot of people who also have the same craving. And the best part of the audience is the very small children. They never cry, but they climb all over you, smear you with orange peels and candy, and make themselves completely at home in a most appealing and trusting fashion. For a broader audience there are story tellers who hold forth in little restaurants and recount the ancient legends and folk tales. Their gestures are wonderful and so are the intent expressions on the faces of the street people who listen.

March 18 / Last night Arthur Sabri came to dinner. He says he is going back to Sinkiang with his father, Mai Ssu Wu Teh, who has been appointed as the Central Government Inspector as a result of the January 1 agreement with the Ining Junta which recognized Chinese sovereignty along with Ining local autonomy. Father seems to get along well with everyone. He is a member of the Kuomintang CEC, has close relations with the sources of power in the Ili River Valley (Ining), is a Moslem, and a leading advocate of Turki autonomy ("Turki" being a generic term for Central Asian peoples). Sabri thinks the going will be tough in Sinkiang. Tai Li secret police agents have it well infiltrated, but the Government had better implement the agreement unless it wants more troubles. The most important factor is that Ining is keeping its own troops as a Peace Preservation Corps and that the Government must reduce *its* troops which he estimates at a quarter of a million. (An unlikely figure.) I asked Sabri if Ining had any foreign support and he said they received supplies from the Soviets on a barter basis in exchange for cotton, wheat, and hides. He added they could get more if necessary. He continually referred to the Ining Government as "we."

[*Among the many problems of the Kuomintang, Sinkiang played an important though, at the time, minor role. Two thousand years ago it was a major seat of civilization and the overland route between China and India and the Middle East. It has declined slowly and steadily since then. Its pri-*

mary importance in modern times has been geographic, since
it is bounded by Tibet, Soviet Central Asia, Siberia, and
China proper. The population has been reduced to nomadic
tribes and a few settled towns. The people are more closely
related to those on the other side of the Soviet border than to
anyone else, but China for centuries has held sovereignty over
them, with varying degrees of actual control. The Chinese
record with minority peoples has always been bad.

The Nationalists never established much more than nominal rule. This was sporadic and tended to get weaker the farther west you went. Agents of the Government either were
ineffectual or tended to set up satrapies of their own, to the
annoyance of the Kuomintang. In the far west the border
with the Soviet Union was more theoretical than anything
else, and ties with Russian Central Asian peoples were strong.
That the Russians did no more than they did to extend their
influence can be attributed to preoccupation with more pressing problems.

Until World War II the British had some influence in Ining, the center of the area, largely as an outpost of their interests in Tibet. This lapsed with the independence of India,
and the Indians never attempted to inherit it.

During World War II, Ining (now called Kuldja, not to be
confused with the Ining in South China) established what
was in effect an autonomous government in which geography
and other factors made relationships with the Soviet Union
much closer than those with China. From the end of the war
until 1949, Chinese control really did not go beyond the capital of Sinkiang, Tihwa; the rest of the province was plagued
with a series of tribal revolts about which very little was
known in the outside world.]

March 20 / We don't really know what the CEC finally did.
The English version of Central News has one release which
implies approval of the PCC agreements; the Chinese version
has another which raises questions about Communist sincerity; and the Communists insist there was a secret
agreement to do nothing and are screaming betrayal. The

Kuomintang is being very cagey and is using highly evasive words. My guess is that the Communists are at least partially right and that the cc has been smart and has picked on a highly technical subject, namely, the draft constitution, for stalling and producing a stalemate which in the end will play into their hands. Then, if clearcut support for the pcc resolutions is not forthcoming, details can easily be used to leave people in a fog.

There is a new and different story on Manchuria. Having got nowhere in securing agreement from the Russians to admit our consuls, Marshall decided before he left for Washington to send one in anyway and see what would happen. There were dire predictions around the Embassy which I thought might have some validity due to the difficulty of communications and the good chance that notification would not be received. But instead of that our man reached Dairen, was welcomed with open arms, and was given the keys, if not the information, of the city. Marshall then sent him word he was under no circumstances to leave the place and return to Shanghai for any reason. He was there; he was to make the best of it. Now we hear he has suddenly taken the boat back. Maybe he ran out of cigarettes. If I know anything about Marshall, his excuse had better be good. [*It wasn't, and there is no record his career was advanced by the incident.*]

March 21 / All last evening and night and all this morning I could not figure out why everything has seemed so restless. Now it has dawned on me that for the first time since I arrived in Chungking the wind is blowing, moving the trees and rattling doors and windows. I suppose it is the lack of air movement that makes this place so oppressive in summer and the air so dead all the time.

I had a talk this noon with a professor just in from Sinkiang, which he had left on request. The method of notifying him he was no longer wanted at the university was a farewell dinner, given for him by the Governor. He says the reason is that he would not play ball with the cc and that he thinks Tashkent (in Soviet Central Asia) is a wonderful place. Now he wants us to send him to the States and keep him there until the cc falls from power.

March 23 / There is a new exhibition here by a Chinese cartoonist who specializes in satirizing the Government through drawings of cats. Nobody thought his work quite as funny as he did, but his technique is straight Covarrubias and he is a brave man to do this. He will doubtless be hit over the head some night for it. And Tsao Yu has a new play called *Sunrise,* which is laid in a whorehouse. Rather, it is laid in two whorehouses, one elegant for fashionable groups in Peiping and the other tough. To get his atmosphere correct he moved into one for a couple of months, which scandalized his conservative admirers.

March 25 / Several of us made an overnight trip into the hinterland. By getting just fifty miles away from Chungking we dropped back a thousand years. The countryside, the villages, the little walled towns are all much as they were a long time ago. The people are so intrigued by these strange beings who suddenly appear that they don't know what to make of it and follow you or stand around in large groups just looking. Breakfast in the little open air restaurant was witnessed by at least a hundred interested and respectful people who made me feel like Bourbon royalty. Unlike other meals here, Chinese breakfasts leave me unenthusiastic. This one consisted of watery gruel topped with an equally watery egg.

In one place, I found some pieces of Szechuan peasant cross-stitch needlework which has practically disappeared and is lovely with its primitive designs taken from folklore and superstition. These pieces were being used as tablecloths, and the innkeeper was mighty puzzled anyone should want them.

It will take a tremendous development of communication to bring these people into the mainstream of modern China, owing to the isolation of valley from valley all through Szechuan. But when we deplore that this has not happened

already and think of the people as being on the rim of the
world, we forget that there are a good forty million of them
in Szechuan to whom this is the center of the world. Just
what they would gain from a change of perspective may be
questionable; but I could guess that if the Kuomintang
cannot appeal to what really interests them any better than
it has so far, then no one should be too surprised if someone else does. I doubt if I have ever seen crowds in any
other part of the world where it is so hard to find a stupid
face or an unkind one.

March 27 / For a change, not much is going on these days.
General Gillem dined with me last night. He is a wonderfully amusing person, even if not as discreet as he might be
sometimes. Mostly he talks about the war in Europe and is
alternately funny and acid. This evening the Chinese Ambassador to Moscow, whom I knew there, asked me to have
dinner with him alone. What he had on his mind I don't
know, but I have always liked him tremendously. Maybe he
just wanted to have dinner. It is really terrible the way this
place makes you look instinctively for an ulterior motive in
everything. He was back for the CEC meeting. According to
him the powers are content to let matters drift because
Marshall will come back next month and straighten them
out.

March 28 / The proposed trip to Peiping has been postponed temporarily due to sandstorms which are dumping
part of Mongolia and the Gobi into the city. Local politics
are getting decidedly sour. Both sides continue preparations
for a showdown and in the meantime hurl dirty words at
each other, both making equally foolish charges. Yesterday,
an attempt was made in the Standing Committee of the
PCC to repair the damages done to negotiations by the last
CEC meeting. It almost came to blows, the Communists
started to walk out, and tempers are jumpier than ever.

April 12 / The night before I was finally to leave for
Peiping I did not feel so good, but charged it to a plague
booster shot, plague being epidemic in China at the

MANCHURIA
Situation as of April 15, 1946

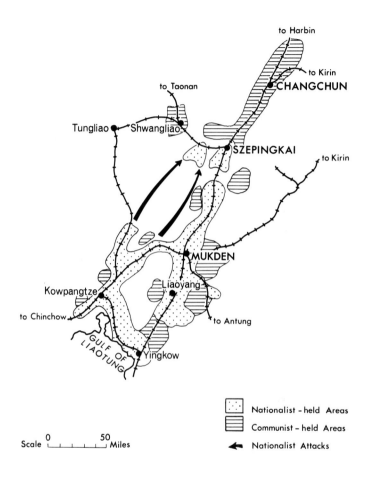

moment. The next morning I knew differently and the
doctor hauled me off to the hospital with lobar pneumonia.
And there I vegetated until the bottom of that lung stopped
looking in the x-rays like a tired swamp. The new treatment
for pneumonia is amazing. After sulfa and forty-eight shots
of penicillin in two days, my temperature was normal; but
after forty-eight shots in the behind, one every hour, by
something that looked like a horse syringe, I never expected
to sit down again—nor did I care. The administering of
the shots varied. Two ladies took turns. One was Chinese,
very handsome and playful, who had a delivery that felt

like a sledge hammer. The other was a shy little Burmese who turned down the lights, went through some kind of ritual with a piece of string and some wooden pegs, and had fingers so deft and gentle I had to watch her to know she had done anything to me.

On the third day, I was enough better that they allowed Sol Adler, our Treasury Attaché, to wander in. The usual cigarette hanging from his lips, he paced up and down and delivered himself of another of his fabulous lectures on Chinese finance, all interlarded with morsels from his incredible store of gossip. Meanwhile, his wife fixed an obviously hoarded can of lobster newburg. Both made pneumonia seem almost worthwhile.

An American Army hospital is quite an experience, at least this one is, where there is no running water. The food stinks, but at least it has the alleged virtue of consistency: pot roast, potatoes, dressing, sprouts, and pie—take it or leave it. The company in the ward was varied. It was all Army except me, one gent with the clap, a youngster with blood poisoning, John Walker of *Life* who has the same thing I have, and a chronic drunk who wandered in on his own and had periodic DTs which were predictable by the moment when he saw the mermaids tattooed on his chest begin to move. He was otherwise convinced he can play an enormous guitar he borrowed from someone. One GI was recovering from chicken pox which will be followed by courtmartial on manslaughter charges for having killed a Chinese while driving drunk. While he waits, he is assigned to guard the drunk and the mermaids. The GI's comments on the Chinese were mostly not fit to print.

The Manchurian crisis

General Marshall arrived back in China on April 18. That same day Communist troops occupied the great central Manchurian city of Changchun in clear violation of the ceasefire agreement of January 10 which, although vague on most matters concerning Manchuria, definitely did provide that areas under effective Soviet troop control were to be taken over by Nationalist troops as the Russians withdrew.

The Russian withdrawal from Manchuria, originally scheduled to be completed by December 3, 1945, had been postponed until the following February 1 at the request of the Nationalists because they believed themselves at that time incapable of taking possession. Early in March the Government made a formal request for withdrawal; and the Soviet Government agreed to begin the evacuation of its armies on April 9 and complete it on April 29. This was the signal for intense military activity.

Despite the ambiguity of the ceasefire agreement, Marshall had felt very strongly that the authority of the Executive Headquarters should be extended into Manchuria to avoid violent clashes once the Russians did begin to move. As early as January 24 he had proposed that a field team be sent to the port of Yingkow, at the southern tip of Manchuria, where a clash had been reported. The Communists agreed, but the Government refused. On February 20 he proposed the establishment of field teams to prevent further clashes and to lay the groundwork for eventual reorganization and integration of the armies, as had previously been specified. Again, the Communists agreed and the Government refused. It was becoming increasingly clear that the Generalissimo would accept no restraints on his freedom of action in Manchuria, and that he was determined to eliminate any Communist forces he might encounter, even though he did not have the military capability of doing so. It was not until the day Marshall left for Washington, March 11, that the Generalissimo actually agreed to the deployment of field teams in Manchuria, and then he attached so many conditions that the directive for the teams was not concluded until March 27 and was so narrow that the teams had authority to do little more than observe.[1] Several truce violations within China proper were further embittering the atmosphere.[2]

All during this period the Generalissimo was massing his armies around the periphery of Manchuria, although he received no cooperation from the Russians, who denied him access to the railroads and refused him permission to enter the strategic port of Dairen. At the same time, the Communists had been infiltrating the rural areas, which the Russians had not even tried to occupy, with guerrilla units and political organizers. As the Russians subsequently withdrew place by place, the Communists continued the same process, this time being able to seize the military materiel stockpiles of the Japanese Kwantung Army which the Russians, more interested in other prizes, had left behind for them.

The scramble for Manchuria at the same time caused a virtual impasse in the political negotiations. Communist troop movements increased Government suspicion of collaboration between the Communists and the Russians and strengthened the position of those elements in the Kuomintang which opposed the PCC resolutions. The Communists resented the obvious intent of the Generalissimo to assume full power in all Manchuria, including areas under their control. When it became apparent that no political decisions could be reached while the Man-

1 *China White Paper*, pp. 145, 146.
2 *Ibid.*, p. 146.

churian problem remained unsolved, the National Assembly, which had originally been scheduled to meet May 5 to initiate constitutional government, was indefinitely postponed.[3] It was not until April 8 that the field teams actually gained entry into Manchuria. As the Russians withdrew they further hampered Nationalist troop movements by again refusing them the use of the railroads, a refusal which could be considered, though somewhat dubiously, a violation of the Sino-Soviet Treaty of August 1945 which gave Russia joint ownership and control with China. At the same time, the Communists strongly protested Nationalist use of American transportation facilities to the north, even though the limitation on the number of Nationalist troops in Manchuria under the military reorganization plans was not to be effective until the end of twelve months. But it was a useful subject of propaganda attacks.

This, then, was the shambles into which Marshall found his work had fallen during his five-week absence from China. He discovered shortly after his return that the Communists were still willing to negotiate future military dispositions and local political reorganization if the fighting were stopped.[4] He also discovered that the Generalissimo was not, on grounds that he had a right to go anywhere he liked in Manchuria to establish Chinese sovereignty and hence would not discuss any political question until he had full control of the railroad mentioned in the Sino-Soviet Treaty of August 1945, even though he lacked the military capability of achieving it.[5] When Marshall proposed that the northward march be stopped where it was because of military weakness, he unexpectedly found out that the Generalissimo intended to keep right on until he recovered Changchun and had destroyed the Communist forces in the region. Once he had Changchun, he said, he would talk about anything. But the Communists, flushed with their military victories and confidence because of the captured Japanese supplies, refused the condition; and Chou En-lai, the principal Communist negotiator, urged Marshall to stop American logistical support in moving Nationalist troops in order to force the hand of the Generalissimo.[6]

Marshall now decided that the time had come to tell the Generalissimo exactly what he thought of the situation, even if it meant gravely offending him. He pointed out to Chiang that most of the difficulties he confronted could have been avoided, but now there was only distrust of the good faith of both sides; that he had prevented field teams from entering Manchuria at a time when they might have avoided fighting; that although the Communists were willing to include Manchuria in the ceasefire, he had resisted the idea; that Nationalist troops had attempted to destroy Communist forces in the Manchurian hinterland; and that his own military advisors had shown very bad judgment. Marshall added that on seven specific and important occasions Nationalist forces had taken action which he called stupid and of no benefit to the Nationalists and which, worse yet, gave the Communists good reason to question Nationalist intentions.[7] The Kuomintang could have had peace in Manchuria and threw away the opportunity; now the

3 *Ibid.*, p. 148.   4 *Ibid.*, p. 149.   5 *Ibid.*, p. 150.
6 *Ibid.*, p. 150.   7 *Ibid.*, pp. 150–52.

Communists were taking advantage of their successes, were daily becoming stronger, while the Government was daily making a dangerous military posture worse by overextending its lines and its forces.

That Marshall had correctly estimated the increased Communist confidence was revealed when Chou En-lai informed him that the previously agreed upon ratio of troops in Manchuria would no longer be satisfactory.[8] In reply, Marshall said that in his view the fundamental difference in the positions of the two sides was the question of sovereignty in Manchuria; that sovereignty meant control and there could be no Nationalist control without Changchun; that he thought the Generalissimo had made a concession in agreeing to negotiate everything else if only the Communists would evacuate Changchun. In view of the impasse over Changchun, he added, matters had virtually passed out of his hands and he did not see that there was anything else he could do.[9]

Having spoken his mind to both, General Marshall announced to them his withdrawal from formal mediation.

8 *Ibid.*, p. 152.
9 *Ibid.*, p. 152.

April 18 / Chungking / Marshall has just returned. It is about time, to judge from the Manchurian news. It is the usual thing, with one very serious exception. The Communists have occupied Changchun, the major city in central Manchuria, on the heels of the departing Russians. It is another indication the Soviets at last have what they want and are pulling out in force. The way the transfer of control has taken place is not going to help the negotiations in the least.

[Marshall's return to China coincided with the transfer of the capital from Chungking back to Nanking, whence it had been driven by the Japanese in 1937. All Chinese, except those who were native to west China, loathed Chungking with a passion—as did most foreigners: it was unbearably overcrowded, insufferably hot for six months of the year and unremittingly cold and clammy the other six, distressingly isolated from any other part of the world—and the symbol of defeat and humiliation. I thought it had a great deal of charm and interest, but then I only lived there for six months.

As soon as Japan surrendered, the Chinese who could do so began to drift back to the coast and to the north; and Chungking slowly slipped back into its Confucian feudal past. It also became apparent that unless the Nationalist Government was to vanish piece by piece it would have to be moved in one vast exodus. It was a formidable undertaking since the only feasible means of transportation were by air and by junk or steamer through the treacherous rapids of the Yangtze. April was the month selected. It would have been a disrupting experience in any circumstances; at this critical time it meant that no one, except the very few who did not have to pack their baggage, did anything except take care of himself.

Peiping for centuries had been the traditional capital, but Nanking had been the capital for the Nationalists ever since the Generalissimo had made the disconcerting discovery during the twenties that the people of Peiping, quite possibly the most sophisticated people in world, laughed at him as a sort of Chinese hillbilly because he was unfamiliar with literary Chinese. Not even his acknowledged talents were adequate to cope with ridicule.

So it was back to Nanking, where the basic differences from Chungking turned out to be no crowding, no charm, and only somewhat better communications with other places. Chungking rather quickly became legend, to the regret of very few.]

April 20 / Since I got out of the hospital, life has centered almost exclusively on preparations for the return of the Government and the diplomatic corps back to Nanking, which takes place in a couple of days. The great wonder is that a move of such magnitude, most of it by air, is not more of a mess than it is. At least none of us was able to bring more than the absolute minimum of personal belongings to Chungking; nor is the furniture worth moving. The Embassy files are a very different and imposing problem.

I am afraid some of us scandalized part of the community last night. We decided to have a farewell party, which turned out to be respectable enough, but we unwittingly selected Good Friday for it. It may sound silly, but in Chungking how are you supposed to know such things?

Even Marshall came and thought nothing of it. Two interesting new people were Robert Payne and his wife. I
gathered that he is sorry he ever wrote *Forever China*.
Opinions no longer are what they were when he wrote it.
He looks almost old enough to vote and teaches literature
and naval architecture in a Chinese university. I liked his
wife, who has the magnificent lines of the Manchu she is.
Rose, in addition to being beautiful, used to be a guerrilla,
writes poetry, conducted a smuggling business through the
Japanese lines, speaks a dozen languages, and was educated
in Boston.

April 24 / Nanking / With a great heave, the diplomatic
corps was pulled out of Chungking yesterday and dropped
into the walled city of Nanking. Despite the surface chaos,
it was really quite a feat of organization. It was drizzling
when we arrived, as it had been for four days. Such paved
streets as there are had vanished beneath the overflow of
ooze.

The city gives a curious first impression of vagueness
after the crowding and bustle of Chungking. The rather
brooding quality of the massive wall which surrounds it, the
greatest one in China, dominates the atmosphere. The
silence is somehow sinister after the endless chatter upriver.
Little has been done to repair the formidable damage done
during the great Taiping Rebellion in the middle of the
nineteenth century or by the Japanese sacking of the city in
1937. The old Manchu Forbidden City still lies in ruins,
and most of the rest is composed of alternating blocks of
rather nondescript buildings and cultivated fields which
give the place a rural feel. The occasional red, blue, and
gold buildings scattered throughout look a little lonely. The
people are subdued and self-centered; everywhere Japanese
troops are in evidence, quite cheerful and undefeated. The
wisecrack is that their surrender was taken by a corporal's
guard, a band, and a public relations man.

The job Ralph Clough, who headed the advance guard,
has done with practically no supplies and one borrowed jeep

is superb. I daresay the deficiencies will be remedied in time, but one can anticipate that the housekeeping details of life will preempt attention for some time to come.

April 28 / The continuing overcast gave a lot of people some bad hours this afternoon. The remaining brass from Chungking, including Marshall, arrived over the airfield, as did General de Gaulle. Fourteen layers of planes were stacked up in blinding weather to be talked in and down one at a time. As luck would have it, de Gaulle was high in the air and hence low on the list to land. This annoyed his self-appropriated sense of priority and he peremptorily and repeatedly demanded of the hapless lieutenant in the control tower that all others be sent away until he had landed. Finally, an exasperated Marshall broke in: "General de Gaulle, this is General Marshall. The lieutenant is in absolute command of this field. You will do exactly as he tells you. This is the last I want to hear from you." The ensuing silence was impressive.

Later on I went down to the waterfront to see about some supplies which had come up from Shanghai on a Navy LST. Not far from the entrance to the wharf there was a small police substation with a half dozen policemen loafing around on a front porch. At one end a coolie with his arms drawn behind him, his shoulders dislocated, was hanging by his thumbs. We stopped to find out why. His license to pull a rickshaw was not in order.

"How much longer will he hang there?"

"Thirty-six hours more."

May 1 / The calendar says this is May Day, but nothing else says so. For one week there has been unbroken rain and an endless flow of people and things into the city. Necessarily all attention has been focussed on the innumerable problems of moving too many bodies out of the weather and into far too little living space. Despite the influx Nanking retains its air of emptiness and detachment. In a way it is a relief, although probably a temporary one, from the morbid Chungking preoccupation with political events.

For the time being, only a very limited number of officers can send for their families due to the housing shortage. One who can was complaining bitterly about the rats in his house. The Military Attaché looked at him unsympathetically: "What did you expect, chinchillas?"

I spent most of the afternoon at the airport waiting for a plane to come in from Chungking with some of our baggage. Instead it was filled with Communist personnel and groceries. Anyway it was fascinating to sit in the control tower and listen to planes from all over China getting out of the muck and onto the ground anywhere they could find openings.

May 2 / The newspaper correspondents are all living in the Nanking Hotel. I was there last night with them. Marshall had given a press conference and they were discouraged because they found him so depressed and worried. When that tight mouth of his says, "The situation is serious, critical, and dangerous," it means just that. But he keeps repeating that this thing must succeed. I gather that when the Generalissimo recently started pressing him for more troops for Manchuria, he received a royal roasting for his pains. The Generalissimo is not always as intuitive about Marshall as he might be. I am almost certain now the Generalissimo is convinced he can settle China by force alone and intends to do just that.

Herbert Hoover will be in town tomorrow for the day. If no one is excited about it, it is only because no one here is excited about anything, except a new officer who arrived this morning: his car was stolen by noon. . . . This morning at Marshall's daily briefing the Military Attaché, who is famous as something of a character, started out his part by quoting from Elbert Hubbard. It is the first time I have seen Marshall disconcerted.

May 3 / Nanking has been filled with the great and the would-be great today. Former President Hoover, assorted admirals with pompous staffs, the Generalissimo, Chou En-lai, and others all descended at once. The visiting Ameri-

cans all left this evening, having been briefed. Since the
Navy takes care of its own, the Naval Attaché was able to
give a luncheon which was very elegant and chit-chatty. As
is becoming almost routine, the conversation was largely
limited to plans for the coming war with the Russians, all
with an appallingly casual acceptance of it and what it
means. The soldiers and sailors are quite openly bored to
tears by peace.

The latest scandal: with thirty million Chinese on starvation rations and the Government crying for more foreign
aid, it is now coming out that certain well placed per-
sonages, using Government funds, are cornering the rice
market, and the godowns in Shanghai are crammed with it.

There is a bird here, lots of them in fact, that flies around
in circles in the sky, always in a hurry without getting anywhere. Its song sounds like "One more bottle, one more
bottle!"

May 5 / This is Double Five Day and it is to be a gay day,
for the Government announced that today we celebrate the
"triumphal" return of the capital to Nanking. It is a fitting
day because it also commemorates the Chinese student
Renaissance of the early days of the Revolution. For a
decade China has waited for this day, but the "triumph"
must be bitter ashes in many Chinese mouths. Japan is
gone, but there still is no peace, nor any in sight. The
weather is doing its best to put a good face on life since
it is sunny and pleasant after steady rain.

May 7 / The Sunday Double Five reception by the Generalissimo was done in true imperial style. It was held in
Government Headquarters, which is old style, filled with
red lacquer columns and very effective. He was a fascinating study, with a freshly shaven head that gleamed in the
light, and reminded me of the Tartar envoy in the Russian
opera, Ivan Grozny. Stiff-kneed, rocking a bit on his heels,
elbows out and hands close in, head back and face immobile
except for the bright eyes that darted about like those of a
snake, he was the perfect picture of a Mongol emperor. I

wonder if he fancies himself as that because in a sense it is an un-Chinese stance. The complete self-confidence somehow conveyed the limitation of outlook. Nobody here has ever been known to disagree with him and get away with it. This makes it difficult because some people close to him give him a lot of bogus advice which he accepts. It was the first time I had ever seen every important name in the Government together. Oddly, they are all mild looking, all except T. V. Soong. General Ho Ying-chin, Minister of Defense, is a surprise: the lower half of his face is soft, womanish, and cruel.

The Generalissimo and Marshall were distinctly cool to each other. They have been having some very harsh exchanges recently and there is a rapidly growing distrust of each other's motives and judgment. The negotiations have reached complete stalemate. Sometimes I suspect the collapse will come through fragmentation of the Kuomintang. If nothing else, the economic condition could bring it down. In Nanking I become increasingly aware of the economic aspects of the whole problem. Chungking, with its location and almost unassailable agricultural abundance, was such an economic world apart from the rest of China that it seemed of little relevance to politics. Here I can see how economics will dictate politics, unless something drastic is done. For example, just in the last three or four months the currency note issue has reached astronomical proportions. No semantic juggling in committee meetings can change what this does to people.

May 10 / Yesterday afternoon the airport was loaded with stars as General Eisenhower and staff arrived for a day. My job, however, was to meet three planes from Chungking with part of our Chinese staff and their families, most of whom had been airsick. The planes also brought beer and pillows, both items being non-existent in Nanking.

This is a beautiful spring day, warm with great fluffy clouds in a bright blue sky and the rain forgotten. The trees are all out and the fields are green and very much alive.

Always the sounds are new and exciting, from the new birds to the small boys who sit in ditches and tootle on bamboo flutes.

May 13 / It is hard to realize that we have been here only three weeks; the memory of Chungking is already becoming dim and nostalgic. Very little work has been done. Almost all time is taken up with housekeeping. We have too few houses, no furniture, little food, no cars, no nothing, and the inflation is so appalling no one can afford to buy anything. But we manage to camp around and get by. And it is raining again and is cold, which happens to be all right with me since my summer clothes have not yet arrived.

It is still odd to see so many Japanese around the streets living and acting as though nothing had happened. They are doing a good job of ingratiating themselves, working hard, being friendly, and speaking good Chinese and English. One Japanese youngster I talked with the other day grew up in Brooklyn. And labor is no problem. Any job that needs doing always has more than enough volunteers. It is quite a sight to see the young ladies of the Embassy straw-bossing crews of grinning Japanese soldiers, including one whose father, a top man in General Motors, probably never thought his cheerful young daughter would give orders to enemy troops as to how to clean up a back alley in China.

Next I make my first visit to Shanghai in a day or two to see for myself what is there and to reason with my Chinese press monitors—Shanghai is the best center for our press translating service—who occasionally break out into a rash of playing boy detectives, and I suspect even more serious and compromising activities, to the intense annoyance of the local constabulary. I can sympathize with the monitors, but they have to understand that an Embassy is not only not supposed to be a cover for such activities, it is actually not even an effective one in this kind of situation.

A Saturday night session with the Russians was a rough deal. The caviar was fine, even if red, the cheeses and

In crisis situations an American embassy cannot assume that the loyalty of its many native employees to the United States transcends their loyalty to their country, or that they are not under duress to act as informers. We seldom found out whether our Chinese employees were working for the

Nationalists or the Communists—or both. We could only assume each worked for someone, and then take such precautions as were possible to keep them from fabricating stories designed to please their various employers. The only alternative would be that of the Russians, who employ only Russians in any capacity, no matter how seemingly innocuous.

sausages likewise. But it started with beer, was followed by straight Argentine gin during the meal, the devil's brew if I ever met it, and ended with a green Ukrainian brandy. A Russian eating and drinking party is well and good in Moscow where it is done with good vodka, but this combination is murderous. I got lost going home in a driving rain; but there was something soothing and reassuring about the deserted city at four in the morning and for a spell civil war seemed very far away. I spent the next day cursing the whole race of man, and myself in particular. A long walk on top of Nanking's magnificent wall—it is twenty miles in circumference—helped a bit. I can even feel something of the assurance that the men who built it long ago must have felt, taking in its commanding view of the purplish hills in the distance around the semi-valley in which Nanking is located.

May 14 / I read so much Chinese press I sometimes get a little soggy. Presumably this is my own fault since I am primarily responsible for having it all translated. Not that I really regret this. I learned in Moscow during the war how much you can learn from a controlled press, once you know how to read it, however dismal the process may be. Taken literally the Chinese press is today one of the great sources of misinformation of all time and bids fair to become more so as the Government is step by step closing down or breaking into harness all papers with any pretense to independence. It is a long, dull chore, as it was in Moscow, but everything put in print says something if you know what to look for. Even the reports on the last riots in Canton which expressed outrage that the raiders left behind them two very active and aggressive beehives can have a good deal more than amusement value.

May 19 / Shanghai / Shanghai is a great sprawling, shabby city that makes me, after six months in the back villages, feel like a country boy who has come to the big town—street cars, filling stations, the latest styles, big buildings, bars, and smart restaurants. One part is slick with too much

money, elegance, and callousness. Another side is sordid
with horrible slums, starvation, corruption, opium, and
more streetwalkers than I have ever seen anywhere. The
better ones know the right people and do not have to walk.
Filtered throughout are the thirty thousand White Russians
who have a finger in everything. And yet, despite the uneasiness and the inflation, the city is listless and somewhat
lifeless, hopeless, cynical, uncertain. So far nobody is doing
anything about it, and even the Communists are apparently
still watching and waiting warily.

There are vague stories here about peasant revolts along
the coast, in the southeast, and in Sikang, northeastern
Tibet, where a couple of hundred thousand people are
reported to have been killed in an uprising against some
undefined opium decree. Chinese peasant revolts are bloody
affairs. These are seemingly not against the landlords, but
against the pao-chia chiefs who are the local political
bosses and can be vicious and vindictive. There has never
been a word about them in the local press, although the
evidence is good that the stories are true. When I asked the
foreign correspondents why they have never reported them,
they just shrugged their shoulders and said that there is no
use doing it since the American public is not interested in

China and no paper at home would print the stories. There are a lot of things in this world that I do not understand and one of them is that peasant revolts are usually put down.

There are several strikes going on in the city, including the garbage collectors. Not many places in China have any garbage; in most of the country the pigs take care of what man cannot consume.

May 21 / The thick oppressiveness of this place is wearying. The cynical tone is set by the exclusive preoccupation everyone has with his own personal gain. People are fatalistic about it: thus things are and nothing will be done about it. Who cares anyway? The White Russians are the worst and make me think of leeches. Nothing is beneath or beyond them. Just why the Soviets want them back is beyond me, unless it is a sense of shame.

A substantial number of White Russians were later repatriated voluntarily and have not been heard of since; neither is there information as to what happened to those who remained behind.

Sunday afternoon I had tea with Madame Sun Yat-sen. She has played a brave and daring role here in trying to liberalize the Kuomintang, curb its excesses, and make it more representative of her husband's ideals for China, and she has done it in opposition to her relatives. The famous charm was there, but she seems to me basically a cold, hard, ruthless woman who knows what she wants and how to get it. Maybe she even wants the right things. She is a good listener and told nothing, quite possibly because someone had informed her I was a secret FBI agent.

Madame Sun's brother is T. V. Soong and her two sisters are married to Chiang Kai-shek and the late Dr. H. H. Kung. She later became a Vice Chairman of Communist China, although her present influence is unknown outside China.

General Morris Cohen, for many years Dr. Sun's personal bodyguard, was also present. He is Canadian Jewish, with a heavy Irish accent, and looks like a Chicago gangster. He is back here involved in various Soong-Chennault business deals and imports whiskey. He quite irrelevantly and too frequently told Jewish stories, none of them funny. After that I had a bad Russian dinner. All Shanghai meals, except the Chinese, are expensive and unappetizing.

Lunch yesterday with Ed Rohrbaugh, who has recently been reporting from the Communist New Fourth Army area north of Shanghai, and Bill Powell, son of J. B. Powell who was the most distinguished American editor in Shanghai

Bill remained in Shanghai until after the Korean War and on his return to the United States was tried for collaboration with the enemy because of stories he had published which supported Communist Chinese charges that the United States had used germ warfare in Korea.

before the war. The latter has completely broken with his father, who is hopelessly ill as a result of his internment during the war, over China. At the same time I saw a group of Manchurian politicians, all very liberal, very full of advice, and insistent that the United States do something constructive for China, without specifying what they had in mind.

Dinner with Ralph Olmstead, whom I knew in Moscow where he was Deputy Director of the War Food Administration. He came here originally with UNRRA and is now deep in I don't know what varieties of private enterprise. We were joined by an ex-admiralty lawyer from Boston who is in business with Chennault and obviously knows whatever it is you have to know to make your way here, and a former naval officer who is promoting some fishing scheme. This is Shanghai for you.

Having learned of a cheap way to acquire a new supply of whiskey I went down to the Customs House to clear it just in time to get in the middle of a customs strike which was breaking up furniture because the employees cannot live on their salaries in the inflation. This seems to be a daily routine.

May 23 / Nanking / It is a relief to be back here in the rural atmosphere of Nanking, even if my secretary has lost my keys in my absence and then banged herself up in a jeep accident. I hopped a ride back with Admiral Murray who is one of the nicest guys in this world, and then went into a long session with the new Minister-Counsellor, W. Walton Butterworth, whom I met in Shanghai. I am impressed with him; he is hard headed, intelligent, a good listener, and I think he will be a good influence around here.

I dined last night with Dr. Tao Hsing-chieh, a brave man and a gentle one with progressive ideas about education. He has worked out a new system of spreading literacy by using grade school children as what he calls "little teachers." Rather touchingly, he got the idea from watching his six-year-old son teaching grandmother to read and

write after his parents had said they were too busy to do so. Then we went to a Chinese dramatic adaptation of Tosca which was really very good. The leading lady is married to the director, both friends of mine; they rehearse by day, play by night, and then ride home many miles on bicycles.

Yesterday was a fine day and the hills beckoned to a group of fifteenth-century Ming tombs which lie below Dr. Sun Yat-sen's ugly mausoleum on Purple Mountain. The Ming custom was to line the road to the royal tomb with huge stone figures of warriors, horses, and other animals, including turtles which in China are either the symbol of fertility or an unrepeatable obscenity, depending on the mood. All the figures are spectacular and some are quite magnificent, strangely reminiscent of early Aztec.

Today has been a welter of papers and humidity and tonight there is an official dinner given by Academia Sinica, an official organization of the leading scholars in all fields which produces most of the best academic work in China.

May 29 / The Academia Sinica dinner had a rather startling finale for me. It was a good dinner, with lots of rice
wine and friendly conversation. I was sitting next to an
astronomer and when it was all over I had the loan of an
observatory. They have one on the top of Purple Mountain
with a marvelous view of the entire valley. The Japanese
gutted the place, but left enough of one building intact
for a residence. Since no money is presently available to
restore it, I am welcome to move in until they can find
the money. All I have to do is figure out transportation and
how to get water since the pump was also destroyed. It
sounds a bit like taking an option on the Brooklyn Bridge,
but I am determined to live in it.

The Minister of Information under the Wang Ching-wei
Japanese puppet Government is on trial now. A few of the
puppets have been tried and shot; most have been forgiven
and taken back into the National Government. In his
defense statement, Lin has admitted all charges against
him and said he has no regrets; he did what he thought
best for China; he knew he would be shot and some day
history would prove him to have been right to work with
the Japanese against the white man, but some sacrifice
had to be made now to placate him—and the audience
cheered.

The observatory plans move ahead. Several yards down the mountainside I found a spring and so I have water. I also found an elderly and gentle old man who can cook and so I shall have a place to get away to from the awful heat and depression of this town.

The June truce

Although General Marshall had withdrawn as a formal mediator, this did not in any sense mean that he had become a mere spectator of events. It did mean he would not again be a party to or sign any agreement unless he was reasonably satisfied that the two contending sides intended to implement it in good faith. What he was saying, in effect, was that each side had become so distrustful of the other that it no longer believed anything the other said, and hence must pursue its own interests by any means available. Neither he nor the United States would be an accomplice. He was also quite obviously beginning to have more than a strong suspicion that each side was increasingly convinced it could win on its own terms and that therefore genuine interest in compromise was waning.

As an experienced military man, he could see this hardening of attitudes as leading into protracted civil war, with all the horror that would entail. He may even have been fairly certain who would win in the end; but he certainly never gave any indication of it, although as he complained more than once the repeated charges by each side that he was favoring the other made his difficult position even more difficult. But he was so appalled at the prospect he foresaw that he was willing for the time being to consult with both sides, act as a channel of communications, and offer suggestions. In other words, he was returning to his original role of the previous December of making his good offices available. As long as he thought there was any slightest hope he would keep on trying.

In fact, during the period from early May until July 1, he was more active than he had been at any previous time. He was in daily and continual contact with representatives of both sides and of any other group which thought it might have something to offer. The proposals made from all directions were endless, infinitely complicated, and often contradictory. It would serve no useful purpose here to spell out in any detail the course of the negotiations, nor would they be of interest to anyone except those who were involved in them or to those involved in comparable situations, as a case study indicating how difficult and susceptible of misunderstanding such problems can be.

In retrospect, there were a few patterns in the welter of conflict which should be interesting and instructive. The most immediate objective of all participants was the termination of hostilities in Manchuria, as the basis from which serious consideration of other problems could begin. The apparent simplicity of the general desire ended here. The events in Manchuria, rightly or wrongly, had in large measure ended any belief the Generalissimo might have had in the good faith of the Communists, at least until he felt himself in a position sufficiently strong that such faith would be irrelevant. He left little doubt of his attitude when he informed Marshall that he was leaving on May 23 for an eleven-day trip to Manchuria. Marshall protested strongly, urging him to let his generals alone for a change. In the end, Marshall reluctantly agreed, when the Generalissimo assured him there would be no further Nationalist troop advances.[1] Marshall, incidentally, made the mistake of loaning him his own plane, an act which further damaged his position with the Communists. The Generalissimo arrived in Manchuria in time for the occupation of Changchun on May 23 by his own troops, following the evacuation of the city by the Communists.[2] He quickly pleaded with Marshall to believe he had been unaware this was about to happen, and assured him there would be no further advances; but the fact soon emerged that his troops were not only scouring the countryside for Communist units but advancing north along the railroad toward Harbin, the last major city in Manchuria still in Communist hands, and east to Kirin.[3] As it turned out, he had not issued the orders for the cessation of offensive action, as he had promised Marshall he would do.

These actions did very little to reassure the Communists. The respective roles were now reversed: the Generalissimo was on the offensive militarily, and this was reflected in the negotiations. When he returned to Nanking on June 3, he agreed to a ten-day truce, stipulating to Marshall that this would be the last opportunity he would offer the Communists to prove their good faith to him. Chou En-lai asked for one month and agreed to fifteen days. The truce was announced on June 6, to be effective at noon the following day. It was simultaneously announced that the fifteen days would be used to arrange complete termination of hostilities in Manchuria, resumption of communications throughout China, and prompt implementation of the February 25 agreement for military reorganization.[4]

During the truce period, which at the last minute was extended to June 30, Marshall resumed formal mediation. The slow progress of conversation amply demonstrated how easy it was in a situation with so many important and interrelated problems to reach agreement on almost everything and then have it break down over a final point. It had been clearly understood at the outset that any agreement was contingent on mutual understandings in all three major areas spelled out in the June 6 truce announcement. There was relatively little difficulty on the first two.[5]

Military reorganization was the stumbling block, and it was further complicated by the outbreak of sporadic and violent hostilities in north China, some of which had obviously been planned by both sides well in advance. The Generalissimo was arguing from his new position of strength and demanding that in troop

1 *China White Paper*, p. 154.   2 *Ibid.*, p. 155.   3 *Ibid.*, p. 155.
4 *Ibid.*, p. 158.   5 *Ibid.*, p. 159.

disposition the Communists give up some areas they presently controlled. The Communists, now on the defensive, were prepared to make some concessions on this point, but they were not willing to concede any of their civilian controls.[6]

When it became apparent that reorganization and troop disposition were simply too complicated for solution within the truce period, it was decided to implement the first two agreements at once.[7] On July 1, both the Government and the Communists announced that they had issued orders for the immediate cessation of offensive action. If the Manchurian crisis had not been finally solved, it had at least receded into the background in the face of more urgent problems. It would more or less remain there until the final stage, and then it would be decisive.

6 *Ibid.*, pp. 162 ff.
7 *Ibid.*, p. 162.

May 31 / Nanking / We spent all yesterday morning with Marshall battling it out as to what the American course should be. There is something unreal about a group of men sitting around making sweeping statements when they all know none of them has to accept responsibility for anything. No one is going to change any basic history, but one action or another can have a good deal to do with whether more or fewer people die in the process. Marshall as usual gave no indication of what he will do next, but I daresay we will find out in time. Americans are still being attacked from all quarters, and each side thinks we favor the other. We hear that a group of Congressmen at home is about to break a campaign attacking Marshall for favoring the Communists. This is pretty foolish and will not help matters any.

The only light touch is that someone else besides us has some troubles too. For several days there has been much noisy publicity about a visit to Nanking by Admiral the Lord Frazer, Commander of HBM Navy in the Pacific, who is leaving for less troubled waters and wishes to bid farewell to the Government. The plan was he would sail up the Yangtze on HMS Newfoundland. On arrival the foreign colony and important Chinese would be invited to repair aboard for inspection and cocktails. Came the happy day and with it the news that HMS Newfoundland was aground on a mudflat. There she stayed covered with slime and confusion until she could be pulled off ignominiously. When she did arrive we were informed by someone, no one is quite sure whom, that the party was indefinitely cancelled. This morning we hear that it was held yesterday with everyone else present, but not a single American. Relations at the moment are distinctly frosty, and the British are convinced we did it on purpose.

June 3 / The Generalissimo gets back tonight from ten days in Manchuria during which he masterminded himself into a worse military position than he was in before he went. This means he will get some very harsh and unpleasant words in a situation which is already tense almost to the breaking point. Marshall is beginning to get the idea he is being pushed around, made a tool of, and he doesn't like it at all. Nor is he a man to play a losing game. In short, he is about as angry as anyone I have ever seen.

June 5 / This has been one of those days filled with too many various things, ranging from a Danish treaty of friendship, commerce, and navigation, to what to do about Macao, to the vagaries of the Chinese press, to the "situation," and back to the Indian Agent General who is sore at me about something. It *would* end up with a party given by our outgoing Counsellor and our incoming Counsellor, a monster affair, with everybody invited, and those showing up being mostly British—the HMS Newfoundland incident is forgiven—and Chinese. What happened to the others is unclear. There was a panic for a while when no Russians appeared, and no explanation. He who had received the message forgot to tell the others that President Kalinin had died and the Russians were in mourning.

Outside my bedroom window there is a large field of terrific cabbages, obviously fertilized as usual, a Japanese concrete dugout, and several thatched huts set under an erratic row of willows. An untold number of Chinese of all ages live there, along with some pigs and dogs and a few chickens. It matters not what the time of day or night, something is always going on with utter lack of self-consciousness. That life is also quite unaware of and indifferent to any world beyond that cabbage patch. There are endless untapped human resources in that field, but China will not change too much until the peasants begin to look out instead of in. The Communists seem to have made some major changes in this respect in their areas, which may be the reason some people who have been there come back talking to themselves.

June 7 / The new fifteen-day truce should fool no one. It just gives a little breather for the licking of wounds. Due to the continuing military deterioration, Marshall really thinks of it as the last chance to salvage the February military reorganization plan and to prevent all-out civil war. The Kuomintang has told the press this is the last chance for an agreement, and I think they mean it this time. Chou En-lai in his press conference as much as said he no longer trusted Marshall. Maybe something can be patched up for Manchuria, but I can't believe it can be very much or for very long; maybe just enough to get Marshall out of the country.

At literally the last moment Wedemeyer's designation as Ambassador was cancelled at Marshall's request.

The payoff is that General Wedemeyer is supposed to arrive here next week, presumably as the new Ambassador. It is inconceivable that the Communists will make or abide by an agreement if he is involved.

June 8 / Having had some trouble in locating a man who shares my enthusiasm for my hill, I finally have one who at least does not mind it. Tomorrow we shall spend the day eliminating the detritus of war from the place. I have little furniture for it, and probably will not have much later considering the local prices. But that does not matter as long as the floor is clean—and it is away from the city.

Marshall, whose patience seems infinite at times, is really getting short tempered and tries to control himself with lengthy digressions on irrelevancies. This morning we were treated to an involved discussion about the problem Madame Chiang is having with termites in her basement.

June 10 / I went up to the mountain and started two

coolies cleaning it up. Then I went the rest of the way to
the top and got a good windburn. The drive up and down
had its moments. The car I had wanted never did turn up
from the Army, which is having trouble with its drivers.
The Army, here at least, is not exactly noted for its deftness
in handling Chinese labor. So I commandeered the biggest
truck in the place. It was too long to take the hairpin turns
without backing and starting. I won't try that one again.

June 12 / I finally spent the night on the mountain and
almost froze to death, so great is the difference between
there and the Nanking steambath. The more I see of the
place the better I like it, for the view is magnificent and
the effect of sun and moon on the plain spectacular. True,
it has its limitations, chiefly in the absence of toilet facilities,
which is remedied with a bucket, a plain white bucket
which cost fifteen bucks US. I like the method of bathing.
The spring down the hill a way is surrounded by ferns and
is ideal for al fresco sponging off. Coming down the mountain this morning I saw a barking deer. It is about the size
of a large dog and makes a noise like a low bark—a beautiful miniature toy.

Back of the Embassy garages the guards have hatched
themselves out a flock of ducks which keep running under
passing cars. So they have built a little enclosure in which
they have raised a wondrous crop of grass, and they spend
most of their time squatting around to watch the ducks.
It is a question whether they or the ducks are more enter-
taining.

A wonderful fight is going on now. Grand plans have
been made for a state diplomatic dinner as a farewell for
the British Ambassador. Now it is all fouled up and stale-
mated because the Russians maintain that the Soviet
Ambassador is the ranking diplomat in China, and the
French who are doing the seating maintain that Marshall
ranks. And neither one will yield. I don't see why they
don't settle it by having both stay home, since Sir Horace
deserves something better than this kind of dinner anyway.

June 14 / It is now only seven days to the end of the truce period and there is much wrestling over some kind of agreement no one really thinks will be reached. The stream of accusations and recrimination from all sides is overwhelming and endless and I doubt if anyone, even the one who makes it, really knows how much truth there is in any statement. Suspicion and tension have corrupted all judgment. Meanwhile, spontaneous evacuations begin, and people and warships move aimlessly here and there. Some people who have just come from Peiping and Tientsin say those cities are armed camps, and the tension grows as armed forts spring up all around. Everywhere small peasant revolts are breaking out. And during the last few days prices on most items in Nanking have trebled; the Government apparently believes that the economic situation is so bad anything, even war, is preferable. One man just in from Washington says that all the talk is of war with the Russians—not just the Army, but everybody; not that anybody wants it, but all are passively and despairingly accepting it as fact, without taking much interest in finding the causes.

The Australian party last night was the usual nationality day mob scene at which the only interest was a long talk I had with Ch'en Li-fu. He told me a story about himself I had heard before, but never quite believed. He says it is all the fault of John L. Lewis he is back in China. He went to school in the States and then worked in the Pennsylvania coal mines. He liked it so well he planned to spend his life there. Then came the big coal strike of 1925 with no foreseeable prospect of ending; so he came back to China. He is still a member of the United Mine Workers and showed me a valid membership card to prove it. "It was in Pennsylvania that I learned the real menace of the Communists. I have spent eighteen years fighting them, and will spend another eighteen if necessary. Obviously you cannot trust them in negotiation and therefore nothing will come of the present series of talks; but that is all right because they can easily be destroyed. This will not mean

Ch'en Kuo-fu, Ch'en Li-fu's brother, was the real power and mind in the cc *clique, and when he died after the Nationalist withdrawal to Taiwan in 1949 the clique fell to pieces. Ch'en Li-fu lost favor with the Generalissimo, retired to Long Island, and devoted himself to raising chickens and to Moral Rearmament. At the time it was impossible to see him as other than unmitigated evil; and yet he was doing what he really thought was best for China, however wrong his assessment of the possible*

*was. No foreigner ever
got to know enough
about his brother to
make a judgment on
him one way or the
other then or now.*

civil war. There will be no civil war unless you think there
will; there will be no general war unless you think there
will. I do not think there will." I am convinced he really
meant what he said, despite the seeming paradox of his
obvious key role in sabotaging the negotiations. He has
become a convert to Moral Rearmament, and he can hold
conflicting views with equal conviction. The cc clique is
the best known and most notorious faction in the Kuomintang. The basic philosophy of its leaders, the Ch'en brothers,
is a kind of Chinese Fascism which has great appeal for the
Generalissimo, who has never displayed any understanding
of economics beyond Confucian feudalism. The brothers are
adamant in their opposition to any agreement with the Communists. Force is the only answer. They can usually count on
the support of a group of generals whose sole objective is to
protect their looting of military funds. It is a formidable combination and, skilled politician that he is, the Generalissimo
does not dare ignore their wishes too much. Perhaps he has
never really wanted to do so. It is this coalition which is
meant whenever anyone in China refers to "reactionary elements in the Kuomintang."

Outside my window a pig is squealing in the alley in
protest at being dragged along on a string.

June 17 / At long last the rain has stopped after endless
hours of downpour which put much of the city under three
feet of water. Now the sun has made it a Turkish bath.
But it was pleasant, cool, and sunny up on the mountain
yesterday. And it was peaceful and very far away from
Nanking. My cook is good and turns out a presentable
meal; he is also casual and is bewildered and a little hurt
when I insist he shall not dump the garbage and the can
in the front yard. I think I finally have him persuaded,
but he is still reluctant about not hanging his underwear
on the nearest convenient bush. It is a satisfactory compromise; I really have nothing to complain about.

I had lunch this noon with the Minister of Information
and assorted henchmen. The conversation was mostly non-

sense, loose and ugly, about the "situation." Either they are desperate or the rest of us are morons. He has, however, a wonderful cook from Fukien (famous for producing the best), who turns out as good a meal as I have ever had anywhere. Food is one of the endless delights of China.

The Government has held a state funeral for Tai Li, whose memory only a few lament. There was a good band which played only three tunes and played them over and over again. They were "Nearer My God to Thee," "Stop Your Tickling Jock," and "Pore Jud Is Dead."

June 20 / Two more days to the end of truce. Doubtless something is going on, but I am sure I do not know what it is. The rumors and the fairly well founded stories are not encouraging, but I no longer believe anything I hear. So I have in an exasperating day made an analysis of the new Mongolian constitution. Example: one article says all land shall be state property. The next one says all private property in land shall be protected. I cannot figure out whether someone had a sense of humor or whether the formidable climate of Mongolia is not propitious for constitution writing.

Tonight I dine with a Chinese medical general who wants to show us a pagoda and is mounting a campaign to have himself named as the official liaison with Americans on cultural matters. Chinese dinner invitations are fun. They are always decorated with flowers and read something like this: "The gardenias are in the water bowl, the chopsticks have been washed since the last time they were used, the wine is hot and waiting for you at such and such a time and place. We hope the first dishes will make you wish to leave the rice alone. . . ."

June 21 / Life continues to be a walking nightmare and is getting worse as the deadline approaches. It is hard to see just what will happen because too many factors are unknown, but the outlines seem clear enough. The best hope for the Communists is prolongation of the truce to stall hostilities as long as possible. The Generalissimo seems

The American plane in which Tai Li was returning to Nanking in a heavy overcast struck the summit of Cowshead Mountain a few miles from the capital, due to faulty radar equipment at the airport. It was said that the Generalissimo wept when he heard the news, as well he might because he never again found anyone who would serve him as effectively. Others, who did not share this sense of loss, noted that Cowshead is in the ring of hills around Nanking which includes Purple Mountain on whose slope stands the mausoleum of Dr. Sun Yat-sen. It was widely alleged that in fact the spirit of Dr. Sun had risen up in anger and struck Tai Li down.

undecided for the Government. The best information is that the generals are committed to war, as is the cc clique. All other groups want peace, and every available missionary is being brought in to exert pressure in that direction.

Marshall is deathly tired, so tired he is fumbling and the initiative has passed to the Generalissimo, who is not tired. I suppose it depends on whether either side can nerve itself for the final break and accept the unpredictable consequences. Part of it also depends on what sort of advice about American opinion the Generalissimo is receiving. My guess is there is a slight edge for prolonging the truce for a few days. If an extension is made, then the stalemate can be dragged out.

John Leighton Stuart

One might well wonder at this point how it was possible for conditions to have become as chaotic as they were and still permit important negotiations to be seriously pursued. One might well wonder how a realist like General Marshall could still entertain serious hopes in an atmosphere that approached fantasy. Certainly in any western context even a pretense of negotiation would long since have been abandoned. But the difference between the West and China was as important then as it is now.

The mere presence of Marshall, and hence by implication that of the United States, undoubtedly created a certain restraint between antagonists who otherwise might have been even less restrained than they were. But there was more to it than that. Two factors were vital. For one thing, the top leaders of the Kuomintang and of the Communists were not basically evil men – at least not in the sense that Hitler was evil. Assuredly they were ruthless, and frequently devious; they had to be to have arrived where they were. Many of the men at secondary levels were evil, and they caused a vast amount of mischief. The top men without question were revolted by some of the things they felt they had to do and by the continuing slaughter, but they also passionately believed that their particular views of society and how it should be run were the only correct ones, that their actions were indeed inevitable. The Mandate of Heaven was inexorable, and current misery was the price for the future. Each could hope against hope that his Mandate was so apparent that the other would sooner or later recognize it and come to terms. History may very well label this single-mindedness as stupid and self-defeating, but not evil, as the more extreme protagonists of one side or the other were then and are now inclined to view the opposition. The devil theory of history is too simple.

The other and more subtle factor goes deep into Chinese tradition. Both the Generalissimo with his Christianity and Mao Tse-tung with his Marxism had avowedly discarded the Confucian ethic which had formed the basis of Chinese society for the better part of two millenia. And yet, having been born and reared in it, they could not altogether escape its influence any more than any other man can totally deny his past. Compromise and peaceful adjustment of differences directly between antagonists are basic in the Confucian way. Agreement to accept the decision of a third party, as in a western legal system, or resort to violence, is the admission of the failure of reason. It is the ultimate humiliation. Both sides probably knew in their hearts, as they frequently suggested, that their differences were too great for compromise, but they could not yet bring themselves to acknowledge finally that the time-tested way of their ancestors had failed.

These two factors were directly relevant to the next step which General Marshall took when he asked President Truman to nominate Dr. John Leighton Stuart as Ambassador to China.

The reaction in the Embassy to the appointment of Dr. Stuart was largely dismay. As a young man, he had come to China forty years before as a missionary and had been there ever since. His interests were a good deal broader than this, as he demonstrated in his years as President of Yenching University, supported by Protestant churches, which had made a significant contribution to Chinese education. This role distinctly set him apart from the run-of-the-mill missionary, and he was certainly more sophisticated in Chinese politics than were most foreigners. For example, his activities during the Japanese occupation will probably never be known, but what is known was that he spent it in the kind of gilded internment which permitted him to commute between Peiping and Chungking largely at will in the hope of restoring peace.

A word must first be said about the importance of Christianity in China during the first half of the twentieth century. The roots of the American missionary movement there go deep into the nineteenth century, doubtless having originated from interest in the country stimulated by the very considerable clipper ship trade of the early part of the century which was the foundation of many a New England fortune. The proselytizing zeal of the Puritan followed trade, even if in this instance the flag did not. And yet, despite all the effort that went into it, by 1948 there were probably no more than two and a half million Protestants and five million Catholics out of more than a half billion Chinese. The effort could have seemed wasted except that the Protestant influence went far beyond its numerical strength.

For almost a century, there had been few American Sunday School children who had not contributed their pennies to the movement, few congregations which had not from time to time heard missionaries on home leave preach. There were few college graduates who had not known a Chinese student, or who did not at least know that one was on campus. In brief, a broad range of Americans had some kind of awareness of China and even some personal involvement with it, beyond the traditional Chinese laundryman. In China itself, the influence was even more decisive. When the United States returned its share of the Boxer Indemnity to found and support Tsinghua University, the Protestant churches followed suit. For decades, the missionary-supported middle schools and colleges provided the main centers of modern education, and sent their best students to the United States for further training. In the process, a large number of these students understandably became Christians.

It was the Generalissimo himself who crystallized the matter. Although not western educated, he found it expedient at one point during his rise to power to be converted in order to marry a sister-in-law of Dr. Sun Yat-sen and thus not only inherit the mantle, but also ally himself with the powerful Shanghai Soong banking interests which had been founded by an early convert named Charlie Jones Soong. The motives of the Generalissimo at the time may have been suspect, as apparently even the missionaries felt, since the only one who could be found to perform the marriage ceremony was a YMCA secretary; but there is no reason to doubt that, at least with time, his Christianity became a sincere and deeply held article of faith. And of course Madame Chiang has always been a devout believer, with great influence over her husband.

One consequence of all this is that ever since the Generalissimo assumed power a significant proportion of influential Chinese leaders were always practicing Christians—and Protestants, seldom Catholics. Parenthetically, during this period one of the ablest and most influential military leaders, General Pai Chung-hsi, who at one time or another held every top job except that of the Generalissimo himself, was the leader of the Moslem community. It can also be argued, I think, that the missionary movement has had more influence in shaping American attitudes toward China than any other single factor; and it paid handsome dividends to the Kuomintang. It is not irrelevant, incidentally, that the missionaries tended to be rather more fundamentalist than liberal.[1] Dr. Stuart, however, was definitely of the liberal persuasion, and I can remember his telling us with a certain amusement of the time he defeated heresy charges against him. As Ambassador he was rather maliciously pleased by the scandalized reaction of his more orthodox colleagues when he served them cocktails, and he thoroughly enjoyed a drink or two himself before dinner. But he never did learn to smoke gracefully or as though he liked it.

It was this background which made the Embassy more than a little skeptical of the appointment; but General Marshall, who had something very different in mind, did not share the skepticism. He had come to the conclusion there was

1 I do not think that the combination of religious and political conservatism had much influence on Chinese thinking at the time. The liberal missionaries for the most part were never really aware of the disparity between the protestations of the Generalissimo and his actions. The conservative attitudes had their impact on American opinion when the missionaries were repatriated and quickly aligned themselves with the most extreme anti-Communist elements in the United States.

little more of a constructive nature that he had to offer; at best he could only be a restraining influence for a while. Another kind of person was needed, if anything was to be done, and Dr. Stuart had what he was looking for. His personal integrity was beyond question; his knowledge of China and Chinese ways enormous. He was acceptable to all shades of Chinese opinion. A great many Nationalist and Communist leaders had been his students and, given the tremendous importance of the Chinese teacher-student relationship, in which the teacher is revered as all-wise, all-knowing, and beyond error, he could say to and do with them things no one else could. Not the least of his qualifications was that over the years he had learned how in negotiation to be just as oblique and, when necessary, just as devious as any Chinese. It was no mean accomplishment.

During the next three years those of us who had had reservations came to have great respect for his ability and deep affection for him as a human being. I think what affected us most was the growing realization that he so passionately loved the Chinese people and was so heartsick over what was happening to them that he would do literally anything that gave any kind of hope of stopping the slaughter to which they were still being subjected. Nothing else moved him, not even the august Department of State, whose instructions he on occasion did not bother to read.

The situation into which Dr. Stuart walked in Nanking toward the end of July would have daunted anyone less determined and cheerful. The July 1 truce had been received with little more than momentary skeptical relief. The events of the next three weeks would dampen even that temporary aberration. The common denominator in these events was anti-Americanism, which found expression in mass demonstrations, press campaigns, and mob action.[2] The Communists began charging that legislation, then being considered by the Congress to authorize military aid once the February 25 military reorganization plan had been implemented, only encouraged the Government to pursue a policy of force and proved that aid for the Government would be forthcoming regardless of whether there was a political settlement. Marshall finally felt compelled to inform Chou En-lai that if this propaganda barrage continued it would end any remaining usefulness he might have.

Paradoxically, the reactionary Kuomintang elements were even more extreme in their denunciations, with charges that American activities were only a sinister plot of the United States to create chaos and pave the way for an American takeover of Chinese economic interests—otherwise why would Marshall try to restrain the Government from exterminating the Communists? As the number of military clashes throughout the country increased, the Generalissimo added his bit to the confusion by leaving on July 14 for his summer residence at Kuling, which was sufficiently inaccessible that any negotiation was seriously handicapped.

Two incidents symbolized what was happening. Two prominent members of the Democratic League, one of them a distinguished university professor, were assassinated by secret police officials of the Kunming Garrison Headquarters

2 *China White Paper*, pp. 170–72.

as part of the mounting campaign of terrorism by the Kuomintang against the Democratic League and other liberals who disagreed with right-wing policy. Then, in mid-month, the Communists kidnapped seven US Marines east of Peiping and held them for several days. This was followed toward the end of the month by a deliberate Communist ambush of a Marine motor convoy carrying UNRRA supplies between Tientsin and Peiping during which three Americans were killed and twelve wounded.

July 8 / Nanking / Although he has often enough been annoyed with Chou En-lai, today is the first time I have seen Marshall really angry with him. It was the Communist statement yesterday which intemperately charged the United States with favoring the Government. The implied assault on Marshall's personal motives did it: "Don't you think my position is hard enough without this which you know is a lie just as well as I do?" Chou looked a little sheepish and said nothing. In distinction to almost everyone else here, Marshall has always thought that Chou, however much they disagreed, has never played games with him. The incident illustrates the confusion since it comes just a week after the extension of the truce without a time limit.

July 10 / The naming of John Leighton Stuart as Ambassador has produced an atmosphere of unmitigated gloom around this place. He is a missionary, President of Yenching University where a great many of the leaders of China, Kuomintang and Communist, were educated, which in China has great meaning due to the relationship of teacher and student, is a close friend of the Generalissimo, has been in China for forty years, is very pro-Kuomintang, and will probably run his show his own way because his background and contacts give him a unique asset in being able to talk to the Generalissimo as probably no one else can. The speculation is it means Marshall will give up soon, go home, and we will continue to dilly-dally along without taking any very definite line of policy on anything. Most disturbing is that Stuart is reportedly sold on the line that Kuomintang lip service to democracy means what it says. Anyway, he speaks Chinese.

July 11 / It is by now quite plain that there won't and probably can't be even an interim substantive agreement, that desultory talks will go on endlessly while both sides jockey for military position, and the Kuomintang is confident it can bring the Communists to their knees militarily in six months. So we temporize, stall, put off the evil day when we make up our minds—if we ever do.

This morning Marshall marched in, announced he had trouble with refugees, and wanted an answer in two hours to the land problem. There has recently been much loose and vague talk about a land reform which would compensate the landlords. I believe it is historically correct that there has never been a land reform movement which was successful in buying off landlords on a voluntary basis. I doubt if in China even forced redistribution of land is any answer because of population pressure. It will take some new scientific breakthrough to feed all these people. The current flurry, I think, comes from a growing realization by a lot of people, including Marshall, that the answer is only marginally and temporarily one of stopping the fighting. A whole new social deal is needed and these same people are finding to their bewilderment that it is not as easy as they would like to think. Marshall's voice this morning was that of a hopeless old man.

July 21 / This is a broiling Sunday afternoon on the hill and it must be hell down in town. Last night there was a cloudburst. When I got up this morning it was still storming and fun to watch the clouds bouncing into the front door, out the back, and over the crest of the hill behind the house. Below, none of the valley was visible. Now all the mountains in the distance are covered with a blue haze.

Political tension this past week got a new lease on life with two murders in Kunming. They were only a couple of reasonably innocuous scholars with long beards, but they had committed the crime of letting it be known they did not like to see people pushed around. Nor, incidentally, has the recent kidnapping and detention for several days of American Marines by Communist troops near Peiping been calculated to improve anyone's disposition.

July 23 / The rumors today are as thick as the heat. Apparently, the Communists have just finished administering a pasting to their opponents at Nantung across the Yangtze from Shanghai. That is getting close. The other night I could hear the artillery fire across the river from the top of my hill. Ceasefire or no ceasefire, reports of sporadic fighting all over the country have become so persistent and numerous during the last three weeks that there must be a great deal to them, even if any one story bears little measurable relationship to the truth.

I took Nathaniel Peffer, the Asian scholar from Columbia University, up the hill for dinner last night. When we arrived one of the biggest storms I have ever seen broke, with the house seemingly in the middle of it. The rain was so heavy it seemed solid. The most spectacular part was the lightning which streaked all around the place, in and out of windows, leaving the air heavily charged with electricity. It seemed like a good atmosphere in which to sit and discuss *Götterdämmerung*.

The whole question of the right of political asylum has always been a difficult and embarrassing one because every instance represents some measure of interference by one sovereign state in the internal affairs of another. Practice has varied widely from one time and place to another, except in Latin America, where the right has usually been recognized.

July 25 / The Kunming murder incident has been thoroughly fouled up from our standpoint because the Consulate has given asylum to other potential victims and now has a refugee colony of at least a dozen professors.

As a result I have been elected as one of two from the Embassy to go there on a hatchet job to see if we can get the Consulate out of its predicament and at the same time get some assurances that when the Chinese leave the premises they will not shortly make a quick trip to another plane of existence. All this is a follow-up to last winter's Kunming student strikes. And now another Democratic Leaguer, Dr. Tao, who has done such wonderful work with literacy, has died of fright and strain in Shanghai. He was a terrific man.

Now it is raining—somehow soothing—and there is something intimate about it. That is one thing that amazes me

about the hill. The more time I spend there the more the
vastness of the view, its impersonality, its detachment from
anything except space and sky weigh on me. I find myself
wanting a garden, a tree, and some grass, something close
and personal, something I can touch.

July 28 / Kunming / We flew clear across China to the
foothills of the Himalayas in a few hours and landed here
nine months after I first landed in Kunming on my way
into China. It seems a lifetime ago. The airport was a
strange sight because there were only two other planes on
it; one year ago it was the busiest airport in the world and
now it is the end of the line. The valley must be one of the
loveliest spots in the world, with much the same charm as
several spots I know in Colombia and Mexico. Being over
six thousand feet high, the air is clear, the sun shines, and
it is cool. And even if the city itself is dirty, it is the sort of
place where one could live and be happy. The trouble is
that a lot of people here are not happy.

When we arrived the men who had taken refuge were
a dejected lot, not daring to leave the premises, not knowing how to get out of the province. One of them said it
meant the end of the Democratic League; and somehow I
had the feeling this is where I came in.

The next morning we haggled with the leading military
personage, a smooth and very tough man and a cousin of
General Ho Ying-chin, Minister of Defence. He blandly
ignored the issues and so did we. In the end an agreement
of sorts was reached. It did not seem to mean very much
until suddenly this morning Governor Lu Han appeared
from Peiping and Indochina and called on us. He commanded the Chinese troops who at the end of the war
occupied north Vietnam. His principal accomplishment before he withdrew was to loot the area of almost everything
movable. Since he arrived by way of the Generalissimo and
obviously with orders that this business had caused more
trouble than it was worth, everything was settled in a
moment with regrets on all sides and flowery speeches and

good will. The refugees will be given safe conduct to Peiping.

My guess is the local authorities had thought they could handle their political problems quietly and had not antici-pated that the proposed victims would run to the Consulate. Just how much encouragement they had received to do so is unclear and is best left that way. So tactics had to be changed. After all there is more than one way to skin a Democratic Leaguer. Tomorrow there will be a gala ban-quet given by the Governor at which everyone will get very drunk and something else will start. All this is as much local Yunnan politics as it is national.

For centuries the province of Yunnan has been a great warlord stronghold and the effort to bring it effectively under the Central Government has been of doubtful suc-cess, even during the war when the Government was next door in Szechuan. It is a pity such a lovely province should be so continually messed up and so much the prey of conflicting personal ambitions. As usual it is the peasant who pays in money, blood, and torture. A good part of last night someone in the neighborhood was screaming out his life or else it was a good imitation. Either one may have been for our benefit.

Kunming itself is a good example of what happens. It is charming and it looks ancient; yet it is not more than seventy years old. Less than a century ago there was a great Moslem revolt in west China which lasted twenty years. Millions upon millions of people were butchered and almost every city in the province was completely destroyed. When it was over there was not a living soul nor a building left standing in Kunming. I have never seen a reference to this in a western textbook.

This afternoon the Air Attaché and I went out for a picnic with an elderly German couple, ex-German Foreign Service, whom Hitler fired for impurity of race. They have lived in China most of the time since 1901. We went several miles down the Burma road to three rather imposing Buddhist temples which always amaze me. They are always located in beautiful spots. In the villages along the way the Chinese population quickly gives way to aboriginal Yunnanese tribes, cousins of the Tibetans. Physically they are different and their clothes become much more colorful. The villages also become increasingly cluttered with Buddhist and Taoist priests who wander around and live off the local people. Where the Chinese predominate there is very little of this.

July 30 / The happy party with the Governor unfortunately did not turn out to be the usual Chinese celebration. He decided to do it western style in his conventional western house. His living room was ornamented with the following: A Venetian mirror, a large photograph of the Venus di Milo, a painting of September Morn, and another one of Napoleon's Retreat from Moscow. The meal was strictly church supper, except for two items. He produced a bottle of finest scotch drinking whiskey and a vintage Bordeaux such as I have not seen since before the war. There are advantages to looting French Indochina. Among those present was General Ku Chu-tung, Commander in Chief of the Chinese Army, who is about as tough as anyone I have ever seen. There is one thing about generals like him —they know exactly what they want, how to get it, and never scruple about the niceties.

This afternoon we went shopping and found little. I ended up with some green pottery, coolie glasses, a battered brass tea kettle, a mandarin skullcap, and a pair of Indian clubs. Just why I bought the last item I don't know. But it was fun sloshing around in the mud.

The August doldrums

Dr. Stuart lost no time in becoming active in the negotiations which went on during the oppressively hot dogdays of August. Even a mild summer in Nanking is dreadful, and the extreme of this one seemed to fit the mood of the times. On August 1 he proposed a special five-man committee to seek immediate organization of the State Council, as agreed the previous January, which would govern until a new Constitution had been adopted. On August 10, in order to force the issue, Marshall and Stuart made a public statement which simply recapitulated the known points of difference between the two sides, and added an exhortation for conciliation and good faith. Privately, Marshall told the Generalissimo his present course, especially in military affairs, would "probably lead to Communist control of China."[1] To another high official he emphasized that the "United States will not underwrite a civil war in China."[2] President Truman added his weight by sending a message to the Generalissimo which deplored the drift into war and added that unless it was stopped he would have "to redefine and explain" the American position publicly.[3] On August 13 the Generalissimo replied publicly to the Marshall-Stuart plea and blamed the Communists for all the ailments of China.[4]

On August 22, Chou En-lai agreed to participate in the five-man committee which Dr. Stuart had proposed. Five days later the Generalissimo also agreed, but only reluctantly and without giving any indication of a willingness to compromise on any point or even to halt the advances of his troops. He obviously remained confident of his ability to obtain a military solution, as he indicated when he replied to President Truman on August 28 and only repeated what he had said on August 13.

What happened next can only be regarded as a bad mistake in judgment by Marshall. On August 30 an agreement was signed between the United States and the Nationalist Government for the transfer of surplus property which had been stockpiled on the islands of the Pacific in anticipation of a longer war against Japan. The sale was part of the overall liquidation of Lend-Lease, which had played such a vital role in the prosecution of the war. Being quite aware of the repeated Communist charges of American partisanship, Marshall tried to reassure Chou En-lai that the material had no military value, that it consisted only of medicines and other equipment for economic rehabilitation which would benefit all Chinese, and that

1 *China White Paper*, p. 176.
2 *Ibid.*, p. 174.
3 *Ibid.*, p. 179. The understanding was that the United States would train and equip China's new army. The arms embargo which Marshall had imposed early in the spring was not lifted until he returned to Washington in 1947. Although at the time no one took exception to the embargo, it later became one of the key points in the China argument. The charge was that it seriously handicapped the Kuomintang in its fight against the Communists. There is no military evidence for this argument, which, moreover, conveniently ignored the fact that, rightly or wrongly, American policy at the time was to encourage a political settlement, and not to assist one side militarily against the other. No one then had seriously objected to this policy. Economic aid was largely limited to UNRRA relief supplies and was important. Direct American economic help would not even be requested until later. American troops were limited in number owing to large-scale post-war demobilization. In any event, experts on China would agree that the more American troops in the country, the greater would have been the anti-American feeling and the swing of public support to any group opposing the presence of foreign troops on Chinese soil.
4 *Ibid.*, p. 177.

no equipment envisaged in the February 25 reorganization agreement would be available until that agreement was implemented. Since the wartime agreements had long since been completed, Marshall did in fact at this time order an embargo on any shipments of military materiel.[5] If Chou En-lai was persuaded, he gave no sign of it.

The President on August 31 sent a message to the Generalissimo in which he said bluntly that unless the hostilities stopped there would be no more aid of any kind. If the Generalissimo believed this warning, he too gave no indication of it – or perhaps he thought it would make no difference.

5 *Ibid.*, p. 354.

August 2 / Nanking / The trip back from Kunming had its moments. We blew a tire on takeoff and were delayed for hours while the damage was repaired. The plane was overloaded by a couple of thousand pounds after a group of Chinese gendarmes hitched a ride with an appalling amount of baggage which included a bicycle. In that condition we just barely made it off the ground and over the telegraph lines at the end of the field. But the flight itself was wonderful dodging in and out of towering clouds and playing peekaboo with spectacular thunderheads.

When we got back we found much snarling and irritation over an ambush of a Marine convoy taking Executive Headquarters and UNRRA supplies over the Peiping-Tientsin road. Three Americans were killed and all sides are frantically pointing fingers at someone else. Actually, geography alone in this instance makes the Communist claim of innocence look pretty feeble. Marshall is setting up an investigating team from Executive Headquarters, but unless something radically different has been introduced into China I'll bet the three sides never agree on a finding. [*They didn't.*]

Last night the Communists gave a farewell dinner for one of our officers who has been transferred. Among those present was a young man named Liao Chung-sze whose father was one of the early holies of the Kuomintang and who has himself fallen from official grace. The amazing thing about him is that he spent four years in solitary confinement without light or reading material—and still he

seems quite normal. I also learned that Li Li-san is in
Manchuria after a twenty-year exile in the Soviet Union
and is seemingly the top man there. It must mean the
Russians are trying to reinforce their position.

August 6 / I am beginning to get my ears above the paper
water level that rose while I was away in Kunming, and
then I shall take off for Manchuria—at long last. One can
hope it will be cooler there. I never knew I could be so
uncomfortably hot or feel so much like a grease spot all
the time.

Anyway the work has had the effect of preventing too
much thinking about too many things. The political pot
still simmers, though we don't know much of what goes on
beyond what is in the papers. I talked yesterday with one
of the Kunming refugees who are through here en route
to Peiping. He was in a low frame of mind, and I gather
that many of the liberals will now either recant or go into
exile. Some of course will go over to the Communists. But
whatever it is, the position of the liberal has now become
hopeless and I would be surprised if many of them could
not be persuaded to enter a coalition on Kuomintang terms.
At the same time, it must be admitted that their choices are
limited. They are learning that no party can survive without armed force behind it, and at the same time many
cannot honestly go along with either of those having power.

Life has taken on one normal aspect. We really are
getting the Shanghai newspapers only one day late and
containing Terry and the Pirates, Dick Tracy, and Dorothy
Dix. . . .

August 8 / The recent Joseph Harsch article on China in
the *Christian Science Monitor* was excellent in pointing out
how little we are really doing here. People who keep talking
about all the aid forget that military aid apart from wartime commitments does not begin until the February agreement has been implemented. The other aid could be put in
a beer mug, being all on paper anyway. There are not
enough American troops here even to defend themselves.

There is a wondrously black storm high in the north. It should bring some relief since the rain is only a block away and smells good. There is an almost complete rainbow. Coming in from Kunming the other day we flew through the middle of a complete one. There was a great storm to be seen in the distance from the hill last night. It put on a magnificent four-hour display of lightning.

August 12 / Mukden / The flight up here was dismaying. All north China is under yellowish, turgid water which is broken only by ridges and occasional spots of high ground on which countless people and animals cluster motionless. No one will ever know how many more lie beneath or have been washed away. And Mukden is as far north as we will get because Changchun is also flooded and Harbin is in Communist hands.

South Manchuria, which is not flooded, is a great and lovely land. It makes me think of our Middle West and the "beauty of fertility." Lacking the human crowding of China within the wall, it has great stretches of fields and trees to the horizon, splashed over with a piebald pattern of light and shadow as clouds play across the face of the sun. Now it can only be enjoyed from the air because Manchuria has the same pattern as the rest of China—the Government holds the large cities and the lines of communication; the Communists have the rest. Mukden was never exactly a distinctive or beautiful city; now it is mediocrity turned to ruins and shambles. It has been gutted by bombing, end-of-the-war vandalism, Russian looting, and now Chinese neglect. The great factories and public works are empty and silent, and the scars of fire are already beginning to be softened by the encroaching vegetation. The houses wear the tired look of disrepair and the streets are dangerous at night for lack of maintenance.

Trade centers largely in stalls along the sidewalks or where sidewalks once were. There is little in them beyond a few art treasures which survived the looting and the cloth and iron tag-ends of a junk collection. The Americans are rapidly buying up everything of value.

The people move—or don't move—aimlessly, listlessly.
They are shabby and the pinch of hunger begins to show
in pale faces and defensive eyes. Only the troops General
Stilwell trained in India stand out as men and exceptional
soldiers. Even they are beginning to show signs of deteriorating morale from inaction, incompetent leadership, and
the watering down of their ranks with the usual Chinese
military product. Still, however, they are so much a breed
apart as to be considered foreigners by the local people.

There is little evidence of military activity or preparation
for it. The troops are crowded into the city and kept here
by the baffling harassment of Communist guerrillas whenever they venture past the outskirts. The accent is on the
negative in all things.

August 16 / Peiping / I don't know the reason, but I was
quite unprepared for Peiping. It is obviously China, and yet
another kind of China. It is everything people say it is, a
truly imperial city full of yellow, red, rose, blue, and green.
The Forbidden City, palace of the Manchu emperors, is
spectacular and breathtaking; the Temple of Heaven must
be the most beautiful building in the world with its simplicity, perfect proportions, and the brilliantly contrasting blue
tiles and the long white marble causeway.

The setting also surprises me. The countryside, with the
Western Hills in the distance, is distinctly semi-arid and
conveys the sense of soil and people felt wherever life
depends on inadequate rainfall and partial irrigation—a
meeting point for the Gobi to the north and flooding rivers
in the south, the desert having something of an edge. The
city bustles: automobiles and camel caravans mingle with
easy familiarity, and the people who ride both do the same.
They have a kind of robustness and gaiety which have been
little affected by Japanese occupation and the slowly closing
noose of civil war. There is an obvious pride and conviction
of personal dignity which enable them to make the best of
straitened circumstances—after all, this is Peiping and
always will be. The laughter on the streets is still self-
assured and carefree.

Three days are too few to know really what goes on in the universities. Certainly, the faculty people are more solemn than the street crowds. They are involved in the same activities and subject to the same terrorism as intellectuals elsewhere, but somehow they are more sophisticated about it, more knowledgeable, less furtive, with fewer illusions about the intellectual and politics. Wise old Lao Chin at Peiping University said to me with a twinkle in his eye, "What I have most against you rich Americans is that you are buying up all our beautiful old Huang hua li furniture. There will be none left for us. But I have saved up enough money and bought one piece more beautiful than any you have ever seen." He had, too.

Nonetheless, the overtone is here. Last night while I was walking on the wall in the moonlight a sentry fired at me point blank. I did not tarry there long enough to inquire into his motives.

August 18 / One of the purposes of these travels is to look into our information programs and what we are trying to

The Huang hua li of the Ming Dynasty is at least three hundred years old because it was made from an Indochina rosewood which has been extinct for that long. Its simplicity of design fits in with anything else, and to look into its surface polished with beeswax is like gazing into eternity.

do with them. On this point of objective there is little understanding between Washington and us—which means Marshall. As long as the Marshall effort is the policy, we are faced with a most difficult problem and it will be only with the most skilful effort that we can minimize charges of partisanship. Washington does not seem to understand— at least those who service our information work do not— that we *are* here in the role of mediator and until that policy is changed should work on a nucleus of understanding and give up the present buckshot approach. Specifically, this means abandoning mass distribution and concentrating on groups in strategic or potentially strategic positions, trying to understand what and how they think, and helping them to do the same with us. Of course we have to realize that everyone wants to use us for his own particular purpose. I have even found several instances of our Chinese employees who are finding us a safe shield for various activities on several sides of the Chinese political fence.

There is nothing particularly wrong with any given item of material we put out. It is just that the overall pattern is aimless and meaningless. In Peiping there is currently a technically beautiful photo exhibit of supposedly typical American faces. Every one could have come straight out of "Li'l Abner." The preceding exhibit was on the Italian campaign in Ethiopia. In Mukden we were showing motion pictures of the Iwo Jima campaign and on the inner workings of a modern battleship to thousands of people who have never seen a rowboat. A recent sample newsfile from our Shanghai office contained the following: articles on Hollywood, problems of television, political party responsibility, the Czech economy, oil in the world, postwar Spain, American international economic interests, and the measurement of earthquakes. The Chinese newspaper reading public which is fighting for survival itself could hardly care less!

One Chinese professor, American educated and very friendly to us, put it this way to me: "None of you Americans on either side of the Pacific has ever taken the trouble

to find out why it is that the Chinese think like Chinese
instead of like Texans, or, for that matter, to take into
account even that most elementary of all differences—the
difference in attitudes between poor people who have never
had enough to eat and people to whom hunger has never
really been more than an intellectual concept."

September 1 / Nanking / Along with all the other vagaries
of the summer heat, August turned out to be the month for
high-level heated messages and even more heated conversations. While hostilities were expanding, the political exchanges were designed to break the negotiating stalemate.
It is doubtful that any participant—with the exception
of Ambassador Stuart who is new to this particular form of
frustration and seems anyway to be a great optimist by
nature—had any real hope, even intention, of progress.

September 8 / It is cool now and the hillside is alive with
blue morning glories which blend so well with the pine
trees.

Marshall has one amusing custom. He sees a movie every
night. Midway there is always a break for ice cream. With
him it is rather charming—and how he does like his ice
cream! My admiration for him is tempered only by a wish
that he would stop trying to make me smoke less. Just
because he stopped. . . .

Kalgan-the military zenith

The military developments during September only served to reinforce a growing
impression that the Generalissimo and his generals did in fact believe that they
could win militarily without any help from anyone else. By the end of the month,
Government forces had succeeded in taking just about everything the Generalissimo had been demanding during the June truce period. The political negotiations
of the time reflected the usual pattern of proposal and counter proposal, seeming
to be on the verge of agreement, and then suddenly coming to nothing.

A critical point was reached on September 30 when the Kuomintang Central
News Agency announced that Government forces had begun operations for the
capture of Kalgan, a principal Communist political and military center northwest

of Peiping. On the same day Chou En-lai sent Marshall a memorandum stating that if this operation continued, he could only consider it as public indication of a "total national split." On the following day Marshall replied that although he disagreed with what both sides were doing he was willing to discuss the Chou memorandum with the Generalissimo. He did so on the same day and again on the following day.[1] The burden of the Generalissimo's argument was that the campaign against Kalgan was in the interests of peace because its successful conclusion would place the Communists in a position where they would have to accept whatever terms were offered them and then the prospects for peaceful political settlement, which everyone wanted, would be vastly improved. Marshall disagreed flatly and said that in the circumstances he saw no alternative to ending the American mediatory effort. The Generalissimo apparently did not believe him, since he refused to budge from his position.

The next day Marshall requested instructions from the President to end his mission immediately. When the Generalissimo heard of this he at once offered to halt the advance on Kalgan for five days on condition that the Communists rejoin the political talks.[2] Marshall then asked Washington to defer his recall until further notice.

The Communists refused the truce. On October 8, Marshall and Stuart issued a public statement outlining developments beginning with the Chou En-lai memorandum of September 30. Following this statement Chou on October 9 sent the Generalissimo a memorandum which concluded that if the attack on Kalgan stopped permanently, the Communists would return to the conference table.

October 10, the Double Ten Day, is the great national holiday, the anniversary of the founding of the Chinese Republic. The Generalissimo chose the occasion for a speech in which he called on the Communists to abandon their plot to subvert the country for their own ends and to participate with all other parties in the National Government and the National Assembly. The Government desired only total and permanent cessation of hostilities, but for three months the Communists had consistently refused all proposals. Nevertheless, peaceful settlement would remain official policy. While he was speaking, his troops were completing the occupation of Kalgan. Other key points were captured on the same day, and coincidentally the Government announced the resumption of nationwide conscription which had been ended when Japan surrendered.[3]

Despite these ominous developments, Chou En-lai was still ready to return to Nanking from Shanghai where for some time he had been living. When on October 11 the Government announced unilaterally that the National Assembly would convene on November 12 to adopt a new constitution for China, Chou En-lai cancelled his plans. The minority parties which had also participated in the PCC followed suit.[4]

No one at the time, with the very possible exception of Marshall, knew it, but the capture of Kalgan was the high point of Government military success. There

1 *China White Paper*, pp. 188–90, and annexes 96–98.
2 *Ibid.*, p. 192.   3 *Ibid.*, pp. 196–97.   4 *Ibid.*, p. 197.

would be a few additional victories, but they would be largely symbolic and of no military significance. As Marshall had warned him interminably, the Generalissimo had now so far overextended himself militarily that he had lost the initiative. He would never recover it. The grinding process of Communist guerrilla attrition and strangulation would now take over, and in three years they would be the masters of China.

The three weeks following the October 10 and 11 announcements produced nothing basically new but there were some shifts of emphasis. Marshall withdrew American mediation into the background because the Third Party Group—composed of delegates to the PCC other than Nationalists and Communists—entered the arena in an attempt to find sufficient agreement that the Communists might be persuaded to name their representatives to the National Assembly, which they had consistently refused to do. This series of negotiations in the end was just as inconclusive as previous ones; it mainly demonstrated, as Marshall pointed out to all participants, that mutual distrust had become so deep rooted that he saw very little hope for any peaceful settlement. On one occasion,[5] Marshall told the Generalissimo specifically that he thought the latter's unyielding position on almost any question was unwarranted by the military facts. It was true, he added, that the Government had captured most of the cities and would probably take more; but the Communists were intact, they controlled the countryside, and they were quite aware, even if the Generalissimo was not, that he lacked the troops to change this situation. In the circumstances, it was ridiculous to think they would or had to yield to military pressure.

The Generalissimo remained unimpressed. His troops continued to make advances which looked good in the headlines, and Communist staffs in Nanking, Shanghai, and Chungking were gradually reduced. But early in November the Generalissimo told Marshall and Stuart he thought the time had come to stop the fighting. He was prepared to order an unconditional termination of hostilities, and asked them to prepare a draft of such an announcement. When they did so, he produced his own draft, which was provocative, obscure, and argumentative, and ended by threatening future use of force unless the Communists behaved as he wished.[6]

When Marshall pointed out that this statement would only aggravate matters, the Generalissimo with unusual candor replied that he had to keep three points in mind: (1) Although the Government had previously been divided on the proper course to follow, it was now unanimous that force was the only answer. (2) In the organization of the National Assembly he must give due consideration to the delegates who had been elected in 1936 and not emphasize the PCC resolutions in contrast to the 1936 draft constitution. (3) He had to be particularly careful of morale in the Army, which had recently sustained severe losses and could be expected to react adversely to an unconditional cessation of hostilities which would be interpreted as surrender of previously stated Government positions.

5 *Ibid.*, pp. 202–4.
6 *Ibid.*, p. 204.

The ceasefire statement which the Generalissimo finally issued on November 8 was somewhat more conciliatory than his earlier draft, but still essentially intransigent.[7] Furthermore, the attitude on the National Assembly was such that the Kuomintang would have an overwhelming majority and could simply vote to ignore any PCC understandings it chose. This factor alone seemed to nullify any gains which might have accrued from the ceasefire.

7 *Ibid.*, pp. 205–6, and annexes 107 and 108.

October 1 / Nanking / If August seemed a welter of harsh words producing nothing, September was a dizzy merry-go-round of charge, counter charge, proposal, counter proposal, and committees of three or five or none or steering committees that never met. It will take a very pedantic doctoral dissertation some day to unravel the threads; and the turmoil will prove to have been nothing more than an exercise in the art of how to negotiate when you have no slightest intention of conceding an iota, and doing it at arm's length, since the Generalissimo has been at his summer residence in Kuling and Chou En-lai has been in Shanghai. Absolutely nothing has been accomplished politically, except that an angry Marshall has warned Chou En-lai that unless the Communists stop their attacks on his integrity he will withdraw.

Militarily the picture is very different. The Government is now not far short of having occupied almost all the territory it demanded at the time of the June truce. Yesterday, if it did not exactly cut a Gordian knot, it started something by announcing its intention of capturing the strategic Communist-held strongpoint of Kalgan in north China on which it has been advancing anyway for some time. This has provoked a thoroughly disgusted Marshall to inform both the Government and the Communists today that he totally disagrees with what both are doing and that unless they stop the fighting and get down to serious business on the negotiations he is going home and the United States is through with China.

October 5 / A long conference yesterday produced nothing beyond the obvious determination of the Generalissimo to go on with his attack on Kalgan. So Marshall asked the President to order him home and started packing. In a panic and on his own, Dr. Stuart told the Generalissimo what was happening and the latter hastily backed down with an offer to halt in his tracks if only Marshall would try a little more. He agreed and cancelled his request for orders.

October 7 / Under great pressure the Generalissimo this morning agreed to a ten-day truce on Kalgan. Chou En-lai flatly and at once rejected any truce with a time limit. This is a reversal. It is usually the Communists who make truce proposals and the Government which rejects them. Marshall is going to Shanghai in the morning to have another try at convincing Chou. Then there will be another proposal and its rejection. When the Government takes Kalgan, and it will, there will be nothing left on which to make proposals for others to turn down.

October 8 / Marshall got nowhere with Chou En-lai this morning, who in fact stiffened up his position by insisting he would accept a truce only if the Government pulled back its troops in China proper to the lines of January 13 and in Manchuria to those of June 7.

During the afternoon Marshall called in the foreign newspapermen to give them the story and details of Kalgan with explicit instructions they could not write it until he said so. Before they had even left the house an official Chinese paper carried the full story.

There is a lovely story about the Marshalls at the summer resort of Kuling which the Communists are using against him. They say that once when he should have been working on peace in China he was walking in the moonlight holding hands with Mrs. Marshall. He is tickled by it because it is true.

October 10 / This is the anniversary of the founding of the Chinese Republic and Kalgan has fallen today! The Generalissimo celebrated both events with a speech in which he laid all blame on the Communists, called on them to submit, and reasserted his intention to seek a peaceful solution.

Nat Peffer is back from a two-month trip to the south. He is normally a cagey guy who sees both sides and weighs them judicially. This time he has come back here full of anger and bitterness such as I have seen in few men, saying that whatever we have seen of terror and brutality in such places as Kunming is nothing compared to Canton; that Americans are universally hated; that this is now a government which has only one possible peer—Spain—and that if we think we can build China as a base for another war we will in the end find the enemy not only in front but also behind. Something terrific has happened to him and his story sounds like a passage out of Jeremiah. I think it is a good day to have him tell it to Marshall.

October 11 / I have been evicted from my observatory on the hill because the staff has returned from Kunming and wants to put it back into operation. Anyway I had it during the hot weather and that is a great deal. So back it is to the Embassy slums which afford the privacy of a goat on the main street of this town. Four years of mess life are too much, but the prospects of escape are meagre given the dreadful housing shortage in Nanking.

Having become insufferably tired of the gray monotony of our housing I borrowed a few ideas from the Chinese, and painted the casement windows of my room the mandarin red used in the decoration of imperial buildings and the door the blue of the Temple of Heaven. The results are startling and attractive, and make a proper backdrop for Sir Ralph, my yellow dragon head, early Manchu, which is authentic because I know where I got him in Manchuria. We could learn a lot from the stunning Chinese use of color in their architecture.

Now the shrill voices of politics, the liberals and the third parties, are in full cry with all sorts of foolish suggestions on which a variety of people seize in desperation. Meanwhile the Communists sit back quietly and we all wait to see what Yenan will say. Chou En-lai cancelled his plans to return to Nanking when the Generalissimo unilaterally convened the National Assembly for November 12. It may be a complete break or it may be an indefinite prolongation of suspense. The general objective seems to be to bring about a break in such a way that the blame can be put on someone else.

At lunch yesterday I met a Russian named Rogov, an amusing and interesting man. He has had many years of experience in China with Tass. He was in the States in 1943 at which time he said there was so much pro-Russian feeling it frightened him. And now—he shrugged his shoulders.

October 17 / So help me God, the Generalissimo did it again! That man's ability at political manipulation at times is almost diabolical. He has made a new eight-point proposal which contains nothing new, but consists largely of suggestions made some time ago by Marshall and Stuart and identified as such to give them added sanction. The tricky part is that no mention is made of changed circumstances, such as Kalgan. This will make it impossible for the Communists to accept or probably even to discuss them, which will put them on record before the world as having said "No" twice in a row.

October 20 / One of our Chinese teachers and her husband invited me to spend the weekend at the family home in Changchow, a small town on the Yangtze a few hours away from here. In traditional Chinese fashion they were married without even having previously met. Fortunately, it turned out to be a good marriage, and the war emancipated them. He went to Burma as an engineer and she, who is an artist, turned against the old family and courtyard life and went with him to the jungle where they lived for three years, learning the modern world which they had barely heard of.

The family life is run in the old style. The women live in one courtyard, the men in another, and little has changed. The old grandmother runs the establishment. She has as beautiful a face as I have ever seen.

In a small town some of the problems of China seem more evident. Two things in particular struck me which you don't see in rural and village areas or in a big city like Shanghai. First was the staggering amount of disease. The other was the filth. Among other things, the word shit takes on a new meaning. Boatload after boatload of it floated along the canals in and around the town to the fields outside, and people live all their lives on those scows.

Not once in the two days did anyone in the family even mention domestic politics or refer to the United States. And this from people who are the educated of China. All my questions about China and Chinese ways of living were fully and openly answered with an obvious pleasure that I should be interested, but there was no flicker of curiosity about anything beyond their own immediate lives. Lack of interest in the outside world is hardly unusual in traditional Chinese society, which has always considered that world as barbarian, but it is puzzling there is little interest in domestic affairs which are already revolutionizing their lives and will soon alter them beyond present recognition.

The head of the family took me to see a large textile factory where he is maintenance engineer. The machinery was a German, American, British, and Japanese melange. To my untutored eyes the standards of cleanliness, light, and safety seemed extremely high. Most of the two thousand workers were young girls who had been brought in from the villages and trained at the plant under contract. They live in factory houses of a quality certainly higher than anything they have ever known before and they are well fed. They go to a factory school, but when I asked what they were taught the only answer I could get was "common sense." They can leave the premises only once a week.

The girls return to their native villages when their contracts expire; and they take back a revolution in their thinking—a breaking away from the rigid limits of orthodox country life. For the first time they have lived with strange girls of their own age, they have earned their own living

and, in a great many cases, they have become the principal
source of income for their families. Fei Hsiai-tung, the distinguished sociologist, once told me he thought this impact
on large numbers of girls, and consequently on their families, is one of the larger social revolutions which industry
is causing in China. In the end not even the tremendous
weight and pressure of regimented family life will be able
to prevent the implicit changes. If the family I visited,
however, was aware of what this can and will mean to the
peasant society on which it lives, there was no evidence of it.

October 22 / The last two days have been confusion, quar-
reling, snapping, and snarling from early morning on into
the next morning about even the most routine matters. Life
has not in the least been improved by a deluge of visitors
who live and eat all over the place and leave dirty clothes
around. They also all seem to need unavailable office space.
In addition, an endless stream of trucks has spent a noisy
day unloading five thousand tons of coal in the front yard.

I was so sure Yenan had announced what I could only
interpret as the coup de grace for the Generalissimo's latest
proposal that I did not even bother to follow what developed: Chou En-lai announced he would return and
the talks could and would continue. That did not and still
does not make any sense, especially since he has not changed
his demands for a return to the January 13 battle lines.

Recently the Communists have been particularly vicious
in their attacks on Marshall. From their standpoint I suppose there is no reason why they should except him from
the picture. In times like these the good go down with the
bad. It is just that they have plenty of direct reason to
know where he stands personally and it has been just plain
bad tactics on their part to do to him what they have done.
I more than half supect that Chou's returning now is largely
prompted by a sense of guilt on this point. Marshall has
been a wise and gentle friend to him and he knows it. Anyway, all the Nanking talky-talk has little influence on what

either army does, and the Communists keep on taking the shellacking. They can't be exterminated, but they can be pushed around.

The day was capped by a dinner for the leading intellectuals who are meeting here to discuss the state of learning in China. Mostly it was endless protestation that art and science should be kept out of politics and ended with three totally meaningless speeches by Marshall, Stuart, and Dr. Hu Shih.

Dr. Hu had been a principal leader of the Chinese Renaissance of the twenties, a distinguished scholar, and an effective ambassador to Washington during the war. For many years he had lived on his past reputation. He was typical of many of the leading minds of China in that he could not bring himself to join the Communists, was revolted by the Kuomintang, and still could not give up the prerogatives of official favor even at the expense of ineffectiveness.

October 24 / Chou En-lai today categorically refused to have anything to do with the October 16 proposal. One of his secretaries told me he had just realized that coincidentally with the offer the Government had significantly stepped up its military operations and is continuing to do so. Rapidly the Communist staff here and in Shanghai is being reduced to skeleton size.

October 26 / This is one of those fall days that make me uneasy. It is hot, dry, dusty, leaves yellowing, with a restless wind. The beauty of fall is yielding to the promise of cold and death, and a sense of doom.

A large pig has just run into the compound with a gang of small boys in full chase. It is hard to tell which party is making more noise. The squealing of pigs will always make me think of China; small boys belong everywhere. And across the coal pile in the middle of the yard and beyond the alley the peasants in preparation for the last crop of vegetables before frost are returning to the good earth some of that which they earlier took from it.

October 29 / While en route to lunch today I was standing in front of the Ambassador's house quite happily splashing in a puddle of water with the young and engaging son of our Counsellor. Along came Mr. Henry Luce looking dishevelled and quite unlike his handsome pictures. We stood there exchanging banalities. He was carrying a copy of *Life* with the article on Dr. Stuart and asked me if I would mind getting it to him since he did not know when he would be

seeing him again. Later I found out he was on his way to
have lunch with him. Maybe he thinks a gentleman does
not carry packages.

Later I was talking with Marshall about the new Government offensive in Manchuria which means complete abrogation of the June truce. He said that one took three months
to negotiate and a new one would take even longer: "And
I can't go through it again. I am just too old and too tired
for that."

October 31 / Last night the Ambassador entertained for
Luce and included the obvious people in the Government,
among them Foreign Minister Wang Shih-chieh, who is far
and away the best of the group and does not belong. The
conversation was incredibly unreal. The remarks of the
Time-Life people nearly convince me I have been right as
to what the new line will be—the problem has been solved,
there are only scattered groups of bandits left, and they
don't amount to much. It is, I think, the beginning of the
blackout. And now we have Paul Hutchinson of the *Christian Century* here, who will be followed by Henry Sloane
Coffin and Henry Van Deusen. The legions of the Lord are
being mobilized to give added sanction to the new dispensation.

November 2 / It was just one year ago this evening that I
arrived in Chungking with a soft rain falling and the far
outlines and vistas shrouded in what sometimes came to
seem the eternal fog. It feels a long time ago and a far cry.
The popular mood among the people then was still one of
relief and of joy that at last there was no war, even if the
original taste of victory had begun to sour in most mouths.
The Kuomintang was flushed with self-delusions of success,
but each day growing more panicky. Compromise—if only
temporary—seemed imperative to buy time for a gathering
of strength against the final struggle. The Communists were
weak in arms and military position, but strong in their faith
that the march of history and the inner corruption of the
Kuomintang would win them victory. For them too, com-

promise—if only temporary—seemed necessary while they gained strength; time brought them victory after victory. In between was that amorphous something known as the Democratic League, the intellectuals, the scholars with foreign university degrees and western culture, the liberals and democrats and thoughtful men who would carry on the great Chinese traditions and modernize them with the new they had learned. For them compromise was not something temporary; it was a way of life. They would stand between the two primitive giants and drive them both in the same harness, the superiority of mind and reason over naked force.

Right now, while civil war intensifies, they are making what must be their final attempt to prove their point—and quite possibly ours as well. To recapitulate the last few days:

October 24—Marshall and Stuart demanded that the Generalissimo come back at once from Formosa where he had gone for a brief inspection trip against their advice. Thereupon Prime Minister T. V. Soong at once took off for an unannounced destination himself. If this keeps up the American Generalissimo will begin to think people are avoiding him.

October 26—Chou En-lai expressed great pessimism to Marshall about prospects, saying the Kuomintang was doing everything it should not if it was sincere. Antung in Manchuria was captured and the port of Chefoo in Shantung province was surrounded. A propaganda truce was announced with fantastic fuss in the papers. The Third Parties did the greatest rejoicing, possibly because they have nothing else to show for themselves at the moment.

October 28—The Generalissimo returned and Marshall gave him a royal bawling out for staying away so long.

October 29—Third Party representatives called on the Generalissimo after Marshall had urged him to be conciliatory with them in word and deed because they are afraid of him and need encouragement to speak up. They presented him with three points for his approval: (1) immediate ceasefire on a status quo basis; (2) local admin-

Carsun Chang was a highly intelligent, utopian, ineffectual politician who had a small political party of his own. Any influence he had was due solely to support from his

*brother, Chang Kia-
ngau. The brother was
a real financial and
economic wizard, in-
corruptible in the
Shanghai business
cesspool, who if the
Generalissimo had ac-
tually given him the
political support he
always promised might
conceivably have saved
China. Hu Lin was the
most influential inde-
pendent editor in
Shanghai. His paper
was the* Ta Kung Pao,
the New York Times *of
China. He was beyond
fear and he knew what
China needed. Un-
happily, neither of
these men had an army
of his own.*

*Dr. Sun Fo, son of Dr.
Sun Yat-sen, seemed a
pale copy of his father.
He was Prime Minister
from time to time
when it suited the pur-
poses of the Generalis-
simo for symbolic
reasons. He tried hard
to be worthy of his
name, and his instincts
were good, but he
lacked the wit or the
strength to have any
measurable influence.*

istration to be arranged by a State Council reorganized in accordance with the PCC; (3) the Steering Committee of the PCC to plan at once a reorganization of the Government to include all parties and then discuss the time for the National Assembly and the Draft Constitutional Committee. The Generalissimo told them he did not think they had any business making suggestions to him. If they wanted to be helpful they should persuade the Communists to accept his eight points, at least as a basis for discussion. Feeling this was hopeless, the Third Party people returned to Shanghai. Later in the day, the Generalissimo, through Dr. Stuart, asked Carsun Chang and Hu Lin to see him again. They agreed to do so the next day.

Dr. Stuart's interpretation of this day was that the Generalissimo has decided that he could not bend the Communists to his will and any mediation would be futile. Hence, he was playing to separate the Third Parties from the Communists and to bring them into the National Assembly as followers of the Kuomintang.

Late in the day Dr. Sun told us that he had given the Third Parties' three points informally to the Generalissimo and the Communists on the 28th and had withdrawn them when Chou En-lai said they were unacceptable. Hence, the Generalissimo turned them down on the 29th on the basis of prior knowledge. Dr. Sun also denied the accuracy of Chou's allegation that the Third Parties would follow the Communist lead on participation in the National Assembly.

October 30—Hu Lin saw the Generalissimo and agreed to use pressure on the Third Parties to accept the Government's final offer: a ceasefire if the Communists would name their delegates to the National Assembly. The Communists refused at once, and the Third Party people left for Shanghai.

October 31—A Government spokesman expressed his unreserved confidence that the Third Parties would end up in the Assembly as desired by the Government. Carsun Chang and the Democratic League made a few low noises about postponing the Assembly, but no one listened. Finally, Dr.

Sun Fo announced that Third Party mediation was finished
because the Communists had rejected reasonable terms.
Most people think they will join the Assembly.

This morning at a gorgeous Shang bronze exhibit Marshall was exceedingly cool to the Generalissimo—as he has
been in the last few days.

November 4 / Taipei / This is a long awaited chance to see
Formosa for myself. It has been an interesting trip, even
though it rained most of the time. Coming here we flew
mostly over the province of Chekiang, which from the air
looks like a crumpled piece of paper. One of the great
misconceptions about China is that it is flat. Apart from
the Yangtze Valley and north China it is mostly rocky and
rugged. Small wonder so many parts are isolated and that
millions are so provincial.

Formosa is like stepping into a different world, tropical,
green, lush, and soft aired. The island, two hundred by
ninety miles, has fifty peaks over ten thousand feet, and the
center is still largely an untouchable land because of aboriginal tribes whose main avocation is collecting Chinese
heads. The Chinese have built a fence around the area to
keep them in.

Taipei at one time must have been an imposing and even
a beautiful city. It is not now, after the bombings we administered during the war. Even today there is still a lot of
rubble lying around the streets. The Chinese will make a
terrible mistake if they do not utilize their opportunities
here, for it is a very wealthy place, and already resentment
and hatred of the Chinese are smoldering. General Chen Yi,
an old crony of the Generalissimo, is the Governor and he
and his entourage are doing a highly competent job of
looting. Bad government here is a fine art, and stagnation
is the result.

Our own people are either kept effectively isolated or
else they do not know how to get around. They have little
to offer by way of information beyond what is obvious on
the surface. The only exception is George Kerr, our Assis-

tant Naval Attaché in Formosa and the only American with
extensive experience here before the war. He is bitter about
the oppression of the Formosans by mainland carpetbag-
gers. He predicts an explosion. His colleagues discount him
and his contacts, but through his hysteria he sounds uncomfortably persuasive to me: "For fifty years these people
waited and planned for the return of the Chinese. They
hailed them as brothers and liberators. Now, if they had a
choice, they would rejoin Japan." The Formosan leaders
would not see me—or so he said.

All the several hundred thousand Japanese are being repatriated, and since they are permitted to take only what
they can carry personally the accumulation of fifty years is
for sale at what it will bring. One can hardly be sorry for
the Japanese, but the neglect of the things is shocking in
some instances. For example, Taiwan National University
has a unique collection of oriental books, the finest in the
world, much of it irreplaceable. Now it rots and no one even
bothers to repair the roof of the library to keep out the
tropical rains. A few more months of this and it will be
gone. The Chinese authorities will not allow anyone else to
salvage it.

This is my first experience with a Japanese style house
(fifty years of occupation have left a marked influence). It
is charming, clean, comfortable, sensible, and without much
furniture. The walls are movable partitions, so you can
change the size of the rooms to suit yourself at any time.
The floors are covered with two inches of very fine straw
matting, springy and sweet smelling. Hence, no shoes in
the house. I rather like the idea of living on the floor.

November 5 / Nanking / I heard this morning that Chang
Kia-ngau, who is at present the virtual dictator of Kuo-
mintang-held Manchuria, arrived here two days ago. Why?
Perhaps to bring brother Carsun into line for the National
Assembly. Marshall and Stuart have seen the Generalissimo,
who said he was prepared to issue an unconditional ceasefire and to entertain any proposals the Communists might

wish to make if they would join the Assembly, but he wants to wait for twenty-four hours to see what happens and then he would like to have our suggestions as to what he should say. I doubt if he will use anything we might prepare.

November 6 / Lo Lung-chi (Secretary General of the Democratic League) and Carsun Chang called this afternoon to express their helplessness and their hope that Marshall would re-enter active mediation. They were told there is little we can do now, certainly not unless the Communists make some answer or even an acknowledgment to the last letter sent them, which contained the latest reshuffling of the Government's proposals. Chang is a good example of the men in the Third Parties. Highly intelligent and well educated, he is as unrealistic as his brother is hard-headed. His party is perennially being reorganized, now being called Social Democrats, now Democratic Socialists. The membership can normally be counted on the fingers of three hands and its program is carried around in Chang's head for such periodic mutation as inspiration may dictate.

November 7 / Having celebrated the October Revolution with the Russians in proper style, Chou En-lai and some Third Party people called on Dr. Stuart. Chou was slightly tight and voiced open bitterness against the United States and the Generalissimo. He refused all suggestions, except that he try to get some answer from Yenan to the last letter.

November 9 / The Generalissimo announced a new cease-fire last night, left seats in the Assembly vacant for non-Kuomintang delegates, and offered to negotiate on the State Council and the Executive Yuan. Apparently, all his advisors opposed the announcement. Within hours the Communists turned it down as unsatisfactory, unilateral, and in violation of the pcc. Marshall also was very unhappy about it—it contained nothing of our suggestions, as anticipated—because it did not go far enough and only confuses matters further.

End of the Marshall Mission

After a few days' postponement to allow for further manipulation, the National Assembly opened on November 15 in an atmosphere conspicuous for its lack of enthusiasm over the announced impending arrival of constitutional government in China. Most of the delegates were members of the Kuomintang, although shortly some of the minority group members capitulated, and others slipped out of sight not to be heard from again.

On November 16 Chou En-lai called on Marshall to ask for American transportation for himself and his colleagues back to Yenan. He would leave a few people in Nanking for the time being. He added that the Government was preparing operations against Yenan, and that this really would mean the end. In agreeing, Marshall asked Chou to find out in Yenan whether there was any desire for him to continue his efforts. Chou did not send back a reply until December 4,[1] and this contained only conditions for renewed talks which obviously the Government would not accept, and with no reference to the inquiry about Marshall's role. In effect, the Communists had rejected further American mediation. Thus ended the negotiations which had begun the previous January.

General Marshall did not leave at once. He recognized that by now the generals and the right wing who were determined to continue the war were in full control as far as that aspect was concerned. Hence, there was no prospect of any kind of negotiation, except on an entirely new basis, and there would be no place for him. He remained for two reasons.

In the first place, he hoped his presence would have some moderating influence on what the National Assembly did. Whether or not that was the case, the Assembly on December 25 adopted a constitution which was surprisingly close to what the PCC had recommended,[2] and did it in the face of strong opposition from the right wing, which wanted something much more authoritarian. The Generalissimo had scored a massive political victory within his own party. Marshall, however, was not impressed, since he knew the gap which could exist between declaration of intent and actual performance. As it developed, his foreboding was well founded.

Marshall had something else in mind. He recognized that he could no longer make any impression on the Generalissimo as to his military prospects, especially after one conversation in early December when the latter had assured him that in eight to ten months there would no longer be any Communist military problem, and then all would be well. (The Generalissimo at this point, incidentally, compounded his own position by asking Marshall to become his personal advisor – which only got him the kind of brisk and peremptory reply for which Marshall was not unknown.) Marshall was deeply disturbed by the economic situation. He could see its effects on the Government, but he was basically concerned by what

1 *China White Paper*, p. 212, and annex 112.
2 *Ibid.*, p. 215.

it was doing and would continue to do to the people of China, regardless of how the civil war came out.

President Truman laid the groundwork for this approach with a public statement on December 18 in which he reaffirmed the basic policy he had enunciated the preceding December. The President added that the United States would in no respect become involved in the civil strife, but would persevere in a policy of "helping the Chinese people to bring about peace and economic recovery in their country."

Marshall then repeatedly and in great detail outlined what he saw. Despite substantial UNRRA and other economic help, inflation was out of control. Foreign exchange reserves had been cut in half. Nothing had been done about industrial recovery, and the great Manchurian complex had been stripped by the Russians. Most sources of raw materials were in Communist controlled countryside. Such foreign trade as could exist was being stifled by nationalistic Chinese trade policies. Nothing was being done about agrarian reform, and China was still primarily an agricultural country. All economic activity was permeated with an obscene amount of corruption and self-interest of individual speculators. And, finally, Government military expenditures were rapidly passing the point which could safely be supported by even a healthy economy.[3]

Marshall pointed out that, given their rural base, the Communists had none of these problems, and the ones they did have they were handling effectively. Economic conditions in Nationalist areas were ideal to attract support for the Communists – and they knew it. Even if the Generalissimo was right in his military appraisal – and he was not – the economic situation alone, Marshall asserted, would destroy everything he was trying to do.

It was to no avail. If the Generalissimo was obtuse about modern military matters, contemporary economics simply did not register. He had economic advisors who did know the situation and what had to be done, but he did not listen. Not until he had been driven off the mainland would he accept advice, and even then he did not understand.

On January 6, 1947, the President announced that he had directed General Marshall to return to Washington. Marshall left on January 8. At that moment, the President announced he was nominating him to be Secretary of State. Coincidentally, the Department of State released Marshall's final statement.[4] In it he stated that overwhelming suspicion between the two main protagonists had been the single greatest obstacle to peace. Reactionary Kuomintang and Communist elements had deliberately and from the beginning done all they could to prevent peace. Only when they had been removed from power could there be hope.

It was, in essence, "a plague on both your houses." It would not be long before he discovered that powerful groups in the United States did not agree.

3 *Ibid.*, pp. 211–14, 220–29. Military expenditures at this time were consuming about seventy per cent of the Government budget.
4 See *ibid.*, annex 113, for the full text.

November 10 / Nanking / Butterworth made an interesting remark about China: "The trouble with those of us here who are not Chinese specialists is that we have been schooled and trained in a European type of politics, a politics so highly developed and sophisticated, or even decadent if you prefer, that specific events assume large proportion and significance. Chinese politics, however, operates on a different basis and specific events do not have the same meaning in relation to the whole. Beliefs and convictions are on a vaguer and possibly more impersonal level. Despite the civil war, the Government and the Communists have tea together and Chou walks without guards, while their respective partisans kill each other in the countryside." And I must confess I sometimes wonder if I am not seeing things when, as I did last night, I see Chou En-lai and Ch'en Li-fu patting each other on the back at a party.

Marshall has a curiously ambivalent attitude toward Madame Chiang. On the one hand she makes something of a nuisance of herself, always butting into things, always hanging around. Disliked by some of the Generalissimo's associates and distrusted by others as being too western, she is a desperately lonely woman whose only outlet now is her husband and the Marshalls. And yet, Marshall says she has been of great help in the negotiations and he can trust her. He once told Chou En-lai he would not believe it now but some day he would realize she more than anyone else had worked for what the Communists wanted from the negotiations. He adds that the Generalissimo is lost without her. One result is that both are too isolated, and he is particularly unaware of the world he lives in. Symptomatic is his delight and fascination with Chinese checkers, and her reaction while playing bridge on a train which stopped briefly at Wusih. About the crowd waiting to greet them she said petulantly, "Oh, let them wait."

November 11 / Yenan was even more unimpressed with the ceasefire announcement than was Chou En-lai, and its reply

was simple: return to the January 13 truce agreement; anything else is only cover for more fighting! The PCC Steering
Committee has met for the first time since last spring. All
spoke for conciliation. No agreement was reached. The Three
Man Committee also met at the Generalissimo's request.
No agreement on anything, not even on another meeting.
Since Chou En-lai was not prepared to discuss anything
unless the Assembly was postponed, Mo Teh-hui (the delegate from Manchuria) was named to urge the Generalissimo to postpone the Assembly. Nothing came of this either.
Wang Bing-nan told me this afternoon that only postponement would be proof of sincerity. Even adjournment after
convening would not be satisfactory.

November 12 / Late last night Hu Lin and several associates saw the Generalissimo again to urge postponement.
He offered a twenty-four-hour delay if the Third Parties
would send delegates. They compromised on three days,
even though Chou En-lai said it was meaningless. Dr. Stuart
thinks the Communists still will not make it a formal break,
even though they will stay out. I agree. So instead of an
Assembly this morning for which China has waited since
1911 two more plane loads of Communist officials took off
for Yenan. This brings the total to 450.

I always thought the Third Parties would eventually join
and not stay out with the Communists, but I did not think
they would capitulate so easily under pressure. Now they
have three days to compose themselves for what can only
be their execution. They of course deny any such thing has
happened, which only helps to confuse matters further.

Winter really is upon us, and it has brought back the
whistling pigeons, which is nice. This morning I looked out
of my window and across the yard on a little rise of ground
saw a huge cock pheasant strutting in the breeze and frosty
sunlight. The hunters of the Embassy had been out all
morning and had seen nothing; the only one was under my
nose.

November 14 / For the last two days the Steering Committee has kept up its efforts to break the impasse—with the usual results. Yesterday Chou En-lai indicated to Dr. Stuart he thought all was finished and he would shortly return to Yenan, leaving Tung Pi-wu to carry on—if there was anything to carry on. Dr. Stuart feels the time has come to reappraise American policy in the light of the new situation!

Tung Pi-wu was one of the venerables of the Communist Party who had been their representative at the San Francisco Conference. He would become the Chief Justice of the Supreme Court of Communist China.

The Democratic League is still dragging its feet on submitting its lists for the Assembly, but Kao Chieh, a reporter for the Shanghai *Ta Kung Pao,* thinks only League members without any other party affiliation will stay out and face political extinction. He thinks the next Government drive will be on Yenan. In contrast to last weekend, there is a strange stillness here today and all indications are that the Assembly really will meet tomorrow. There is very little interest in it, and less hope. The three-day postponement is publicly hailed as a brilliant stroke of politics by the Generalissimo, but no one can give a reason why, except that it puts the Third Parties over a barrel. The logic sounds a little hollow.

November 16 / The National Assembly was convened yesterday and dutifully reported in the press without enthusiasm. The Third Parties made fussy gestures about postponement up to the last minute, but it was strictly no dice. Dr. Stuart wanted to go to Peiping to see the Communists there and Marshall vetoed the idea. The atmosphere is one of anticlimax. Under pressure from Marshall, the Generalissimo has agreed to send a mission to Yenan for another try at breaking its stubbornness; but he shows all the signs now of thinking of himself as destiny's choice to be the champion against Communism. He is convinced the only answer is physical destruction and likewise convinced of his ability to do the job.

This morning Chou En-lai asked Marshall for transportation for himself and entourage back to Yenan. He will leave a representative here for the time being. He said he now anticipated a Government drive on Yenan and that this would be the end. Marshall agreed it would.

November 19 / The apathy continues amid synthetic oratorical fireworks in the Assembly. About an hour ago Chou En-lai returned to Yenan and now I guess there will be nothing except civil war in earnest and to the finish. Outside of Marshall, I am the only officer who has been here since the end of the war. I suppose coalition had to be attempted, even though it was an impractical notion at best and the very nature of this kind of political struggle has precluded success except on a temporary basis and then only under great stress. I know Marshall now believes he made a mistake in ever thinking coalition was desirable or useful or possible.

November 24 / Yesterday we received approval of some property deals, which means we will shortly start to move and the next month bids fair to be confusion of another kind. Maybe it will be a good substitute for politics at that. The new Embassy is a plush one and covers about ten acres of ground. It was the office and residence of Wang Ching-wei, the Chinese puppet president under the Japanese. Almost every time we look at it we discover another hidden staircase.

It has turned warm again and in the fields around here the fifth crop since April is being planted. It is amazing how fast things grow.

The hall in which the Assembly is meeting has a sound amplifying system. Everybody wants to use it at once with much shouting on several concurrent topics. The only way to stop the melee so far has been to turn off the electricity. During these sessions the Madame sits in the front row, doodling, with a bored look on her face, and from time to time the Generalissimo passes scribbled notes up to the rostrum.

November 29 / Thanksgiving has come and gone and no regrets. On the eve it turned very cold and by morning the city was buried under snow which kept falling all day, very beautiful and sad and wet and uncomfortable. The feature of the day was a memorial service by the Officers' Moral

Endeavor Association. This was conceived and sponsored by Madame Chiang during the war as a morale builder for Americans. It is a very Chinese idea, by which during times of trouble responsible officials visit the people to comfort them and reassure them that the Emperor is still very much on the job. It works for the Chinese and is expected; for American GIs it was only a subject for obscene humor.

December 1 / Marshall has had another one of those endless sessions with the Generalissimo which should qualify both men for the Order of Saint Simeon Stylites. Largely rehash, its main interest was the flat assertion by Marshall that the Communists could not be destroyed militarily. The Generalissimo just as flatly disagreed. He even set a time schedule of eight to ten months and then asked Marshall to stay as an advisor to the Government. This evoked a very firm: "No! If I have been unable to have any influence on you as mediator with the full backing of my Government, how do you expect me to have any as an advisor?"

December 6 / Despite all the work we have to do there is very little of it that is more than time filler and no one has his heart in it. What we do next is the great unknown. Probably nothing for the time being. The Communists have left, the National Assembly goes drearily on its mosaic way, and we wait to see what happens next.

When I was in Shanghai the other day the mobs were savagely knocking out each other's brains. It was messy. As far as I can find out it really did start as a street corner row between two peddlers, whereupon the Shanghai underworld and other groups decided to settle a few scores of their own. The general dissatisfaction is such that anything can set off such incidents, and everyone is agreed there will be others this winter. The air in Shanghai is now one of murder. This is what it means to be "strong, united, and democratic."

Overheard at dinner last night: A lady to one of our Lieutenant Colonels—"You say your name is Murphy?" "Yes, but from Virginia."

December 14 / It is eerie to watch the growing confidence of the Generalissimo and his faith in his destiny. It has been all the stronger since he celebrated his sixtieth birthday, which due to Chinese numbering, superstition, and the normally short span of life of the average Chinese has special significance. It gives you license to stop explaining yourself and to begin acting solely on the authority of age.

The Assembly goes on its chaotic way. The most agitating question it confronts is whether the capital will go back to Peiping. The Generalissimo opposes this move. Mostly the proceedings are designed for foreign consumption.

December 17 / Tomorrow we start to move and I am first. My new quarters are nice, having central heating and a shower, which is real luxury in Nanking. The new Embassy is in a part of town where there are few paved streets, no sidewalks, and consequently a somewhat heightened danger of being trampled to death some night by a pig. I was there this afternoon at sundown. Back of the compound there is a rise of ground on which there is a large Buddhist temple and several rows of stripped trees. Silhouetted against the sunset, the trees were filled with thousands of small crows which from time to time would rise up into the sky and then settle back into the trees. It was lovely and sad, like most winter sunsets, I guess.

Chou En-lai's recent speech in Yenan can only be interpreted as closing the door on negotiation. Actually, I think they somewhere along the line decided they did not want a coalition. It is an ugly sight to watch a country being forced into one extreme or another.

Nat Peffer has returned from a trip to Manchuria in the low frame of mind of everyone who has been there. Most people go unbelieving of the stories they hear and then find the facts worse than the stories. They can find neither explanation nor justification for the Russian looting and not much more for the neglect since then. Even the Russians themselves must wonder what it is they thought they were gaining.

Last night I had dinner with the Governor of Jehol, smooth and tough. He really looked and acted like a storybook Mongol, with bright, darting eyes and a great shrewdness. What impressed me most was his tremendous nervous energy which is typical of so many Chinese leaders. It gives you an inkling of what these people will be when they get rid of their worms and have enough to eat. When it happens, somebody is going to be badly outnumbered. . . .

Some of the Sinkiang Turki delegates to the Assembly whom I had known in Chungking came to lunch today. These people have been in Central Asia so long they play for themselves alone and against everyone else. They know they have time and history on their side and will need them unless a miracle happens. Given the traditionally bad Chinese record with minorities, that particular miracle seems improbable. Considering their isolation from the outside they have a surprising knowledge of the world.

December 25 / The National Assembly today adopted the new constitution. It is satisfactorily close to the lines laid down in the PCC agreements, and it is a real political victory for the Generalissimo because his own right wing wanted something very different and much more Prussian in character. Whether it is ever implemented is something else.

The holiday season has been an appalling succession of cocktail parties, all parading the same faces and indifferent drinks. I suppose it helps to dull depression and despair. As the bitterness deepens in this country and suspicions multiply we see less and less of the Chinese and more and more of the diplomatic corps. It is an empty way of spending time. So Nanking becomes worse rather than better as a place to live. The one happy item is a Christmas card from Wang Bing-nan, who is now the only Communist representative left in town. His German is good, but his English is about on a par with my German. His card reads: "To the dearest Mother in the world—and naturally that's you." Bing-nan takes himself so seriously none of us has had the heart to kid him about it.

Peffer leaves shortly in a hopeless mood. Like most of us here he is dreadfully pessimistic about what the future holds, fed up with a corrupt and ineffectual Government, and completely disillusioned with the integrity of the Communists when they speak of doing anything other than provoking whatever chaos may be needed to secure their own ends.

January 1, 1947 / The year ended and the year started on a sexual note. From the north comes the word that an American soldier in Peiping, doubtless moved by the holiday spirit of love, has been accused of rape by a Chinese girl. His version is that the lady wanted five dollars and a hotel room, but compromised for three and a park. The trouble started, he says, when her guardian came along and protested violently. Naturally her version is different. Rape being unarguable, the facts will probably remain obscure. We are, however, already being tried in the press and found guilty, and there are rumblings of protest demonstrations.

January 4 / Like the rains, the riots came. Huge student demonstrations in Peiping limited themselves to noise. In Nanking they were a little earthier, as usual. One was fairly orderly, but the other came to rock throwing and was broken up when the local gendarmes moved in swinging their belts. The brass buckles have a distinctive and sickening thud when they come in contact with a living skull. Both riots were rich demonstrations of the Chinese gift for foul invective—this subject lending itself admirably to a particular segment of the vernacular anyway.

January 5 / The Peiping rape agitation has died down as quickly as it grew, and nothing of consequence goes on except repeated announcements in the press that democracy has arrived in China. I suppose another offer will be made to the Communists and they will turn it down. For reasons of their own, I don't think they will ever listen to anything again. Their stand may be foolish and cost much, or maybe it is just the way they figure; presumably they are prepared for what comes.

January 6 / Marshall was recalled today. The last few weeks he has been staying on in the desperate hope that somehow, in some way, he could modify the course he now admits that Generalissimo is determined to follow and which he is convinced leads only to disaster for the Government. It is a tired, angry, and frustrated man who is packing up tonight.

January 8 / Marshall's farewell "a plague on both your houses" statement has the Chinese vacillating between stunned silence and anguished screams. The dismay is compounded by the announcement he is to be Secretary of State, which leaves them with no illusions as to what they can expect from the United States at this time. It was typical of him that he took off almost unnoticed and that his new job was kept completely secret until he was in the air and beyond reach of supplication.

Rampant inflation

For several weeks after Marshall's departure the Communists and the Government continued rather desultory efforts to renew political negotiations. The proposals and counterproposals made such extreme demands that, in the circumstances, it was clear neither side expected a favorable response and both were so confident of ultimate victory that it made little difference. Both separately assured Dr. Stuart that the other in a few months would be in a military position where it would have to accept any terms offered.[1]

Published Communist statements finally and openly aligned the Party with the Soviet Union on foreign policy, denounced the United States as the heir of German and Japanese Fascism, and stated that it would never recognize any agreements entered into by the Nationalists subsequent to January 10, 1946. For its part, the National Government continued to maintain that, as it always had, it still regarded the Communist problem as a political one which could be solved through reason. Communist intransigence, however, left the Government no alternative except the course it was following, and it must therefore proceed with its own program of political democratization and economic rehabilitation. As his reports to Washing-

1 *China White Paper*, p. 231.

ton repeatedly showed, Dr. Stuart found himself in an agonizing dilemma. He wanted very much to believe that Kuomintang words meant what they said, but the record compelled him to a certain skepticism that words would ever become action. This conflict in his own thinking became particularly acute after the Government on February 11 notified the Communist representatives in Nanking that their presence in Government controlled areas was no longer desired.[2]

One curious footnote was that on March 10 at a meeting of the Council of Foreign Ministers in Moscow, the Soviet Union proposed that China be placed on the agenda. When the United States objected, as did China on grounds this would constitute interference in its internal affairs, the matter was dropped. Even more curious was that on March 8 the Soviet Ambassador in Nanking had proposed that the Nationalist Government take over the administration of the ports of Dairen and Port Arthur in Manchuria which had been given to the Russians in the Sino-Soviet Treaty of August 1945, and that there be joint operation of the railway line from Dairen through Mukden to Changchun. These negotiations rather quickly broke down and were not resumed.

The constitution adopted on December 25, 1946, which would end political tutelage and establish free democracy, was not to go into effect for one year in order to allow time for the reorganization of the Government. This proved to be much more difficult than anticipated. The Communists had made it clear they would not participate, even though a certain number of positions were reserved for them. At a fairly early stage the Democratic League had so far identified itself with Communist views that it too would not participate. This meant the division of positions would be between the Kuomintang on the one hand and the Youth Party and the Social Democrats on the other; but these minor parties were of so little consequence that the important phase would be the internal manipulations of cliques within the Kuomintang itself.

On March 1 the Government announced the reorganization of the Legislative and Control Yuan and of the People's Political Council which gave the third parties and non-partisan members distinctly minority representation, but still much larger than their political strength would have warranted. Since these agencies of Government were of little importance, the announcement attracted slight attention. The critical struggle was over the key agencies, the Executive Yuan and the State Council, and negotiations here were stalled.

Two days later, Dr. Stuart gave the Department of State his interpretation of the attitude of the Generalissimo, which he found ambivalent.[3] In part, he found him truculent and, under pressure from the cc clique on which he relied for rank and file Party discipline, inclined to go it alone without American aid. And in part he believed the Generalissimo did not see that there would be any improvement in Soviet-American relations, and hence he could hope that the

2 *Ibid.*, p. 232. Dr. Stuart was a model of outward self-control. One had to know him well to realize the depths of his anguish.
3 *Ibid.*, pp. 234–37.

United States would in some fashion rescue him from his predicament. This latter theme would become dominant and in the end readily exploitable.

As he looked at the deteriorating military situation, Dr. Stuart's attitude was just as ambivalent as that of the Generalissimo, although for different reasons. He fully shared the general Chinese distaste for reliance on foreign assistance; but he could not agree with the military optimism of the Generalissimo, and he saw only disaster if the cc clique gained full control of the Kuomintang. It may well be that at this point only the Communists and the cc clique were unconfused about what they wanted and how to get it.

The struggle within the Kuomintang was joined when its Central Executive Committee met in March. The conflict was primarily between the loosely knit, liberal Political Science Group and the cc clique which wanted no reorganization at all. The cc lost this round, but kept control at all levels of the Party machinery. The manifesto of the cec when it adjourned on March 24 contained only the usual generalities,[4] and the juggling continued.

During the same time the consequences of eighteen months of practically total neglect of economic matters became glaringly apparent. In response, Dr. Stuart changed the emphasis of the American approach to the Chinese situation. Since it was quite obvious that the Generalissimo would follow no military advice except his own – and in any event Dr. Stuart claimed no military expertise – the Ambassador concentrated his efforts on economic and political problems, especially as it became clearer that without drastic economic reform even an unlikely reversal in the military picture would probably be meaningless. Furthermore, economic reform, regardless of the military outcome, might possibly alleviate some of the Chinese misery.

Although it was natural that there had been strong inflationary trends during the war with Japan, this process did not stop with the end of the war. Actually prices continued to rise until the end of 1946 at a fairly steady rate of twelve per cent a month, and were kept from accelerating largely because of large consumer goods imports, including unrra stocks. In January 1947 the rate suddenly shot up, and was reflected most spectacularly in February when the price of one American dollar in terms of Chinese National Currency (cnc) went from 7,700 to 18,000, largely because of currency speculation.

Urgent new requests were made for American aid. On February 6, Dr. Soong frankly told the Ambassador that his earlier optimism had been unwarranted, that economic collapse was now a distinct possibility. A large commodity credit, he said, had become urgent. Dr. Soong was quite right that the only favorable factor was that foreign exchange reserves, although depleted, were still adequate because of projected unrra shipments and substantial residual foreign credits still in the pipeline. In view of these reserves, the Department of State felt that additional aid would serve primarily political purposes without economic reforms to make aid effective.[5]

4 *Ibid.*, annex 126.   5 *Ibid.*, pp. 361–64.

All during this period, Dr. Stuart continued to stress that military matters could not improve and the endless political negotiation would mean little unless drastic and unpalatable economic steps were adopted and ruthlessly enforced. It made no sense to pass reform resolutions and then let the market, especially in Shanghai, do just as it pleased. Most disturbing of all was the new interest in economic matters being shown by the CC clique, whose activities were soon seen to be directed toward personal enrichment and with no concern for the public welfare.

On March 2, T. V. Soong resigned as Prime Minister, and the Government moved in rapidly to curb speculation.[6] Police measures, however, were successful only temporarily.

6 *Ibid.*, p. 361.

January 17 / Nanking / Life is settling down a bit now. We finally got squared away for the move to the new chancery and it is finished. The night before it started, just as I stepped out of the Ambassador's house, a spectacular cold front moved across the sky. And that was it. During the night it started to rain and has not stopped yet. If there is a thing in this town that is not covered with mud I have missed it. It is hard to imagine how all pervasive mud can be in a city with little paving and no sidewalks.

But even the mud fails to dampen the pleasure over the Marshall appointment. There are only two reservations; his life and its very nature have not given him a basic political mind or intuition—which may, incidentally, have been an element of strength here because if he had had a real sense of history and politics I don't see how he could have stuck it out as long as he did; and he is deathly tired. The local Russians appear pleased with the appointment in the hope that it may for a while ease the tension. The Chinese are shocked and appalled, although the officials dare not say so too openly.

The Government has made a "final" offer to negotiate. The Communists turned it down with the by now usual counter offer of a return to January 13. Thus endeth any hope of any talks. It was accompanied by a spate of attacks on the United States and Marshall which were preposterous. The alternative now of the Kuomintang is hopeless and little less distasteful no matter how you look at it. One can only pray God that the inevitable American revulsion against the Communists will not drive us to foolish extremes. Marshall is of course the best man to prevent that, if anyone can.

January 20 / There is really great relief in the Kuomintang that the Communists are so obdurate in their stand and so extreme in their statements against us. And why not? The more so the greater will be the pressures at home to support the Kuomintang. Dr. Stuart continues to fish actively in local waters, and he and Philip Fugh (his Chinese secretary who has been his confidante for many years) are in constant touch with all the elements of the Kuomintang. Yesterday the Generalissimo asked him to talk over the final Communist reply. Dr. Stuart suggested he make a public statement about it and was asked to prepare a draft. It took considerable argument on our part to break that one up and convince him not to be the fall guy.

The Embassy will operate very differently now. Marshall kept every thread in his own hands. Sometimes we knew the details of what he was doing and reporting, sometimes we did not, at least until later. Now the place is a sieve. The Ambassador works in his own residence and almost never comes to the office. Everything he knows Philip knows. Everything Philip knows is funnelled directly to the Generalissimo. The only way to prevent this is to keep things from Dr. Stuart, which can be embarrassing since he is after all the Ambassador.

Dr. Stuart knows nothing and cares less about how the American Government works, nor does he really know too much about America in general, having been in China for almost fifty years. His Christian and emotional ties to the Kuomintang and all its works are tremendous and get in the way of his judgment all the time. Like others of his persuasion, he can see a lifetime going down the drain and that is hard; but we must remember that this faction is bound to have great influence on American attitudes.

Just to confuse matters, Walt Butterworth, who has no Asian background, runs the Embassy itself and does it very well. If I know anything about him, he will do his able best to discipline Dr. Stuart and Philip; and if I know anything about those two, Walt will find it a hopeless chore. The mystery is why Marshall, who must know of the situation, permits it. Maybe he just thinks it no longer matters. Anyway, I'll bet we never find out either!

January 25 / The second New Year (Chinese) has come and gone. The Chinese one is always a great celebration, very noisy, and lasting several days. This year, however, there was little sign of anything doing, except that everything was closed. To make matters worse it was still raining, and the city kept sinking deeper and deeper into the mud. Nanking is built on an old swamp, which is not much help either.

Every evening at dusk a flight of crows, miles long, comes in from the east, lights in the trees around the Embassy for half an hour, and then takes off for the west. A little snow is falling from a leaden sky on this afternoon's flight. It is a melancholy and even ominous sight.

Chinese New Year is the usual time of year to settle all financial accounts. There were gloomy forebodings and predictions that this year it would be economic disaster. There was a normal number of Shanghai bankruptcies, but nothing else of any consequence happened. The Government did issue a statement formally blaming the Communists for all the ills of China; the negotiations to get the Third Parties into a reorganized government continued on their uninspired way; and it now looks as though there will be no further developments until after the Third Plenary Session of the Kuomintang Central Executive Committee, which is scheduled for March 15.

As a distraction, the press is blowing up a storm about sovereignty over the Paracel Islands which are nothing but sand spits a good many miles off the coast of China. But all Chinese can agree in demanding that the French troops there withdraw immediately under penalty of extreme displeasure. Some Chinese are even being unkind enough to suggest that the French themselves started the argument to draw attention away from their own unhappy plight in Indochina.

January 27 / The Shanghai rumor factory says the Generalissimo has offered the Finance Ministry to H. H. Kung with T. V. Soong's approval, and that T. V. has ideas of going to the States, maybe seeking a loan, maybe as just a general goodwill tour. Another rumor is that disaffected elements, not specified, in the Kuomintang may join the Youth Party—which makes little sense unless it is strategy for undefined ends. I do know Dr. Stuart is urging the Youth Party to join the Government; he is being devious again about it and methinks I smell Fugh somewhere in this particular caper. Actually, I doubt if the Kuomintang will do anything about reorganization for some time, thanks to the political gifts handed to it by the Communists. I think they will also stall with some idea of an overt move on their behalf from the States; but Marshall will be too busy with other things for a while to give much time to China. Since no one else at home who is presently in a position to force action seems to want any, the course will be to sit tight at least for a few months and see what happens.

January 28 / More rumors: O. K. Yui (the Finance Minister and a very able one) will probably be fired, but H. H. Kung will not get the job. Soong might well go to the States on a loan mission. Not rumor: Soong told Dr. Stuart he most certainly would *not* go. But maybe he will. . . . What anyone says specifically means very little.

January 30 / For some unexplained reason Butterworth is keeping it very quiet that there are eighty thousand holdout Japanese troops in eastern and northwestern Manchuria who are fully equipped, fighting the Communists, and want to be repatriated.

Announcement has been made that the Executive Headquarters in Peiping is to be disbanded. There has been no public reaction as yet, but the Generalissimo is delighted since this move will cut off Communist communications with any area not under its control. Wang Bing-nan is non-committal, but obviously worried about getting his people back to Yenan.

January 31 / The Generalissimo has asked that Executive Headquarters personnel not be dispersed so they can be put together again on short notice. Impossible—Marshall's instructions were that the disbandment constituted final termination of his mediatory mission. Should negotiations ever be renewed the conditions would obviously be very different. Chinese Army reaction is that this means approval for war.

The American Agricultural mission made its recommendations some time ago for needed agrarian reforms, but nothing has been done about it despite our heckling. It was ready for publication a couple of days ago when T. V. Soong discovered it had recommendations for devaluation of Chinese currency to encourage exports. He ordered these deleted. Now he must be informed he cannot delete them and if he does we will publish the correct text.

February 4 / I had a long talk the other night with Ch'en Li-fu, who to me anyway has the attractiveness magnificent evil sometimes has. Maybe it is just fascination. He was again expounding at some length his line that what China really needs is a religious revival. The reason for this, he said, is that then it would be easier not to feed the people. And he said it as though he were talking of so many rows of potatoes, even gaily.

The hordes of birds around this place have become quite a nuisance. One of our lads has a rifle he uses on them rather effectively and they are beginning to leave. Yesterday he shot a hawk—or thought he did. In the afternoon I found it down against a wall, well camouflaged in the underbrush. It was very much alive, although badly wounded and with angry green eyes. When given the coup de grace it spread out its wings, rose on its tail, and slowly fell over on its back. For a moment it made me sick at my stomach.

The final evacuation of Executive Headquarters personnel ends a unique experiment in international affairs, something Marshall dreamed of as a great and altruistic example of mutual help in an unhelpful world. I suppose it was implicitly doomed to failure from the beginning, but it hurt him a great deal to have to admit it. Now that the deed is done all China is appalled by the implications. Those who yowled the loudest for American troop withdrawal are now asking us to reconsider, even the students who rioted over the Peiping rape case, the Communists who now have no communications with the outside world (we set up air and radio service all over China for their use at our expense), the Government which suddenly wonders just how much of north China it can hold, and the Peipingites who hated Americans and now see their prosperity gone and their city a prey to bandits. Ironically enough, it was only the cc clique which consistently approved our being here and warned that when we left all shades of opinion would regret it. So now we have gone and the consensus is that it is just another American trick. The only ones who have been largely speechless are the Russians who, with unaccustomed restraint, say only that this marks the end of one phase of American policy—which, after all, is one way of putting it.

One of the more startling results of the whole experiment has been the broken down colonels who made up the American component—known rather unaffectionately as The Thousand Sleeping Colonels of Peiping. None of them is in any sense what you might call pro-Communist. And yet, every one of them who has been in Communist territory has come back rather dazed and muttering, "You can say what you please about their system or what it leads to, but they have something new in China and that something thus far is better than what the rest of China has." American interest in China, I think, is now gone for a while. Later it will be different.

A good deal of attention is suddenly being paid in the

press at home to two English translations which have just appeared of *China's Destiny*, written in 1942 by the Generalissimo. The book has been read by millions of Chinese, and has been the textbook in Government and Party training schools; but it attracted no attention abroad, although the American Army made its own private translation. The interest in it now comes from the fact that the two versions are quite different. The official one was put out by the Ministry of Information and is obviously designed for American consumption. It makes all the "correct" statements about the virtues of democracy and the glories of international cooperation. The unofficial translation, which is the true one, is a real Confucian feudal document. It calls for a return to the traditional authoritarian values in politics and for a controlled agrarian society in economics. In foreign policy it is anti-western, xenophobic, and imperialist. By and large it represents the view of the cc clique and it is incredible that its implications have not been taken more seriously as an indication of what we are up against with the Kuomintang, especially in any efforts for reform and modernization.

But even Dr. Stuart, who normally gives them the benefit of the doubt, has his reservations. What to do about it, even if you knew what you wanted? I think there is much to what one of the Kuomintang liberals said to me: "The trouble with you Americans is that you want to make changes that will take at least fifty years—and you want them in two." He was rather bitter about it. The only trouble with this is that they do not have fifty years to spare.

Three new buildings are going up near my house. The coolies chant as they haul, mostly a monotone with occasional wild outbursts. The effect is almost hypnotic. I guess it is the way all slaves chant.

February 5 / For reasons he did not explain to us, Dr. Stuart sent word to Carsun Chang that he (meaning, Chang assumed, his Social Democratic Party) had better not join any reorganized government. When word of this leaked out, the Youth Party, which really does not want to join anyway, presumably to avoid responsibility, let it be known that they would like the same suggestion to be made to them. Actually, there is growing Kuomintang opposition to having the Youth Party in because it is almost entirely Szechuanese and brings up unhappy memories of Chungking days. Despite its name, incidentally, its membership averages seventy in age.

February 6 / News stories from home say some amazing things about China. From them you would get the idea that mammoth armies were maneuvering across the landscape. Although the Government does have sizeable units, the fighting is much more on a guerrilla basis with small units. Nor is the Government having the victories with which it is credited. There is plenty of evidence that the Government is being hard pinched and is worried about it, especially since it is beginning to soak in that Marshall means what he has been saying lo these many months—that there just are not going to be war supplies for them from us or anybody else. Nobody seems to believe it when you say there has not been anything of the kind since the end of the war. Even the surplus property deal simply did not include anything of value for war. Right now Tass is plastering the Far East with the story that all troops we are taking out are actually being sent to our naval base at Tsingtao in Shantung province. This is a plain lie. God knows Admiral Cooke would like to have them.

The heat is at last on with a vengeance for an American loan and the arguments for it are astonishing. T. V. Soong hauled out Sol Adler at 11 P.M. to tell him that a Communist victory was imminent without a loan, to which Sol replied that the proposition sounded like a poor investment. They have also put Jack Blandford, an American advisor to the Government, to work earning his salary. His argument is that no loan, no pay for troops; no pay for troops and over they go to the Communists. Butterworth so far takes a fishy view of all this.

February 12 / Soong and entourage are dancing around like a bunch of small boys who have to go to the bathroom. They are using every known dodge to get our money—though they must know by now that any loans will not make the slightest difference. Just how thirty million dollars for cotton purchases will be a bulwark against Communism is a little vague—but that is the story. Butterworth remains unimpressed and noncommital.

February 14 / Last night the Generalissimo injected himself into the economic mess by giving Soong a list of things to do which indicated a good grasp of the immediate needs, if not of the long range necessities. The most important demand was an adequate rice supply for industrial workers, Government employees, and students and teachers. The other important one was investigation of Communist penetration of labor unions. Soong claims they are already well penetrated by Government secret police.

February 15 / The financial events of the past week in Shanghai have been disastrous. The new export-import regulations announced to conserve the dollar exchange could hardly have been more badly bungled or less calculated to achieve the desired result: they in effect strengthen the favoritism of financial interests close to Soong. We told them so to no avail. The result was a chain of dollar exchange explosions which in a week cut the value of Chinese currency to one third, while in the same period prices almost trebled. Exchange will of course drop back some, but prices will not. The panic in Shanghai is valid enough, but it will not be definitive since eighty per cent of the people live on the land, consume what they grow, and will not know anything has happened. The peasants look at the sky rather than the financial columns; now is the time for rain and they are getting it.

Butterworth's toughness is most disturbing to the Chinese, especially to Soong, who hates him because he is tough too and does not like competition. Soong is still trying to bamboozle us out of some kind of stopgap but is making no impression on Butterworth, who has decided Shanghai needs to do some more sweating—and that is what it is going to do. Even the plea that the Government will collapse got nowhere. Soong's final argument was that a major loan was essential for China which is now the last hope to prevent a world Communist takeover. The loan would turn the trick. Without batting an eyelash, Butterworth said that if that were so it would be the high point in his career as well as Soong's. For a moment I thought Soong was going to hit him.

Right now there is a large magpie outside my window which acts as though it is trying to relieve a bad case of constipation.

Trouble on the outer marches

During the spring of 1947 two events occurred, thousands of miles apart, which, although tragic enough in themselves, did not have immediate impact on developments in China but were symptomatic of the general malaise and would have unforeseeable consequences in the years ahead. One was on Formosa; the other along the undefined border of Outer Mongolia and Sinkiang, not too far from Siberia.

The first came to public attention on February 28, 1947, when open rebellion broke out on the island of Formosa. By the time it had been suppressed uncounted thousands of civilians had been slaughtered, and the educated and intellectual elite had been decimated. No Formosan who was alive at the time will forget the holocaust, nor will the hatred of the mainland Chinese abate.

Formosa was settled by mainlanders several centuries ago, although it was always somewhat apart from the mainstream of China. It was seized by Japan as part of the settlement of the Sino-Japanese War of 1895, and for the next fifty years was ruled sternly, but not oppressively. Even though its economy was tailored to fit Japanese purposes, the standard of living became in Asia second only to that of Japan itself. But during this half century, Formosan irredentism became the most powerful emotion on the island, and when Japan surrendered in 1945 the Chinese were hailed as liberators. The rejoicing did not last long.

The Generalissimo named an old military crony, General Chen Yi, as Governor. The sole objective of the Governor and his henchmen was to loot the island of everything movable and take it back to the mainland. The Formosans were allowed

Situation as of March 20, 1947

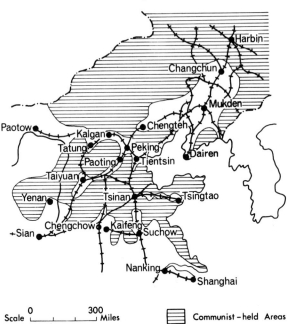

Scale 0 — 300 Miles   ▤ Communist-held Areas

no more voice in their own affairs than they had had under the Japanese. Economic problems, in some measure caused by heavy American bombing during the war, became catastrophic when total neglect accompanied the plundering. By the time of the rebellion, it was not at all unlikely that in a free plebiscite the Formosans would have voted to return to Japan.

General Chen had kept the island so tightly sealed off from the rest of the world that only a small handful of people outside was aware anything was amiss, and the Formosans were unable to get an audience until they resorted to rebellion as their only hope. Suddenly confronted with this appalling situation, the Generalissimo pleaded ignorance of what had been happening, recalled General Chen, and appointed a reform administration.[1] But the damage had been done. When two million mainland Chinese fled to the island in 1949, they found themselves living

1 *China White Paper*, pp. 307–11. George H. Kerr's *Formosa Betrayed* (Boston: Houghton Mifflin, 1965) is the definitive work on the subject. Mr. Kerr was one of the few Americans who was permitted any long-term residence on the island by the Japanese and came to know it intimately. He returned after the war as the American Assistant Naval Attaché and remained until 1947 when the Nationalists decided they no longer wanted expert witnesses present.

as a hated minority in the midst of a population that outnumbered them by at least five to one. It was a precarious position. It was not, incidentally, until 1949 that the Generalissimo would have General Chen shot on charges of conspiring with the Communists to turn over to them his own province of Chekiang, across the Straits from Formosa.

Since the Nationalist Government was driven to Formosa something of an economic miracle has taken place, even though much of it must be attributed to massive American aid and American direction in development programs. There has been, however, no political miracle. Despite all attempts at whitewashing and window dressing, the fact remains that even to this day the Formosans, with an occasional exception, are to be found only in the lower ranks of the Government and the Army. The Kuomintang has effectively silenced all opposition, whether Formosan or mainland; and the large American military presence does not exactly encourage dissent.

Despite all claims to the contrary, no one really knows what the Formosans are thinking or what they will do when the firm hand of the Generalissimo has been removed. Nor can anyone say with assurance what will be the attitude of the Army which in almost two decades has been forced to acquire a heavy percentage of native Formosans in the ranks. The eventual solution of the Formosan problem could take unpredictable turns.

Inklings of trouble in Sinkiang began to filter into Nanking early in the spring, but it was not until June that matters came to a head in the form of the Mongol invasion from the north, and it would be mid-July before details became known at the Embassy. China traditionally has claimed suzerainty over Mongolia and has claimed sovereignty over Sinkiang since the eighteenth century, but in the twentieth century it has seldom exercised much effective control. Large Russian infiltration into Outer Mongolia began in the 1920s when the Soviet Union obviously intended to make it a buffer between Siberia and China. The Sino-Soviet Treaty of August 1945 recognized its independence after a plebiscite, and since then there seems to have been a good deal of ebb and flow of Russian and Chinese influence. Which one predominates at the moment appears a little uncertain.

Chinese control in Sinkiang has been more extensive, although as often as not local warlords have done about as they pleased. Basically, the problem has been that the indigenous peoples on both sides of the Sino-Soviet border have always been racially the same and have tended to look on the border with a certain disdain. From time to time the local tribal chieftains have found that it suited their purposes to play off the two giants which surround them one against the other. The evidence is clear that Communist China has made a determined effort to eliminate any Russian intrusion, although its specific purposes are a little obscure. The evidence is almost as good that this effort is causing considerable friction; and there is reason to assume that the area could become a major source of conflict between the two. It has been at least two thousand years since Central Asia was anywhere except on the rim of history; it would be ironic if it were again to move to the center.

*Ining, headquarters of
the Russian-supported
rebel forces on the
Sino-Russian Central
Asian frontier, was
only a short distance
to the north of Kash-
gar, which had been
the northernmost Bri-
tish toehold prior to
Indian independence
only six weeks before—
obviously a sensitive
meeting point.*

February 27 / Nanking / Walter Graham, British Consul
General, has come in from Tihwa and the tune of what he
has to say about Sinkiang sounds like China in a Central
Asian dialect. He believes the province continues to drift
away from the Chinese and toward the Russians. Governor
Chang Chih-chung, one of the more moderate and intelligent members of the Kuomintang, can slow down the
drift because of his good relations with Ining, but he cannot
change it. Graham is convinced the principal support for
the rebellion comes from the Soviets, but that by no means
negates the legitimate grievances of the Turkis against
Chinese treatment of minorities. He says the Soviets deliberately provoked the 1945 uprising in which whole units of
the Red Army were loaned to Ining, along with aircraft
and pilots, anti-aircraft units, artillery, and ammunition.
Now there are Russian administrators and political advisors
in Ining which make it little more than a Soviet puppet
regime, and the population is unaware there is anything
else in the world besides Russians, Chinese, and themselves.

This fits in with something Arthur Sabri, who is here now
as a Sinkiang delegate to the National Assembly, told me.
He said that Achmed Jan Kasimi, who is Vice Governor of
Sinkiang as well as titular head of the Turki People's Party,
is a Soviet citizen and has been for several years. He added
that many other influential members of the Ining Government are also Soviet citizens. Sabri implied that he is about
to become Commissioner of Public Health on his return
to Ining, which is of interest mainly because of his father's
importance in the Kuomintang CEC.

March 1 / The explosion on Formosa has come. Reports
are too fragmentary and conflicting to give a clear picture;
but it is serious. At the other end of the China axis there
are more riots in Tihwa.

March 2 / The Generalissimo has at last announced the
reorganization of the Government to prepare the way for
promulgation of the new constitution scheduled for next
December 25. It is an indifferent mixture of Kuomintang,

Youth Party, Social Democrats, and non-partisans, which cannot mean much. It was not announced whether Soong would continue as Prime Minister.

Having been informed they were no longer welcome here, the last members of the Communist delegation left today. There was a kind of symbolic sadness about the end of communication; but they seemed cheerful and confident enough.

Their departure highlights another sadness which has been creeping on almost unnoticed all winter. Little by little people we know are slipping away, dropping out of sight. The few still around are wary and uncommunicative. It is personally sad, and officially dangerous in that it leaves us with a narrowing base of information—for the most part only what the Government wants us to know. Around the Embassy this is becoming known as the usually unreliable sources of information.

March 3 / Soong refused to continue as Prime Minister and his resignation as head of the Supreme Economic Council was also accepted with alacrity. Apparently the break came over the Generalissimo's demand for an increase in troop pay and rations to bolster sagging morale. On all sides our military people find increasing reluctance in Government troops to fight an endless war of Chinese against Chinese. Soong obviously could not see where they would get the wherewithal and decided to save his reputation at the cost of his face and skedaddled. A new gold scandal in Shanghai, in which he is *not* involved, is little calculated to enhance the attractiveness of his job.

March 4 / Two of our eager beaver Assistant Military Attachés stationed in Manchuria have managed to wander around someone's picket lines and get themselves captured by the Communists as a reward for their curiosity.

March 6 / Reports are now conclusive that the Formosan riots are being put down by massacre. The trouble was not planned, but started when the Monopoly Police beat to death a woman who was selling cigarettes without a license. So far no armed Formosans have been seen, but the trouble is far from settled.

March 8 / The Russian Ambassador here has asked China to take over the civil administrations of Dairen and Port Arthur, as well as joint administration of the railroad to Changchun. Just what this caper means is less than clear.

Such a towering amount of verbiage is bandied about on the subject of Russian objectives and activities in China that it is curious no one ever thinks of Nanking-Moscow relations which, as far as anyone can judge, are correct, even easy, with a minimum of problems under discussion seriously. The Russians initiate little, if anything, and the Chinese confine themselves largely to protests about events in Dairen, Manchuria, Mongolia, and Sinkiang. It is hard to imagine that Nanking does this for any reason other than making a record, or that Moscow conceives it to be more than an exercise in the gentle art of diplomatic note writing.

In part this comes about because Sino-Soviet relations in practical terms are a by-product of the broader struggle of Soviet-American relations. Nanking has abdicated its unrealistic status as a major power simply because it is in no position to make that status effective. The Far East is the only part of the world in which only two major powers face each other—and neither of them is Chinese or even Asian. The multidirectional relations of major powers in Europe, Africa, and the Middle East are absent. Instead of being an advantage, the absence of complication is a handicap in that it limits the range of maneuverability, especially for us since we are allied with a faction in China which is in the process of losing the Mandate of Heaven. The Russians can afford an amused complaisance since their cohorts give every evidence of picking up the Mandate as fast as the Generalissimo drops it. Too much we tend to look on this as a struggle for power; it is indeed that, but we overlook the third major participant, the people of China, who might just have a few ideas of their own as to what they would like to see happen in their country. In the long run it is they who will decide. We alone maintain the illusion of Nanking as a major power and insist it go through the motions of acting like one, when in fact it can be little more than our third withered arm. China can never be more than that until someone manages to attract the real sources of Chinese power and put them together.

March 15 / The appointment of Chang Kia-ngau as Governor of the Central Bank has been greeted without enthusiasm or even outrage. The Generalissimo has balanced the intention of the Political Science Group (the liberal foreign educated wing of the Kuomintang of which Chang is an influential member) to seize financial control in Shanghai by naming a cc clique man to head the Central Trust. cc has recently been turning a beadier and more interested eye on the money markets. A Control Yuan report has accused Soong's agents of being unduly cavalier and free wheeling in the gold market, while at the same time good newspaper sources report that T'ang En-po, Yen Hsi-shan, and Ku Chu-tung, all top ranking generals, are speculating in the yellow stuff. Against this backdrop, a reshuffling of the Legislative Yuan did not even make the front pages.

March 24 / Government troops have captured the Communist capital at Yenan with a great deal of nonsensical hoopla. Apart from limited symbolic value, it only means the Government is now dangerously overextended in yet another direction.

March 24 / As far as we can tell the first half of the Central Executive Committee of the Kuomintang Third Plenary Session which convened a week ago on schedule has been largely a struggle for power between cc and other groups, mainly the Political Science Group, with the Whampoa clique and assorted generals without strong factional backing sitting uneasily in the middle. The odds seem to be on cc at the moment, as witness its drive to oust Wang Shih-

The Whampoa clique was composed of graduates of the Whampoa Military Academy; the Generalissimo would have favored it had he not needed to balance conflicting groups.

chieh, far and away the ablest if not the most forceful member of the Government, as Foreign Minister, whom even Dr. Sun Fo, an intimate friend for years, has now deserted. cc is also attacking General Ch'en Ch'eng for his bungling of the Shantung campaign, although he seems to have retrieved himself somewhat by his ostentatious capture of Yenan. Along with some visionary economic proposals, the cc boss Ch'en Li-fu has made the too, too innocent proposal that all cliques be abolished in the national interest. Soong has been conspicuous by his absence and Premier Chang Chun skitters nervously between Nanking and Shanghai on foolish errands, mainly unavailing attempts to persuade Hu Lin, Fu Sou-nien, Miao Yun-tai, and Kuo Mo-jo, all ostensibly liberal independents, to sign up with the Government. The lessons out of this chaos can hardly be lost on a group as ruthless and determined as cc, although I doubt if the Generalissimo will allow many of them to sit in the front in view of the known American attitude toward them. This matters little since the Chinese, after all, have heard of puppets too.

The lightest touch has been the effort to get Carsun Chang to represent his Social Democrats in the Government. He has been very much the reluctant dragon. They even got him as far as the railroad station in Shanghai and he squeezed out again. The fact is that Chang, who is very articulate, wants the fun of loud public protest without responsibility and he is aggrieved that there are those who would deny him this.

March 30 / George Kerr is here from Formosa to report on that unhappy island. It was the cigarette vendor incident which sparked the explosion. For the next week Governor Chen Yi temporized while negotiating with Formosan representatives about their grievances over being looted and treated worse than they had been by the Japanese; he promised and compromised, and there were only a few killings. At no time were the Formosans militarily organized or armed.

Then troops from the mainland landed and the slaughter began. Partly it was wanton and random killing of anyone on the streets to induce public terror. In part it was systematic to eliminate leadership, students, teachers—the community and intellectual elite. The total must run into thousands upon thousands and the process is still going on as individuals disappear and fresh bodies are daily being washed up on the beaches and into the harbor at Keelung.

Kerr's report is the first the outside world has known of the magnitude and savagery of what has happened.

April 1 / This morning the Tass man in Nanking, who is witty, savvy, and intelligent, was enjoying the recent Moscow and Communist blasts at us for having a residue of armed force in China. He was even more amused when I pointed out that not long ago we were attacked as irresponsible when we pulled out our main strength, and before that for having anything at all here. "That is right. No matter what you do we will attack as being wrong. Why shouldn't we? You know how it is."

The Soviet Embassy press officer is considerably less light-hearted and takes life and himself very seriously. He has been in China since early in the war and has always been free and easy with Americans. We have all found it possible to talk with him as with none of the other Russians. Most significantly, he has long been troubled about Manchuria, but if he knows the reason for Russian looting there he has kept it to himself. He has even admitted that the Russians had an opportunity to gain much sympathy and threw it away by their behavior. He also recognizes the intense personal distaste of all Manchurians traditionally for Russians, which now includes Communist bitterness over Russian failure to help them in 1946.

Stalin never did understand the role of public opinion in the United States. Undoubtedly many factors went into his attitude toward China. It is quite

As far as Government resentment is concerned, however, he points out—and rightly so—that they stayed in Manchuria as long as they did at Government request and, furthermore, that Government compliance with the 1945 treaties areas it controls has been less than satisfactory.

likely, in his own ideological terms and in view of his past relations with the Chinese Communists, that he really meant it when he discounted their future, at least for a long time to come. It is just as likely that he was caught off balance by the disastrous and publicly forced American demobilization. In his view, major powers simply did not do such things.

Atrocities against Russian railroad workers have been especially nasty.

He has also certainly reflected other and much higher level views in the past that the Chinese Communists had a dim future and so it made sense to leave Manchuria as useless to Nanking as possible. He was genuinely surprised, at first even disbelieving, over the precipitate dismantling of our rather impressive power position in China after the Japanese surrender. Now that Communist victory is almost inevitable it is inconceivable they will accept the role of junior partner any longer than they have to. The Russians will yet have much to regret.

Springtime of discontent

On April 17 the reorganization of the Executive Yuan and the State Council was announced. General Chang Chun became President of the Executive Yuan, or Prime Minister, and Dr. Sun Fo, son of the founder of the Chinese Republic, was elected Vice President. Other appointments were of the same ilk, and a case could be made, on paper anyway, that it was a victory for moderation and reform. The ominous sign was the simultaneous establishment of a separate Kuomintang political committee whose secretary general was Ch'en Li-fu, the leader of the CC clique. The well-nigh inescapable conclusion was that the front-row seats, exposed to the view of the world, were occupied by the moderates, but that the reactionaries were concealed behind them where they could render efforts for reform impotent. This was precisely what happened.[1]

Beneath all the manipulating and maneuvering, something else was developing which was both amorphous and ominous. This was an accelerating decline in morale, especially during May and June, and it found outlets in several different directions. The most significant was the outbreak of the largest and most violent student demonstrations since the end of the Japanese war. Intellectuals in any underdeveloped country play a political role out of all proportion to their numbers and far beyond the role they have in literate societies, simply because they are an elite. China was no exception.

The student riots were of such magnitude and their demands were so uniformly for the immediate ending of the civil war that the only conclusion could be the intellectuals were disillusioned with the Government and were moving rapidly in the only direction they had to move. The riots were murderously suppressed by the Government and the secret police. Doubtless the Communists and the Democratic

1 *China White Paper*, pp. 244–45.

League were involved, but there had to be more to it than that, considering how widespread they were. Paradoxically, there was reason to believe some of the riots had been organized by cc to provide an excuse for eliminating disaffected elements and discrediting the Political Science Group as incompetent. They would probably have been more violent than they were had it not been June and time to close the universities for the summer anyway. There was no reason, however, to suppose they would not be renewed at a later date.

Coincidentally, there were serious rice riots in the major urban centers before the summer crop came in; stocks had run low, and it was discovered that speculators were hoarding what was available.[2] These too were suppressed by the same techniques that had proven at least temporarily effective with the students. Equally serious was slipping morale in the Army caused by inept leadership, passivity, and corruption in the Government, and by inadequate rations, thieving officers, and a growing reluctance of Chinese to fight Chinese when there seemed to be no end to it and little evidence of purpose. Troop morale was particularly bad in the key area of Manchuria, where Government control had been reduced to a few cities, Government troops were doing little more than garrison duty – there are few things more dangerous than idle soldiers – and civilian rations were being cut to a subsistence level. Government capture of the Communist capital of Yenan was meaningless, except insofar as it overextended Government resources in yet another direction. In north China, and especially in the key province of Shantung where the Government needed a victory, activities resulted only in attrition and losses, despite certain momentary gains, which the Government could no longer afford. It was the increasingly familiar picture of guerrilla soldiers, living on their internal resources and needing little outside support, in opposition to a conventional military opponent whose costs of maintenance rose steadily.

If there was any humor in the situation it was provided by the People's Political Council, which had played such a significant and highly respected role in the war against Japan as a sounding board for public opinion and an effective rallier of public support for that war. Meeting on May 26, at its last session before going out of existence, it passed overwhelmingly a resolution inviting the Communists to return to Nanking to negotiate the end of the civil war. The ppc then just as overwhelmingly passed another resolution demanding the continuation of military action to eliminate the Communists.[3] If amusing, it was also highly symptomatic of popular confusion and uneasiness.

Although Ambassador Stuart from time to time felt cheered by what he chose to believe was a growing willingness by the Generalissimo to do what had to be done, he also reported on June 18 that "The growing discontent with or even hostility toward the Government has been stimulated among the intellectuals by the extremely harsh measures against the students and among the unthinking masses by the mounting costs of livelihood. In its simplest terms the complaints center around freedom and food. . . . Actually much of the strength of Chinese Com-

2 *Ibid.*, pp. 368–71.
3 *Ibid.*, p. 240.

munism is due chiefly to the inefficiency and corruption of the Kuomintang and –
with an alarming acceleration – to popular loss of faith in the Government."[4]

On June 30 the powerful Standing Committee of the Central Executive Committee held an extraordinary and previously unannounced meeting, and adopted
three resolutions: (1) continuation and expansion of the "punitive action" against
the Communists; (2) integration of the San Min Chu I Youth Corps into the
Kuomintang; and (3) preparation for the fall elections.[5] Even the declaration of
national mobilization by the State Council five days later could not dispel an
impression that this was a combination of the ridiculous and the tragic.

4 *Ibid.*, p. 246.
5 *Ibid.*, p. 249.

April 12 / Peiping / It is spring in Peiping and very lovely
indeed. When you spend some time in Nanking and then
are here you suddenly realize you had forgotten what a
sorry place Nanking really is. I have bought some furniture
which is extraordinary and beautiful. It is not the Manchu
Dynasty furniture to which we are accustomed, every inch
carved and painted; but Ming Dynasty, very plain and
simple in line. It would go with anything.

One of the fun places in Peiping is an old Mongol
restaurant, famous for its mutton and rice wine, where you
eat and drink yourself silly on a do-it-yourself basis. You
cook your own mutton with oversized chopsticks on a huge
outdoor brazier which has allegedly been in use for three
centuries without having been washed. However old it may
be, the carbon crust on it is at least three inches thick and
exudes a most appealing odor of seasoned mutton fat and
garlic. You also help yourself to the wine from a large jar.

I have also seen some of the faculty people at Tsinghua,
which is the university we financed by returning our share
of the Boxer Rebellion indemnity money for this purpose.
It is a thin life the intellectuals have these days as their
incomes shrink and political control over their thinking
tightens. Most noticeable was the reluctance, really refusal,
of any of them to talk beyond chit chat. Any confidence
they have had in us, and most of them were educated in
the United States, is gone; but enough bitterness creeps out
unconsciously to suggest that any alternative offered to their
present situation with any hope of improvement gets a

sympathetic hearing—witness the slow but steady flow of
intellectuals into Communist areas.

April 15 / Nanking / Lo Lung-chi, Secretary General of
the Democratic League, who is constitutionally incapable
of reticence, was franker last night than I have ever heard
him. I am pretty sure that what he says represents most
non-Communist, non-Kuomintang Chinese, and that we
are making a mistake in not understanding this attitude
better and giving it more weight, whether we like it or not.
He said: "The Democratic League is middle-of-the-road
liberal and opposed to both extremes, but the political
exigencies of the moment require it to follow a course
largely in support of the Communist position. The League
believes the Kuomintang deliberately violated the pcc agreements, if indeed it ever had any intention of carrying them
out, and therefore the Communists are right in calling for

abrogation of the 1946 constitution. The impending new reorganization of the Government will have little meaning except as window dressing for foreign consumption."

When I asked him whether he thought the Communists ever sincerely intended to enter a coalition, he said he thought they did until July 1946 when they lost all hope. When I then asked him whether he thought elements as far apart as the Communists and the Kuomintang could ever really be expected to work in a coalition except under extreme foreign pressure and then only as an interim measure, he expressed doubt. He added his opinion that within ten months all Manchuria and Shansi would be in Communist hands and then there would be a good chance for a coalition in which the Communists would eventually have dominant, though not complete, control.

Lo thinks the United States could stop the fighting by stopping aid to the Kuomintang, and even if this did mean Communist ascendancy it would be no threat to Chinese sovereignty since the Chinese people would fight Soviet control just as they now fight American control. He added: "As between a fascist Kuomintang supported by the United States and a Chinese Communist Party supported by the Soviet Union, the League will support the Communists because they are fighting the greatest menace of all, Fascism. Furthermore, even though Communism in China would allow no more scope for the activities of the liberals than does the Kuomintang, still Communism means greater good for the mass of the people and should be supported, even though the League would prefer to see the liberals in power and believes this is the group which should have American backing." He did not, however, have any specific suggestions as to just how this policy could be implemented in the circumstances. He finally repeated his belief that the Communists would never in the long run tolerate Russian interference because they would always be Chinese first and Communists second.

April 20 / The Executive Yuan and the State Council have

been formally reorganized and this time democracy has been born in China. The Generalissimo said so.

April 26 / While the weather tries to settle down to being warm in the valley, it is also raining, which plays havoc with sinuses. Around the Embassy we identify people not by their footsteps but by their coughs. Doubtless Dr. Freud would have some observations, but we like to blame the weather, which, incidentally, has managed to paralyze us for the past week. The monsoon effectively keeps a lot of planes on the ground and no one can get anywhere.

My garden is coming along as well as could be expected in our clayey soil, and the new spears of corn are as pretty as they always are. A lot of flowers are in bloom, including the wisteria, but few have any fragrance, or if they have they find it difficult to compete with the current new laying on of the Chinese variety of fertilizer. This plus onions really sets the prevailing odor of China, although it is amazing how you get used to it and never notice it. The United Press man here has a dog which the other day somehow managed to fall into one of the vats in which night soil is ripened. He hit bottom, bounced out and made a beeline for the house, dashed around the living room, shaking himself all the time, and settled on the sofa.

April 26 / Rigg and Collins, the American Army officers captured in Manchuria by the Communists early in March, are finally back, thus ending a weird case. I had thought they would be given the royal treatment, but I was wrong. They were kept in solitary confinement the entire time except for a lot of questioning.

April 30 / It is wonderfully quiet around here today. The weather finally broke and six planes took off in six different directions with half the Embassy and most of the visitors. It is also becoming unseasonably hot.

Life has been appallingly democratic these days. As part of the campaign to demonstrate that the reorganization of the Government means radical changes really have taken place,

everybody is being formally introduced to everyone else at
tea parties to the accompaniment of a lot of snickering. The
first time the Generalissimo wanted something done Soong
came out of retirement, moved in over the head of Prime
Minister Chang Chun, and did it himself. On the whole, the
Chinese are the least impressed with the new order, but they
are distressed that Marshall also is not impressed.

The prize story of the week has come from a Foreign
Office spokesman at a press conference. A large number of
Germans who were scheduled for repatriation conveniently
escaped at the last minute and most have not been heard of
since. The Foreign Office says the Government knows
where they are, but is not picking them up because of the
housing shortage in Shanghai.

May 8 / One mistake we all make is not paying enough
attention to Communist theoreticians, though God knows
it is dreary reading at best. One good example is the New
Year's analysis of international affairs by Liu Ting-yi, which
has just been publicly released and to which he gave the
catchy title of "Explanation of Several Basic Questions
Concerning the Post-War International Situation." It is
written in the usual soporific Marxist verbiage and contains
most of the expected cliches, but it also has some interesting
new material. Due homage is given to the Soviets as the
authors of everything good in this world and proper vilifica-
tion is heaped on us as the source and leader of all evil,
along with assurances that good naturally conquers evil.
The victory will come about because the real conflict in the
world is not between the Soviet Union and the United
States, but is the internal struggle among the capitalist
states. Proof is found in the leftward swing of peoples all
over the world and in the impending American economic
crisis.

More original than this dreary routine, however, are several suggestions, both specific and implied, that there has been
considerable independent thinking and practice in Yenan
which is not about to be toned down by all the anger of

the Kremlin. Notable among the points are the views that the internal capitalist struggles decrease rather than increase the danger of war, that capitalist encirclement does not exist, and that the sharpness of internal capitalist controversy gives the Soviet Union security and hence the opportunity of remaining aloof from the world squabbles. Also interesting is the repeated appeal to the authority of "Marx, Lenin, and Mao." This won't make Stalin happy! This is also the first major declaration which makes no reference to Mao's 1945 doctrine in *The New Democracy* that Communism is a far-off goal. Rather, the assumption is an immediate drive for Communism along with the abandonment of any hope for coalition.

Although the analysis is the most outspoken declaration to date of support for the Soviets, even this loyalty is expressed in curiously reserved tones. There are even suggestions of wariness as to where Russian ideology ends and Russian nationalism begins. We have all seen too many examples of Russian, even official Russian, contempt for the Chinese as Chinese to assume that the Communists have not noticed it too. Traditional Chinese pride and xenophobia will make their acceptance of Russian nationalism, however cloaked in ideology and theories of national treatment, the neatest trick of the century unless the Russians shortly improve their manners and increase their tolerance of what someone else might happen to think about his own life. Every overtone in this analysis only confirms that the Chinese Communists—whatever weaving they may do through necessity—will in their ideas, attitudes, and actions be guided by their own years of struggle and experience, not by the struggles and experience of anyone else.

Recent visitors to Communist areas have observed a good deal of local autonomy. The general directive comes from on high, but its implementation is left to local discretion. Furthermore, the general directive is largely limited to traditional Chinese peasant desires, namely land reform, relief from exorbitant taxes, and some opportunity for individual expression. To the average untutored peasant the reforms have nothing to do with ideology, which is just so much meaningless verbiage to him. He consequently proceeds to carry out permissible reforms with great gusto and turns on his former landlords and bureaucratic supervisors with all the cruelty and ruthlessness they formerly used on him. There is some evidence that in a few cases Communist leaders have attempted to check excesses, thereby bringing down upon their heads the same wrath previously reserved for the landlords. It may be that the indigenous peasant revolution is outstripping the Communist revolution. In the end, of course, only that government which can satisfy minimum peasant aspirations will secure and retain peasant loyalty. Herein lies the greatest failure of the Kuomintang.

May 13 / The last few days have dropped into the doldrums of an unduly early and terrible heat. The sky is like tarnished copper and the gardens are already wilting, including my lettuce. But in the willow outside my office window a dove hatched out her first this morning and has been chortling about it ever since, a pair of golden orioles has been swooping around, and the bottle birds are back. And I do have my own mint bed and the luxurious satisfaction of pruning it. So it could be worse inside our wall, though not much worse outside. There are rice riots in cities all over the country, universities are on strike, and civil war spreads, inflation mounts, and nothing is right with China today. Not that it should be deduced, as many have deduced, that any final collapse is imminent. This country has a tremendous absorptive power for punishment. It is eighty per cent agricultural, and the peasant population lives not much more miserably than it always has. Unless the rice crop this year is a failure the situation can drag on for a long time.

May 15 / Rice prices have more than doubled in the past two weeks and the riots are spreading even to the countryside. Students and teachers are becoming increasingly violent and a good many heads were cracked in the Nanking demonstrations today. It is getting to the point where no one bothers to inquire into the cause of the average-size demonstrations any more. Only the big ones inspire much interest.

It is now quite apparent that the military campaigns of the last few weeks have been larger than anything seen in China for a long time. Not only did the Kuomintang want, it desperately needed, a major victory in Shantung. It did not get it. Despite Government claims, it never had things its own way, never wrested the initiative from the Communists, or damaged Communist ability to attack or withdraw at will or cut communications as suited them. The Communists took the initiative in Manchuria and forced their way to the gates of Changchun. They were, to be sure, finally turned back and in this sense suffered a territorial defeat; but if the objective was a serious drain of Nationalist strength they succeeded. Casualties were high on both sides and all signs point to a diminishing willingness to fight among Government troops. Somehow the Kuomintang still fails to instill any sense of purpose in its troops and there are increasing instances in which Communist appeals are resulting in defections.

May 20 / In the wake of the long series of disorders the Government has banned all public gatherings. The students go right ahead and riot anyway. The riot yesterday was frightening, with thousands of students and troops involved, barricades all over the city, and many people badly injured. It is not known whether anyone was killed. The earlier riots were cc inspired and based on frivolous demands such as stopping examinations or dropping this course or that one. Then the Democratic League moved in and the motivation changed quickly to demands for economic relief because of dwindling rice supplies, skyrocketing prices, and speculative hoarding. Outside our compound the troops are continuously on the move and the city looks more like an armed camp than anything I have seen in a long time. The Government is showing some signs it means to stop demonstrations.

June 1 / My farming is coming along nicely. The main problem is that the Embassy gardeners keep doing what they want to do despite anything I say. They seem to have a feeling this is beneath me, and more importantly that I do not know what I am doing. That may be true, but I have fun making mistakes. The one thing they will not touch is the row of corn across the front yard. The lettuce is now edible, the rambler roses have thousands of blossoms, and a small gardenia tree is in flower.

The *Time* article extolling the virtues of Ch'en Li-fu is causing an uproar and I am suspicious of what is behind it. A lot of Chinese in high places, and certainly none of them flaming liberals, are most disturbed. They give it more official standing than it deserves, but still. . . . One said to me rather bitterly: "Do you have to go to such extremes?"

[*One of the more unfortunate determinants of the American image around the world over the years has been* Time *with its enormous audience both in and outside the United States, due in large measure to its extraordinary readability and quick, comprehensive coverage of news. Although it has seldom been possible to question its factual accuracy, it has been a frightening example of how news can be "managed" by discreet selection of facts and the use of adjectives and descriptive phrases. Sometime during this period the Director of the United States Information Service in China was simply characterized as "big, beefy Brad Connors." Brad was "big" and he was "beefy," but the mental picture left by the conjuncture of these two words had nothing to do with those qualities which made him one of the ablest and most effective officers the United States had in China.*

There has long been an impression that Time *was the mouthpiece of Washington. Unquestionably it has more often than not reflected the views of the power establishment with which Henry Luce had intimate ties. In China this view was especially strong because of Luce's China missionary background. But* Time *has never hesitated to express different opinions when it held them. In this parti-*

*cular article it reaffirmed its unswerving support for the
Generalissimo and suggested, in its dismay over the disarray
of developments, that the doggedness, personal integrity and
austerity, and uncompromising anti-Communism of Ch'en
Li-fu were what he needed. This view may have been
acceptable to the China Lobby, but it most assuredly was
not the consensus in Washington at that time. True, it would
become that, but only much later.*]

There is a kind of lull before the storm which is scheduled to break tomorrow if the students have the guts to
walk into the face of sudden and violent death. It is a
general strike which has grown out of the so-called Nanking
Incident. A few days ago they decided to demonstrate in
favor of an immediate and negotiated peace in the face of
Government decrees forbidding such goings-on. On the
appointed day troops mounted machine guns around the
university grounds to keep students in; but they then
formed a close-order phalanx and marched out singing a
Chinese version of the Battle Hymn of the Republic. The
troops let them go. The palace gendarmes, however, who
are a tougher crowd, were called in and what happened
after that was appalling. Since that time there have been
killings, beatings, and hundreds of arrests. Our reports indicate the same thing happened in Canton. Much depends on
how bitter the students feel and how effective the Government has been in rounding up the leadership. The new
troops coming into town today are plug-uglies and there are
many signs the boys and girls are wavering. If so, they are
lost because the initiative is the only advantage they have.

June 3 / The general strike fizzled yesterday.

June 7 / Butterworth has just come back from Manchuria
and confirms what we had been hearing, namely, that the
Government structure is collapsing except in three or four
cities. To all intents and purposes the Communists are in
control of the whole area. In Shantung, which is a vital
stronghold, the Government is bogged down to its neck, and
some of our people have even seen Communist artillery

beginning to move toward Shanghai. The entire air force
is being used to evacuate the generals and their impedimenta while their troops are abandoned to their fate. And
now comes the decision in Washington to lift the embargo
on munitions. This will make us hated by everyone except
the most extreme reactionaries.

June 16 / The headline news is the Mongol invasion of
Sinkiang. Doubtless there was a scrap, maybe even a big
one; but then this sort of thing has been going on for centuries in that uncharted and desert region. As for Soviet
complicity, doubtless the Russians are interested in the area
and doubtless it will fall into the Soviet orbit unless the
Chinese do something more effective than they have for a
long time; but the Mongol army was trained and equipped
by the Russians and it might conceivably have acted on its
own. The Ministry of Information admitted to me that the
hoopla is designed to help force a loan from us and to dis-
tract attention from the disasters in Manchuria which are
real disasters. The gentleman in question did not even smile
when he said it.

This trip and others like it were fact gathering missions, made for the same reason that a good newsman leaves the cocktail party circuit in the capital to observe events for himself.

June 22 / *Tsinan, Shantung* / The Military Attaché and
I approached Tsinan—the capital of Shantung province—
flying low over the Tsin-Pu railroad beginning some fifty
miles south of Taian to see how much damage has been
done by the Communists. Their guerrilla activities have
been especially successful in disrupting railroads, which are
essential for the more traditional and conventional type of
warfare practiced by the Nationalists but have little relevance for Communist tactics. The Nationalists have yet to
learn this lesson and act accordingly. Although there has
been more reconstruction than we had expected, there are
long stretches between Taian and Tsinan where even
the embankments have vanished. Taian itself has almost
vanished as a functioning center.

Here we have been the guests of General Wang Yao-wu
who has filled our time so completely we suspect he would
just as soon we did not forage for ourselves. He staged a

review of the Ninety-sixth Army for us. By usual Chinese standards the troops seemed well fed and fairly well clothed, although not more than half the men had arms and fewer had helmets. The men seemed tough, mean, and sullen, and their discipline indicated good leadership. Wang gives an impression of competence not ordinarily associated with Kuomintang generals. He is confident of his ability to hold out despite the long siege; but there is little military activity in the area because he and the Generalissimo disagree on what should be done next, and so nothing is done.

We visited one of the largest textile mills in Shantung whose general appearance and methods of operation are practically identical with those in the Yangtze Valley, except that it is working at only half capacity due to a shortage of raw materials. Then we went to a model Kuomintang school for war orphans. The director is the head of the Party Women's Organization for Shantung and the wife of the provincial Party chairman. She is an extraordinary woman, a large, raw-boned Shantung type, with great energy, a most attractive personality, and she can drink like a trooper, which is unusual for a Chinese. What she has done with the school and in building up the children in two years is most impressive. Although she denied it emphatically, many of the children looked half Japanese. After considerable coy evasion she finally admitted the school is cc affiliated and is designed to train Party workers. Something about the place made me think of the Hitler Jugend.

Cheloo University is a sorry spectacle. It is physically rundown—even the grass needs cutting—and enrolment is small. The siege and financial troubles are largely responsible. The biggest effort is being made on the medical school, which before the war was noted for its training of rural doctors.

There is a general and intense bitterness here against the Communists such as I have seen nowhere else in China. Not a single person has had one good word to say for them, although there is also no great confidence in the

ability of the Kuomintang to do what is necessary. Power
locally appears concentrated in the military and the CC.
Typical of the attitude was the Secretary General of the
Command, a former private secretary to the Generalissimo,
who suggested that perhaps the time had come for a change
of leadership in Nanking. But there was nothing to suggest
any lack of faith in local military leadership.

The classic and monumental account of this obscure and fascinating footnote in history is Chinese Jews *by Bishop William Charles White (University of Toronto Press, 2nd ed., 1966; New York: Paragon). The good bishop also put together and absconded from China with the nucleus of the Chinese collection at the Royal Ontario Museum in Toronto, quite possibly the finest Chinese collection in the world outside of China itself.*

June 24 / Chengchow, Honan / We flew from Tsinan over
the yellow loess plains of north China and the ancient seats
of ancient cultures. This is where China began. Kaifeng
was especially interesting from the air because we had a
perfect view of the old walled city. We could even see what
is left of a synagogue dating back to the original Jewish
communities in the eighth and ninth centuries when T'ang
semitic traders flourished. Vague legends still speak of the
Lost Tribes, and people whose faces show semitic traces
still practice some of the forms and customs of a religion
whose source and meaning they have long since forgotten,
shadows and echoes out of the long past of turbulent men
in middle Asia. Nor is this just imagination: many T'ang
tombs have yielded burial figurines which are unmistakably
Jewish.

Here near the gap in the Yellow River we are staying
with O. J. Todd, UNRRA consultant on closing the gap and
a great Yellow River authority. Todd, to put it gently, is
something of an eccentric and his insistence on driving a
jeep with his eyes closed can only be classed as insanity; but
he is a wonderfully dynamic man who talks about the river
as he might about a mistress. At the closure site we stood
on the loess flats and watched thousands upon thousands of
coolies in endless lines pushing squeaking wheel barrows
with their little piles of dirt and equal number of mule-
drawn carts slowly moving up to the top of the dikes, inch
by inch raising the level of the land against the sky and
against anticipated summer floods. There are long stretches
of the river where even during normal times the water level
is several feet above the surrounding countryside. It has
taken many centuries thus to contain China's Sorrow.

During the war the Government cut the dikes of the Yellow River to stop the Japanese Army advance. The principal result was to drown hundreds of thousands of Chinese and to flood millions of acres of some of the best farm land in China. The Japanese advance continued on schedule.

It is apparent that relations between Todd and the local
military are not good. The Army wanted the gap closed
earlier than planned in order to cause a premature flood
downriver in Shantung before the Communists would be
able to evacuate peasants in areas under their control, and
it took intervention from Nanking in order to prevent this.
For this and other reasons, every faction accuses Todd of
being the tool of someone else, but I suspect he would be
most unhappy if he did not have trouble of some kind on
his hands. I would be astonished if he had ever been anyone's fool.

The Chief of Staff who commands in the absence of
General Hu Tsung-nan can only be described as sly, incompetent, corrupt, and degenerate. Missionaries we have
visited are completely useless as sources of information and
might as well be living in Patagonia for all they know of
local conditions. I am afraid that all too many western
missionaries in rural areas live such isolated lives and concentrate so exclusively on their proselytizing work that they
become this way and still have little success in conversion.

But the river and work on it dominate everything. Surely,
it must have been this way in the building of the Great
Wall and the Pyramids—or even the great B-29 bases in
west China during the war. It is that infinite patience and
fatalism in the Chinese peasant, and even in the humblest
an instinctive and atavistic sense of the continuity of history. It makes Nanking seem fatuous and trivial.

June 25 / Sian, Shensi / Sian dozes in its desert sun and
shade and the thinning memories of an ancient Chinese
capital, surrounded by a timeless range of hills—a beautiful
piece of real estate. Far removed from any immediate Communist threat and little concerned with contemporary China
on which, in any event, it has largely turned its back since
China long ago moved slowly out of the west and toward
the east to meet the ocean, it seems preoccupied mainly
with its own problems.

Northwest University is typical. Started during the war
as a combination of three Peking universities in exile, it is

continuing on its own. The physical plant is impressive, but
the faculty is mediocre, the student body indifferent and
well disciplined by the Kuomintang Youth Corps, and academic standards to all intents and purposes non-existent.
The library is small and poor in quality. There are gran-
diose plans for a National Library of Sian, but the President
is vague as to what it will consist of, when, or why. The
principal interest in Sian is still archeological, except when
the contemporary world intrudes as it did when we were
shown two Nationalist aviators who had made a forced
landing in Communist territory. Before being sent back
here, their hands had been cut off and their eyes cut out.
They came tied onto mules. Having no air force of their
own and experiencing air power only on the receiving end,
the Communists are terrified of it and resort to this kind of
atrocity to dampen the enthusiasm of the Nationalist Air
Force. It works rather well. Air power against the Communist kind of warfare can be no more than a negligible
military factor, but it does have psychological impact.

There are few troops here, although those we have seen
gave a better appearance than any so far, even being
equipped with leather boots. Economic activity is negligible
and the crops this year are good. Political interest is so slight
that reaction to the recent Mongol foray into Sinkiang is
amused indifference. Like the Italians, they have seen
all this happen many times before. The political bosses
are concerned primarily with preserving their own local
satrapies, and the Kuomintang chairman admitted he had
not even looked at the new constitution.

June 27 / Chengtu, Szechuan / We flew south to Chengtu
and then up to the foothills of the Himalayas—foothills
here would be mountains anywhere else—and ran into some
really nasty weather that put our Air Attaché on his mettle.
It was only through that unfailing skill in the seat of Handsome Haney's pants that we escaped spending the rest of
time in this incredibly beautiful valley.

Almost overnight, isolation has dropped Chengtu back

The world would, indeed, intrude sooner and in ways no one at the time foresaw. The great semi-desert area that begins at Sian and extends westward has become the site of Chinese nuclear development, close to the Russian heart, and next door to Soviet nuclear centres in central Asia.

where it was before the Japanese got the idea Asia was their destiny. There is something symbolic in the fact that here the biggest air bases in the world were built for the great B-29s which could strike directly at Japan. The airstrips were built by a half million Chinese coolies, each with his little hammer making little rocks out of big ones; and the strikes never came off because there was never enough gasoline to get the planes to Japan and back again. Hankow on the middle Yangtze was as far as they ever got and they made rubble of that great river port. Today the bases are abandoned and grass is beginning to grow up between the rocks. The main local concern is the struggle among the local gentry for personal power.

Governor Teng Hsi-hou is trying to consolidate his hold on the province militarily and economically and is not exactly dainty in the way he goes about it. Landlords and gentry oppose him. Last spring's rice riots came out of this conflict when the gentry withheld stocks from the best crop in years in order to embarrass a Governor who represents Nanking in their eyes. A few well placed and prompt executions put down that maneuver, but there is no evidence the struggle for power is by any means over. Some say Teng has the province under his thumb; others that his control extends little beyond Chengtu itself. The truth is probably somewhere in between. Teng is hardly simplifying matters for himself by trying to muscle into the Sikang opium trade which has for some time been controlled by his principal rival, Liu Wen-hui—this being one of the time-honored perquisites of the west China warlord. The immediate result of this particular fight is an outbreak of tribal warfare which has cut off the caravan traffic from Tibet and makes rural travel unsafe. Meanwhile the bandits are having a field day.

Not surprisingly, conditions at the famous West China Union University demonstrate once again that centers of learning are among the casualties of civil war and chaos. The physical plant and the library are in good condition. Main emphasis is on the medical school. But a second look shows that, as at Northwest University in Sian, the faculty is at best mediocre; it is composed mostly of WCU University graduates, not one of whom has made any contribution to anything. The student body is apathetic and wholly controlled by the Kuomintang Youth Corps whose Chairman is also President of the University. The relatively good economic condition of the students here is not conducive to political activities, which are kept slightly below the simmering point along with academic standards. And of course there is always the threat of the Army conscription gangs we saw prowling the back alleys and whose advent always produces silence and vacant streets. If and when it seems desirable the gangs can raid schools as well as slums for raw and bleeding recruits.

Even the local leaders of the Youth Corps and the CC are pessimistic about the future of the Kuomintang, which they say not even massive American aid can now save. Since the right wing now has the military power, there is no chance for the liberal elements and only a long period of disintegration and fragmentation can result, along with growing Szechuanese autonomy from the central Government. Unless the Kuomintang is rejuvenated, they say, the end product will be Communist victory; and the timetable for that depends largely on when General Li Shih-nien chooses to move out of the northwest and into Szechuan.

As it turned out Li knew better than to make the usual mistake of the Generalissimo by overextending his lines. Once the Communist victory in central China was assured, the west China warloads would hasten to make their peace with him.

The brightest spot in Chengtu is the West China Border Research Society and its museum, which have a vague kind of relationship with the University. The work this group is doing on Sino-Tibetan border society and culture would be an ornament in any academic institution in the world. The credit belongs mainly to Cheng Te-k'un and Li An'chi, who are not only first-rate scholars but are also as alively aware of contemporary events in their own country as any Chinese intellectuals I have met.

One of the most hazardous jobs of the war was flying the Hump over the Himalayas from India to China which for most of the war was the only line of communication into China. The height of the mountains and the uncertain weather resulted in high casualty rates. Few men survived being forced down, but some of those who did met a weird fate. On the Chinese side of the mountains there is a vague and fluctuating line between the Chinese and the Tibetans who have long feared and hated the aggressive and absorptive power of the Chinese. As a protective measure the tribes in the foothills have had an absolute ban on intermarriage with the Chinese; and as a result, since the tribes were small and had little contact with each other, too much inbreeding tended to produce the usual results. To help counteract this a few Americans who survived bailing out over the Hump were made slaves of and used for stud purposes. I have never heard of anyone who survived this experience, but the tales of reliable travelers in the region are too numerous and detailed to be dismissed as fantasy. Of course Americans are not the only beneficiaries of this hospitality, since slave raids into neighboring areas could serve the same purpose, but an Anglo-Saxon strain in Tibet is an intriguing genetic variation.

June 28 / Chungking / Everybody once said that Chungking would revert to the status of a sloppy river town once the capital moved. In fact, the boom is amazing. A new sewer system has been installed, all the streets have been repaved, tunnels have been built through the hills to shorten communications, and a new modern hotel with a chrome decorated bar has been built at the tip of the peninsula. New store fronts are being put up and all is clean and orderly. Even the rats seem to have gone elsewhere. The city fathers are obviously spending the loot they hoarded during the war years.

Teng Hsi-hou may control the Chengtu Valley, but Chungking goes its own way. Business is booming, crops are good, and a highly efficient and ruthless Garrison Command has reduced the thriving wartime intellectual life to stagnation. About the only remaining source of information from the outside world is now the United States Information Service Library which we may now have to close thanks to the infinite and penurious wisdom of the Congress of the United States. Academic circles are in consternation at the prospect. So am I.

Even allowing for the softening effect of time and distance, Chungking makes me nostalgic for the particular kind of good life that it was and for its very real simplicity, hard but clear, because the objectives of life were relatively uncomplicated and the ugliness of the present was still in a sense a shadow on the horizon. Today it is warm and sunny and exciting with the promise of the past.

June 29 / Hankow / Despite some reconstruction, Hankow, the second port of China a thousand miles up the Yangtze, is still in the grip of an advanced stage of dry rot which is all too familiar in China. The waterfront, once a showplace of wharves and commercial and office buildings, remains largely the rubble which our B-29 strikes made of it at the end of the war. The local administrations, both civil and military, are stagnant, corrupt, and inept. Deterioration is the password. The university life has suffered along with the rest. It has the lowest standards in China and the students are restless, undisciplined rowdies who lack direction and objective, and are the victims of a tactless military oppression. As in Chungking, about the only outside contact is the United States Information Service which is trying to branch out southward into Hunan in the Changsha area. There are many reports that middle Yangtze political unrest is increasingly centering in the Changsha area and away from Hankow. The venerable, if heavy and somewhat decrepit, hand of Governor Cheng Ch'ien doubtless has something to do with this.

The only cheerful note in Hankow is a kind of corn which the Governor served us. The full-grown ears are only about an inch and a half long, a dozen or so to the stalk, and are eaten boiled, cob and all. Very delicious. The Governor says it grows in only one part of the province.

July 1 / Nanking / The trip was instructive, even if the

information and impressions were only variations on and confirmations of the expected, namely, despair and decadence and corruption and the absence of any idea of what to do about China. All anyone knows is that disaster is not far off. The other discouraging fact is that away from centers such as Shanghai and Peiping the only Americans are missionaries most of whom have been here for decades. There are two kinds. One group seldom strays from its compounds and has not the faintest notion of what is going on in the vicinity. The other, the politically minded group, is invariably allied with the right wing of the Kuomintang and accepts its dicta without question.

Back here I find myself in a most unfortunate mess. With the cut in United States Information Service appropriations I have to decrease the China operation by half. It is a nasty and unpleasant job. One especially unhappy result is that Chinese employees we let go find it almost impossible to get other work and become our bitterest enemies.

I am sorry I missed the big junket of American newspapermen. From reports, their reactions must have been interesting ones. I understand they gave the Mayor of Shanghai a rough time of it, especially since K. C. Wu knows better than to claim the millennium has already arrived. They did not like what they saw, but they also could not figure out anything else to take its place that they would like any better and that had a chance of coming to pass.

July 15 / The uproar over the Mongol attack in the Peitashan range in northeast Sinkiang which filled at least half of the press for almost two weeks last month has been forgotten, but we do have now as much of a report on what happened as we are likely to have. Our Vice Consul in Tihwa went to see and hear for himself and is back. Peitashan is a desert range of ten-thousand-foot mountains which runs east and west. For centuries the edge of Mongol-

occupied areas has been a fluctuating one, depending on the
relative power and fortunes of the Mongols and the
Chinese. For some years now Peitashan has been a sort of
de facto boundary—whoever drew precise lines in a nomad
region? The Mongols were north and the Chinese south.
On April 15 Kazak troops under someone named Osman
Bator from the Chinese side went into the mountains and
found no Mongols, although there was a garrison and an
airstrip some twenty-five kilometers to the northeast. Decid-
ing to keep the Mongols out of the hills, Osman Bator
posted Chinese patrols on the northern slopes. On May 13
there was a clash and two Mongols were captured. On
June 3 a Mongol detachment appeared under a white flag
and demanded the return of their men. This presented
problems because they were quite dead. Since the Chinese
were unable to comply with the ultimatum, Mongol cavalry
and five airplanes attacked Chinese positions on June 5.
Both sides withdrew after three days of fighting. Chinese
casualties appear to have been two men and thirty horses
killed; Mongol losses are unknown, but a good deal of
Russian equipment was captured. As of now the Mongols
are on the northern slopes where they were in the first
place, and the Chinese are on the south and sitting on the
crest where they were before. There is no evident disposition
on either side so far to make anything more of it, nor is
there any action beyond the normal and generally accepted
trigger happy reaction of a man on horseback to a rustling
in the underbrush.

Who put whom up to what bids fair to remain one of
these trivial mysteries with which history is filled. Certainly
the Mongol side will remain closed to us. An American
who works for the Ministry of Information did tell me the
target of the publicity uproar was American opinion and
that they were sorely disappointed by the "reserved judgment of the Secretary of State and of American editorial
opinion." The shades of the great Khan must be amused—
and a little sad.

The eye of the storm

On July 4, 1947, the State Council passed a resolution declaring that the Chinese Communist Party was in open rebellion against the National Government and therefore called for total national mobilization to suppress it: "We have never attempted to castigate Communism as a theory or an idea . . . but nothing has succeeded in dissuading the Communists from staging a rebellion." And thus ended any pretense at compromise. It was typical that the resolution called for, among other things, "the acceleration of economic reconstruction, the reform of local governments, the mobilization of manpower and resources, the improvement of food and conscription administrations, the maintenance of social order, the mitigation of the people's sufferings, the protection of their basic rights, the practice of thrift, the increases of agricultural and industrial production. . . ." In speeches on July 6, both the Generalissimo and Prime Minister Chang Ch'un agreed that all these measures were essential. In order to do these things it had been necessary to declare national mobilization.[1]

On July 6 Secretary of State Marshall sent a message to the Generalissimo, through Dr. Stuart, which repeated the condemnation in his final statement of the preceding January, adding that the Generalissimo "was forewarned of most of the present serious difficulties and advised regarding preventive measures," and warned that only the Chinese themselves could undertake the kind of reforms which would make any sort of American assistance in any sense relevant. The Generalissimo replied that he understood fully, and that appropriate measures would be taken.[2]

On July 11 President Truman announced that, pursuant to the recommendation of the Secretary of State, he had instructed Lieutenant General Albert C. Wedemeyer to proceed at once to China and Korea on a fact-finding mission, and to make clear "that the United States Government can consider assistance in a program of rehabilitation only if the Chinese Government presents satisfactory

1 There had been other possibilities. In 1946 the Export-Import Bank had earmarked five hundred million dollars, at the request of General Marshall, for Chinese domestic development programs. No projects had been approved, since the Bank doubted the ability of China to service any loans in view of its inaction and the growing corruption. When no acceptable proposals were forthcoming, the Bank cancelled the earmark on June 30, 1947. In the meantime, the Government had made a request for a loan of one billion dollars, and was informed that the United States could not agree to any such thing "in principle," but would certainly give serious consideration to any proposal made in detail as to how it would be used. On May 20, Marshall had informed the Congress that he did not expect to request any further aid for China during the current session. This, of course, did not preclude Export-Import Bank loans if there was reasonable prospect of repayment as required by the Bank's charter. No such proposals were forthcoming.
2 *China White Paper*, pp. 251–52.

evidence of effective measures looking towards Chinese recovery and provided
further that any aid which may be made available shall be subject to the supervision of representatives of the United States Government."[3]

Whether it was so intended or understood at the time, this mission marked the
beginning of a significant change in American policy. The announcement came as
a bombshell to the Embassy, which had had no slightest inkling of any such
development. The Nationalist Government was equally puzzled, but interpreted
it as meaning that immediate and substantial military and economic aid would be
forthcoming. It had reservations, however, about possible conditions. Liberal and
dissident groups were bitter in their opposition.

We never did learn the real reason for the mission. The alleged one of finding
the facts was nonsense; they were already on record in scrupulous detail. What
made it strange was that at no time during his entire sojourn in China had there
been any criticism of Marshall or of what he was trying to do. The only exceptions were the editorial page of the *New York Times* – in marked contrast to its
news columns[4] – and *Time-Life*, which questioned the possibility of success and
suggested that in the end the United States would have to throw its full support to
the Kuomintang.[5] No adverse statement had been inserted in the Congressional
Record. Coverage, in fact, had been minimal.

Even after Marshall returned to Washington there was no great outcry for a
change. Public comment generally deplored the breakdown of negotiations, was a
little appalled by the spreading of hostilities, but at the same time did not see that
there was really very much the United States could usefully do. Certainly there
was no disposition for any particular involvement. Still, something had obviously
happened to cause the Mission.

In the United States the Communist coup d'état in Czechoslovakia in February
1948 was viewed as an ominous and sobering event.[6] The Greek-Turkish Aid Bill
had been fiercely debated and finally passed after President Truman and Senator
Vandenberg, senior Republican member of the Senate Foreign Relations Committee and long a leader of the isolationist faction, reached an agreement on
bipartisanship in foreign policy and the necessity for opposing Communist aggression. The Marshall Plan for Europe was in the offing. Vandenberg, in agreeing to
support the Administration, was reported to have said that the President would
have to scare hell out of the people. The latter might have had second thoughts
had he had any idea how successful he would be in this respect and how much he
would be contributing to the emergence of McCarthyism. None of this, however,
as yet necessarily included China – except for one factor somewhat beneath the
surface.

As early as 1940, T. V. Soong had organized in Washington the nucleus of what

3 *Ibid.*, pp. 255–56.
4 *New York Times*, January 8, 1947, p. 22, col. 2; January 13, 1947, p. 20, col. 1.
5 *Life*, January 22, 1947, p. 22.
6 See Eric F. Goldman, *The Crucial Decade* (New York: Knopf, 1956), pp. 76–81.

would later become known as the China Lobby. Initially its objective was more American aid against Japan which, after all, was the common enemy; hence Chinese activities could assume an air of legitimacy. But the organization and the contacts were still intact after the war. The appeal of the Kuomintang could be widespread. Church groups were firmly committed to it. Business could eventually be persuaded that Communism had not been and could not be sympathetic to free enterprise. As the Cold War deepened, others could be frightened by the threat of an international Communist conspiracy whose aggressive intentions had to be stopped as the only way of preventing a third world war. As it finally emerged, the China Lobby was an amorphous coalition of individuals, groups, and interests whose only common tie was dedication to support of the Kuomintang. The Lobby quite obviously had enormous sums of money at its disposal, although there has never been any legally provable evidence as to where it came from.[7] There is every reason to assume that it intensified its efforts as soon as Marshall returned, and that it had been quietly active while he was still in China.

Since Marshall seldom told anyone what he was thinking, we shall probably never know whether, despite his July 6 message to the Generalissimo, he had decided a more positive American attitude was now indicated, or whether he thought a new appraisal by Wedemeyer, who had made no secret of his sympathies with the Kuomintang, might lessen some of the pressures for drastic action. If the latter was the case, Wedemeyer's own reactions while he was in China were at least partial justification for this view.

Wedemeyer spent one month in China. He visited almost every part of it open to him; he talked with an astonishing range of people. His staff was without exception able and knowledgeable about China. He was openly aghast at what he found out.

On August 22, he addressed a joint meeting of the State Council and the Ministers of Government at the invitation of the Generalissimo, who urged him to be frank and candid. He was. He criticized the military effort and the corruption and inefficiency in it; in substance, the Government could not defeat the Communists by force—only political and economic reform which had never been implemented could do that. Those present, beginning with the Generalissimo, were deeply offended by his remarks, although as he protested later they had been made "courteously."[8] No one who has ever known Wedemeyer personally could doubt that he would invariably be tactful, regardless of what he said.

Two days later, as he left China, Wedemeyer made a public statement which summarized his views and concluded: "To regain and maintain the confidence of the people, the Central Government will have to effect immediately drastic, far-reaching political and economic reforms. Promises will no longer suffice. Performance is absolutely necessary. It should be accepted that military force in itself will

---

7 Cf. Ross Y. Koen, *The China Lobby in American Politics*, referred to on p. 100, note 3.
8 *China White Paper*, p. 259.

not eliminate Communism."[9] The reaction was unfavorable, except among the liberal opposition, possibly because the possibility of large, immediate aid seemed diminished. The Ambassador concluded that the remarks had been "a rude shock to the Chinese Government . . . but most politically conscious non-partisan and liberal Chinese undoubtedly largely endorse all that the Mission has said."[10] Subsequently, Wedemeyer expressed to the Ambassador his regrets that he had said what he did; in retrospect, he thought he had harmed more than helped the situation.[11] Certainly he had at least slowed down efforts to get more help quickly from Washington.

There was more confusion ahead. When Wedemeyer presented his report to the President it was discovered that, although his analysis of the situation contained nothing which had not already been reported to Washington, he had made a recommendation for immediate action to place Manchuria under a guardianship of five powers including the Soviet Union, or a United Nations Trusteeship. He had made a similar recommendation in 1945. The President believed that any such recommendation, if made public, would be unacceptable to China as an infringement of its sovereignty and as indicating a belief that the Government was incapable of ruling its own territory. Furthermore, it was believed that the United Nations, with all its other problems, was not yet in a position to implement any such proposal. The Generalissimo was confidentially informed of this recommendation and, hence, of the reasons why the report could not be made public. He made no comment. The fact was that the program which the State Department did propose and which Congress later approved included all his recommendations except the Manchurian one. But the suppression of the report had two other consequences. It reinforced the suspicions of many that something devious was going on inside the Department; the suspicions would remain long after the Wedemeyer Report had been forgotten. In China it was used to strengthen the reactionary factions within the Kuomintang and to weaken the reform efforts of the liberal elements, as became apparent at the next session of the Central Executive Committee of the Kuomintang.

9 *Ibid.*, p. 258.
10 *Ibid.*, p. 258.
11 Wedemeyer would in a fairly short time find it possible to forget what he had seen and become a staunch supporter again of China Lobby views. One of the perplexing and discouraging aspects of the period from the departure of Marshall to the final collapse of the Nationalists on the mainland was that all visitors to China left appalled by what they had seen and heard and in despair over the future of the Kuomintang. With but few exceptions, they all sooner or later managed to forget what they had seen and act as though it had never happened. The expert blandishments of the China Lobby somehow managed to persuade them that what was happening was unnatural and easily reversible if only the United States would stop vacillating and agree to all Chinese requests without questions or conditions. Certainly no other foreign pressure group anywhere has ever had nearly the control over American policy that the China Lobby has exerted. Besides Ross Koen's *The China Lobby in American Politics*, to which reference has previously been made, there has never been any good explanation of this phenomenon.

July 24 / Nanking / The Wedemeyer Mission arrived with
all appropriate honors and every top Chinese who could
make it was present. He could not have been more cordial
or more noncommittal. The Chinese divided rather evenly
between those who are still puzzled as to what this is all
about, and those who remember that he was the one elected
to soothe the raw sores General Stilwell left behind him
during the war and take this return as the answer to all
their problems. The attitude of this latter group somehow
managed to create the distinct and visible impression that
each one had arrived at the airport carrying a gunnysack
into which to put his share of the gold bars with which
Wedemeyer's plane was unquestionably loaded. Now they
are puzzled too because he did not have any with him.

The plan is for a few days of briefing in the Embassy, a
quick swing around the country, and then back home with
the word. He has a good and knowledgeable staff with him.

Last night one of the houses inhabited by several young
ladies of the Embassy was dark. Either the generator was
staging one of its periodic strikes or else the gloom was
deemed more suitable for the intensive courting which was
going on in the downstairs living rooms. Out of the
steaming night a tall slender figure appeared at the front
door. A young Air Force captain hastily welcomed him:

"My name is Captain Reece. What is yours?"

"Wedemeyer."

Probably for the first time in his life no sound came from
Fly Boy's open mouth.

July 26 / Wedemeyer listens well, asks the right questions.
He is more than a little shocked, almost unbelieving, to find
for himself that what he had heard about conditions is if
anything understatement. And he is visibly annoyed by
Chinese pressure tactics, especially the justly famous charm
act of Madame Chiang. He may well be the only living
human being on whom it does not work. She tried it on him
once before during the war and it did not work then either.

At the briefing session this morning, Ray Ludden, head
of the political section, was sounding off with couplets of
doom. Wedemeyer in asking a question called him Jack.
A horrified young aide quickly whispered something to him.
Wedemeyer smiled and said, "Since three of the four State
Department officers with the Dixie Mission at Yenan during
the war were named John, I thought I was entitled to have
the fourth one wild to make it four of a kind." Remembering
his hostile attitude to the four at that time, the laughter
was a little forced; and it was ironic later to see him pacing
the lawn with his arm around Lud's disapproving shoulders.

July 29 / With all the excitement, the idea is only now
beginning to soak into Chinese consciousness that Wedemeyer is here for exactly what he said he was coming for—
to find out for himself what is going on. The flap is quite
unnecessary. There is nothing sensational about the mission
and is not likely to be.

On top of everything else China has been having one of
its worst heat spells in fifty years. Summer in Nanking is
really quite frightening at times. The heat and humidity for
four months are appalling. What makes them unbearable
is that there is never a breath of air stirring. It is hard on
tempers, foreign tempers anyway. I do not mind the heat,
but I do mind the first case of prickly heat I can remember.
I look as though I had an old social disease. The only good
thing about the steam blanket over the city is that it puts
the town to sleep and the usual official social round drops
to nothing.

I have, however, enjoyed sitting around gossiping with
Bill Bullitt, the first American Ambassador to the Soviet
Union, whom I had known slightly before. He is doing an
article for *Life*. Whatever else he may be, he is a good con-
versationalist, which is rare in the wilderness that Nanking
has become. Nobody stays here unless he has to. Bullitt said
he thought the place would be intolerable unless one had
some attractive sin lined up. Unfortunately the choice of sin

is as limited as everything else. Like most others he is
appalled by what he has seen and heard. He keeps muttering, "Someone has not been telling the truth."

Sunday we had a visit from a group of American pub-
lishers and I squired them around. They were somewhat
bushed, but managed to get through the day. I took them
to have tea with Madame Chiang. The Generalissimo came
in for a few minutes and put his foot in his mouth with
biting criticism of the American press. Madame was most
embarrassed and tried to tone it down in translation. I was
amused at Ben Welles of the *New York Times,* who went
with us and was very much that side of his father (Sumner
Welles) which is not so well known as his usually rather
austere exterior. He sat on one side of her and I on the
other. She was wearing a lovely pale blue Chinese style
dress. In front of her an electric fan on the floor slowly
billowed her skirt up and down. Ben was so fascinated he
never heard a word the Generalissimo said and afterwards
sighed, "That is the best looking pair of legs I have seen in
a long, long time." I had to agree.

August 9 / Midmorning I went over to my house which is
in the same compound as the office to see why all our
Chinese gardeners were standing around it. In one of the
bedrooms I found Wang, my number one servant. He had
hanged himself on the transom. Suicide is common and
very honorable in China. It is the final protest against
injustice or a way of dramatizing your troubles to force a
solution. Wang had been having trouble with his son who
for some time now has been showing an alarming and
disturbing preference for the sing-song girls instead of going
to school where he belongs. This is one way of straightening
him out.

One corollary to the tradition is that if you hang yourself
in someone else's house he becomes responsible for all subsequent financial liabilities. The police would not allow the
body to be removed, nor would the relatives accept it until
I had paid all funeral expenses in advance. Still to be

negotiated is the extent of any future financial responsibility. Tradition or not, it has been an upsetting tragedy,
to put it mildly. Wang was a nice man, albeit a moody one.
I hope the son decides to join some relatives upriver.

Trouble comes in bunches. In the last two days some
American soldiers in Nanking drowned two Chinese, apparently the outcome of some horseplay; in Shanghai
another shot one; in Tientsin a Marine did the same thing.
And in Sinkiang a Chinese plane crashed killing all aboard,
including Barbara Stephens, a young reporter I had known
in Chungking. She was a lovely girl. The Chinese are not
even trying to get to the wreckage, saying that no one of
importance was aboard; but there is reason to think there
were some whom they are just as glad to be rid of on
account of political activities they considered undesirable.
A rather cryptic message from Barbara just before she got
on the plane in Tihwa suggested as much and that she was
following some lead for a newspaper story. Now we will
never really know.

August 18 / Life is a bit disjointed these days with the
announcement that Walt Butterworth, who had been called
home on consultation, will stay in Washington as Director
of the Far Eastern Bureau. He is an excellent choice for
the job, but will be sorely missed here because he was the
one who really made this office function. The Wedemeyer
Mission is on its last legs—the effect of the heat on Wedemeyer, incidentally, having done the Kuomintang no good.
He is feeling none too happy about what he has seen in this
unhappy country. When we get the Mission off we start
getting ready for visiting Congressional groups, though we
still do not know which ones will come to the Far East. It
sounds as though the entire Congress expects to spend the
late summer abroad.

Luckily the rest of life is quiet. No one has the energy for
much more than an occasional picnic on the mountain
where it is a little cooler. The other evening a group of us
dilly-dallied too long in the breeze and were locked out of

the city for the night, since the gates close at nine-thirty and are so massive the guards inside can hear no amount of noise outside. The cobblestones on the road make a hard bed.

I have discovered that one whole bed of something unknown in my garden is red peppers, which are now ripe and crimson. For some foolish reason I am very pleased with myself about it.

August 25 / Wedemeyer left yesterday morning in a cloud of suspicion and harsh words. It has been extraordinary to watch the change in his attitudes and ideas during his month here. We still know nothing of the genesis of the Mission or its purpose beyond the avowed one, if indeed there was another. His arrival was most enthusiastically heralded by many Chinese, and Wedemeyer himself reached Nanking filled with optimism. Both reactions changed quickly. Chinese opinion was soon convinced this was no free lunch which had descended upon them and that if any aid was to be forthcoming it would be delayed and would have a series of unpalatable conditions attached to it. The more places Wedemeyer visited, the more people he saw, the more despairing he became about this Government and about the possibilities of giving aid which could be effectively used and avoid crippling dissipation. If he had any definitive and positive conclusions when he left, he kept them to himself.

His last two or three conversations with the Generalissimo were angry ones in which neither man minced any words and in which no common understanding was reached. The Generalissimo was particularly infuriated by an uncommonly blunt speech Wedemeyer made to the State Council in which he excoriated them for practically every public— and even private—vice ever known. In the end, they parted on not exactly cordial terms. The Generalissimo will of course quiet down in time, realizing that anger right now is a luxury he can ill afford; but the harsh words are bound to have some effect on the attitudes of the two men.

The important question is where do we go from here, and I have seen no signs the Mission is any closer to an answer than we are. Wedemeyer has the advantage over us in knowing the thinking and the practical possibilities at home. The Chinese are increasingly aware of this factor and disturbed by it since they realize that the British economic crisis will necessarily take priority, even if China disagrees and disapproves. Basically we are right back where we started. This is hardly calculated to improve the Chinese peace of mind, and they are being pettish about it with those of us who have to stay behind to collect the dead fish tossed in our direction.

August 27 / This has been a good day. It is the birthday of Confucius and therefore a holiday. For weeks now my toilet has not been working properly and I, foolishly thinking I had better things to do, left it to the professionals, to no avail. But the spirit finally moved and the morning was pleasant while I tinkered on it. Now it works. It is a sorry reflection on our civilization when you feel reassured in finding out you can do such elementary things as fix a toilet.

Then I spent the afternoon floating around lazily on Lotus Lake. There and in the ponds scattered around the city the lotus is in full bloom, quite magnificent stuff. Most of the blooms are the size of a man's head and gorgeous in color, though perhaps a little too imposing to inspire any very personal feeling. The heat and humidity make most vegetation oversize. My cosmos is eight feet tall and flowerless; the zinnias are almost as tall and very coarse. Lettuce died off in mid-July. Maybe the climate is good only for rice. For that it does very well indeed.

On the rim of the abyss

The Fourth Plenary Session of the Kuomintang Central Executive Committee met on September 9, allegedly to consolidate the San Min Chu I Youth Corps with the Kuomintang for the purpose of bringing younger blood into the Party.

The atmosphere was bitter, and there was general speculation about other objectives in mind. The Generalissimo set the tone in his opening speech in which he stated that for twenty years he had attempted to carry out the principles of Dr. Sun Yat-sen and now had to admit failure, but would keep on trying, since he had no responsibility for the failure. He scathingly denounced the shortcomings of the Party, and said the Communists had showed themselves to be abler and more dedicated to the welfare of China. Asserting that China would never again rely on the United States, he implied that closer ties with the Soviet Union should be established. At the time the Embassy interpreted this last item as blackmail; before the year was out it would develop that there was substance to it.

When an elaborate program of reform was proposed during the session, it was generally expected that it would pass until the Generalissimo demanded that it be dropped and that in its place the Party carry out the promises which had been made during the past two years. The final communiqué of September 13 contained nothing specific, but it was obvious that the main result of the meeting was further to strengthen the control of the cc clique through its domination of the Youth Corps, and that disappointment over the outcome of the Wedemeyer Mission had played an important role.[1]

The Ambassador in reporting the foregoing to Washington added his discouraged interpretation that what it all really meant was that the Kuomintang, as it had in the war against Japan, had come to rely entirely upon the United States to bail it out of its difficulties. Increased Communist military activities in north China and Manchuria at the same time only added to the gloom, as did reports from Shanghai that the cc clique was making important headway in ensuring that its candidates for the National Assembly would sweep the elections to be held before the end of the year.[2] During the next month Dr. Stuart found no reason to change his pessimistic appraisal.

The Generalissimo himself revealed much of his attitude when on October 11 members of the Military Affairs Committee of the US House of Representatives called on him. In answer to their questions, he said he believed the Chinese Communists were completely communist, totally dependent upon and supported by the Soviet Union. In repeating his request for American aid, he said the "predicament in Manchuria was an American responsibility." Finally, if the Communists did win, it would not be because of the Communists or the Soviet Union, but because the United States had failed to honor its commitments.[3] If this was perhaps the first time this refrain was played, it would not be the last – in China and elsewhere.

Coincidentally, there were developments with the minor parties. Carsun Chang's Social Democrats split into two groups and for all practical purposes faded away. The Youth Party melted into the Kuomintang. And, after a campaign of rumors that the Democratic League was taking orders from the Communists, it was formally outlawed on October 28. Following negotiations, the League on Novem-

1 *China White Paper*, p. 262, and annex 143.
2 *Ibid.*, annex 144 and 145.
3 *Ibid.*, p. 264.

ber 6 announced its own dissolution; a few of its individual members joined the Kuomintang, most went into political oblivion, and a substantial number crossed over to the Communists. Apart from the Communists, only the Kuomintang remained as an organized political force. On the surface it may have looked like political unity, but the Kuomintang itself was a collection of warring cliques which fought each other as savagely as they fought outside groups, and only the manipulative skill of the Generalissimo made any fiction of harmony at all possible.

The threat which the Generalissimo had made in September about the Soviet Union became the possibility of Russian mediation in December. General Chang Chih-chung, who had played an important role during the Marshall negotiations, told Dr. Stuart on December 20 that he had discussed the matter with the Generalissimo, having first approached the Soviet Embassy in Nanking about the chances of their help in persuading the Communists to resume negotiations on the basis of the PCC agreements. The Generalissimo neither encouraged nor discouraged General Chang from trying. The Russians agreed to try mediation, but when eventually the Communists refused to stop hostilities as a condition for negotiations[4] nothing came of the attempt.

Nor was there much reason why the Communists now should compromise. By early March, the Government controlled no more than one per cent of Manchuria, and perhaps only ten to fifteen per cent of China proper north of the Yellow River. Between the Yellow River and the Yangtze the entire countryside was infiltrated, and Government forces were hard pressed and on the defensive in all sectors. The speculation in Nanking was that T. V. Soong had been sent to Canton as Governor of the province of Kwangtung in the far south to prepare a stronghold to which the Government could retreat from Nanking. The wild predictions and guesses henceforth centered largely on the possibility of salvaging something in the southern half of the country. Anything more was not even included in fantasy, and even this much was assumed to depend solely on massive American aid.

In the meantime, preparations for the elections continued. They were actually held late in 1947. The grassroots work of the CC clique paid off, and they won practically all contests for the National Assembly and the Executive Yuan, to the very considerable embarrassment of the Government, which had publicly committed itself to a certain proportional representation for non-Kuomintang candidates. To extricate itself the Government had to persuade certain successful candidates to withdraw on the basis of an ex post facto declaration that only those Kuomintang candidates would be considered elected who had had prior Party approval. This action would backfire against the Generalissimo when the National Assembly at its spring meeting decided to rebel against him. The CC clique might still not have control at the top, but it was even more firmly entrenched at the working levels.

It was symptomatic of the general discontent that during January and February Shanghai and other major cities were shaken by riots and disorders with some loss

4 *Ibid.*, pp. 265–68.

of life and property. No one thought the disturbances forecast any immediate
overthrow; rather they were seen as the signs of things to come. Against this
background, the focus of attention during the winter months shifted from China
to Washington and to the Congress of the United States.

September 1 / Nanking / Again we are getting an assortment of rumors and reports of more trouble in Sinkiang which suggest Nanking is not doing so well in implementing the 1946 agreements with the rebel regime in Ining designed to restore peace in that area. I suppose there was no real reason ever to suppose they would, despite the apparently honest efforts of Governor Chang Chih-chung and his more liberal colleagues. Granted Nanking has more pressing problems than the border regions, a little more intelligent thought to them over the years could have softened some of the contemporary difficulties. Actually the Mongol areas are more dangerous and serious than Sinkiang. It is much more than a problem of Outer Mongolia alone, which for all practical purposes was resolved by the Russians in the twenties and in the independence plebiscite in 1945. There are just as many Mongols in Manchuria and north China as there are in Outer Mongolia.

Although this was probably true for the Nationalists, especially in view of their frustrating preoccupation with Manchuria which Mongolia adjoins, the situation has been reversed for the Communist regime. Doubtless muted friction still exists over Mongolia, but there is no question who now controls Manchuria.

Russian hegemony in Outer Mongolia, whatever its ruthlessness, did break the feudal stranglehold of the corrupt lamas and saved the rest of the population from probable extinction in their own degradation. The Japanese in Manchuria and north China found much the same conditions, but their policies were economically disastrous and resulted in the death of a large percentage of the Mongol herds on which the economy depends. The return of the Kuomintang has done nothing to improve matters, whereas the Communists in their Mongol areas have done better. And since the word tends to get around—even in Mongolia —large numbers of Mongols, particularly the younger ones, are supporting the Communists, not for any ideological reasons, but simply because they see this as their only hope for physical survival. The undisputed material improvement in Outer Mongolia has propaganda values which are not exactly being overlooked. To say the least, the possibilities of a Greater Mongolia are intriguing. The same is true for a Pan Turanian movement in Central Asia, both Chinese and Russian. Our suggestion that these two movements warranted more attention than we are giving them has been treated by Washington with the silent scorn it doubtless so justly deserves, even if there are others around who take the movements quite seriously.

And so the Kuomintang is harvesting another bitter apple for its barrel. It is the ancient story of Chinese contempt for and ineptitude with minorities. It will be interesting to see if the Communists do anything to alter the unenviable record.

September 11 / Last week was spent in Shanghai. This time I decided the odor of the place is not that of corruption, but of plain decay: the rotting of a whole social order. It may be a nebulous way of putting it, but I think that basically Wedemeyer was right when he said that the only cure is a spiritual regeneration from within. And he was honest enough to admit he did not know how you started it, what caused it, or what kept it from starting. Anyway, I saw a lot of people, none of them cheerful, and had a change of food and water which has cured me of the usual Nanking summer complaint.

As an observer, I am now sweating out a regional UNESCO Far Eastern Conference on Fundamental Education, which is not a success. The Chinese are monopolizing it and using it for their own purposes; and the other delegations, including a fascinating man from Burma in a green shirt and with a perennial mophandle cigar in his mouth, are annoyed by it all. I don't think many of the non-Chinese by now are quite sure any more what fundamental education is. I'm not either. I rather naively had assumed it had something to do with the elimination of illiteracy. From the way the Chinese talk, I now suspect it is a new device by which they hope to pry a loan out of the United States.

September 19 / A member of the Central Executive Committee of the Kuomintang let me see a copy of the Generalissimo's speech at the current Fourth Plenary Session. Some of the things he said differ a good deal from ideas usually expressed publicly by this Government, the Generalissimo included. He castigated the Party for the present situation in China in stronger terms than I have ever heard here; and in so doing he largely absolved himself of any blame for current economic troubles. He then asserted the ability of China to solve its own problems without American assistance, and in conclusion stated his recognition of the appeal the Communists have for certain sectors of the population. He certainly does not talk to us that way!

Ostensibly the meeting was called to consolidate the San Min Chu I Youth Corps with the Kuomintang. Actually a strong reform movement developed and came to nothing. The main result was to strengthen the power of the cc clique.

September 28 / *Shanghai* / Big strikes started here yesterday and the city is half paralyzed. Despite the current wild economic fluctuations and the price jumps, the strikes are not economically motivated. Rather they are protests against Kuomintang and secret police regimentation. In a sense this is more serious for the Government, which has so far taken care to see that labor is fed, and labor is now actually better off than any other group except some of the politicians.

It is a curious sensation to be in Shanghai at this time and read *Man's Fate* by André Malraux, which might almost come out of this morning's newspapers. What hits me most is that, although the book deals with the massacre of the Communists in Shanghai in 1927 by the Generalissimo, only the major character is Chinese. All the rest are foreigners and real persons of the twenties. I cannot help but wonder just how much of the Communist failure in Shanghai at that time—probably the most obscure time and place in twentieth-century China—was attributable to foreign, and this includes Russian, leadership and meddling. The terrorist, the Chinese Ch'en, is the one who rebels against Comintern dictates. It is worth remembering that present Communist leaders were almost all survivors of the Shanghai debacle.

The foreign bungling of that time reminds me of a story Nat Peffer once told me of a telegram sent to Borodin, who was still head of the Soviet civilian mission to the Kuomintang, and signed by Stalin or Trotsky, telling him to put his trust in Dr. Sun Fo—and what a footling role Sun now plays. His only political asset is his name. There is another story that when Borodin and Madame Sun Yat-sen were leaving for the Soviet Union in 1927 the train stopped for an hour in Sian. Borodin was stretching his legs on the platform when a huge barefoot peasant from north China came up to him and said, "If you had made your deal with me, you would not be on this train." And then he walked away. It was Feng Yu-hsiang, the famous and notorious "Christian General" who would later baptize his troops with a firehose. Feng once told me the story was true.

The Generalissimo and his victories must confuse a lot of people. You must announce victories. Apparently the only thing which matters is what something seems to be. Actually, both sides do it. There seems to be nothing inconsistent in announcing the capture of a place once and then doing it all over again in a week. Last spring the Government announced the war would be over in three months. Yesterday the Chief of Staff said Chefoo in Shantung would be taken today, which would mean the end of the war. It has not been taken. The Communists announce the capture of places which never existed and the destruction of divisions no one ever heard of, although Communist communiqués are much more reliable than those of the Government. Of course it is quite possible that since they are winning they can better afford the luxury of truth. If you added up the total of announced casualties it would run into the millions since the end of the war.

General Lucas had previously commanded the unfortunate American landings at Anzio, Italy, during the war.

September 30 / Nanking / Yesterday I went up the Yangtze with the Ambassador to Wuhu to investigate stories of thousands of refugees streaming in ahead of the fantastic sweep of General Liu Po-ch'eng southward from the Yellow River, and to check on alleged atrocities. There were no refugees and there had been none; and the missionaries who had come from the Communist areas north of the Yangtze said there had been no atrocities. The Communists had behaved well.

So, instead of the misery which is synonymous with refugees, we ran into a phalanx of missionaries who were delighted to have visitors and made us inspect schools and churches, have our pictures taken with hordes of odorous and reluctant youngsters, go to receptions, and consume appalling quantities of fruit juice and cookies. It is a tough, isolated, and lonely life they lead. The prize one was an Episcopalian bishop, a lively old gent with a charming wife. He seemed to get a certain pleasure out of blowing cigarette smoke in the faces of the more orthodox and ducking into the kitchen for a nip before dinner.

The trip in a launch on the river was a lot of fun. Seeing the Yangtze this way you get a new dimension of its vastness and a brooding sense it must know how its muddy bulk dominates the entire region. Periodically thousands upon thousands of ducks would fly in low from the north, pause for a while on the banks, and move on south.

October 1 / This has been a rough day because of the story that we have agreed to train Nationalist divisions. The story has been even more sensational because it is untrue. General Lucas, who commands our military advisory group, was shooting off his mouth. He has been drawing up such plans, but without Washington's or the Embassy's knowledge or approval, and he is now on a very hot griddle at an unfortunate moment. Lucas, who is personally a sweet, incompetent old darling, has been a thorn for some time now due to his fondness for extemporaneous public conversation on unauthorized topics.

October 5 / The student body in China plays such an important—and noisy—role in political life that I have been prowling around it here to see what makes it tick. Certainly it is a phenomenon vastly different from anything to which we, as Americans, are accustomed. In any country, of course, which has a low literacy rate the educated man and especially the intellectual has a tremendous advantage and an almost automatic role to play in society. The scholar in China, however, has had traditionally an even more important role. He has always been at the top of the social pile because he has always been the bureaucrat and government administrator. The nature of the language has made this almost inevitable. Although there are many very different spoken dialects there is only one written language—of such formidable difficulty that only those with the highest education have had the skill in communicating which is essential in holding an empire together. One can assume that the scholar has had a vested interest in resisting any simplification of language which would put it within reach of a larger population. In such a situation the military has had no chance for the position and influence it has elsewhere, and indeed it has normally been at the bottom of the social structure.

The University of Nanking is a classic example of the dilemma in which the Chinese intellectual finds himself today, to say nothing of the dilemma for anyone who would command his allegiance. By and large the Nanking student group still comes from the scholarly and the bureaucratic class despite the changes of the last century. Only a few come from humble origins or from the small emerging middle class. They instinctively think of themselves as the natural heirs of power. Generally they have liberal views, but liberalism to them means unrelenting opposition to the National Government and everything it does.

This opposition arises from Government failure to provide adequate financial support for education, while being only too willing to interfere in what the students and teachers consider to be purely academic matters. Both groups are bitter about the efforts to regiment them politically along Kuomintang lines. They supported the Kuomintang in its early revolutionary days when they had an important voice in its activities; now they are just told what to do and the penalties for failure to conform are often dreadful. They resent the failure, as they see it, to uphold the dignity and prestige of China. Thus, in the tradition of their fathers' student uprisings of a generation ago in support of the Kuomintang, they are as much nationalists as anything else.

The small and very active Communist group skilfully leads most political activities; and the majority who have had neither experience with nor much knowledge of the Communists and their ideology admire their success in opposing the Government, and identify with them on these grounds. Most deny any desire for a Communist government. Actually the students seem convinced the Communists will be unable to take over, but that they can and will destroy the Kuomintang which will then permit the intellectuals to assume control. Anything which advances this aim is good; anything which hinders it is bad.

Although genuinely devoted to the United States in the abstract while being critical of specific contemporary American actions, they deeply distrust Russian political motives while uncritically accepting specific actions and accomplishments. They have little understanding of or interest in democracy or civil rights as we know them. Their goal is power for themselves, not the broadening of the base of power; and they assume that the future must be through state planning and some form of socialism, not capitalism or free enterprise—a view they share, incidentally, with the Kuomintang. In brief, the Government has lost the allegiance of the scholar class without which no government has long survived, and that allegiance is rapidly being thrown to the Communists. The students assume the Communists will use their allegiance in traditional ways and, in justification of the view, point out that Communist leadership for the most part is neither proletarian nor peasant in origin,

In retrospect it is clear that the Chinese intellectual was not the only one who harbored this illusion. The lessons of Chinese history, repeated over and over again, seemed to say that coalition was feasible because in it the intellectual would hold the balance. The failure was in not understanding that there were powerful groups in China which did not consider themselves bound by these lessons.

and that even the few like General Chu Teh, the Commander in Chief, who did begin life as peasants somehow managed to get an education early. Whatever validity these assumptions may turn out to have, the Kuomintang has lost support among a group it can ill afford to disillusion.

October 24 / Changchun, Manchuria / Mukden had little new to offer. It is more crowded than before, shabbier, more depressed, more hopelessly resigned to the inevitable prolonged siege and final defeat. The change is quantitative, not qualitative. The Ramgahr Divisions trained during the war by General Stilwell are symptomatic of what has happened. Where once they were the equal of any troops in the world, they now look and act much like any other Nationalist soldiers. Morale and self-respect are gone through the corrosion of poor leadership, indifferent treatment, and the gradual infiltration of their cadres with run-of-the-mill soldiers.

We flew to Changchun from Mukden over the railroad. It was a lovely day and the sunlight was filled with autumn haze. It was also filled with something else that was not so lovely. The sixth Communist offensive is now in progress. Flying high to avoid anti-aircraft fire, we could see that the entire railroad from horizon to horizon was on fire and the roadbed was visibly being obliterated. This is not the first time it has been torn up; but it is unlikely it will be rebuilt again until the civil war is over, even if by some fluke the Government should recapture the land through which it runs.

Changchun is an extraordinary sight. The Japanese laid it out on an endless plain as the capital of their puppet regime of Manchukuo, with great spaces between buildings and some of the widest streets I have ever seen. The Government buildings must be architecturally unique. I don't know how to describe them except as giant tile beehives in somber colors. The rest of the city is made up of log shacks which might be any Russian village. The farther north you go from Mukden the stronger becomes the Russian legacy of the nineteenth century.

The population does not begin to fill up the place now and the few people who wander the streets are overshadowed by its physical facts. In a way this is true of all Manchuria I have seen. The vastness and beauty of the land dominate man, as though daring him to assert himself at his own peril. It must be the same quality our own middle west and plains states had a century ago.

October 27 / Peiping / I had a talk last night with Jack Belden, an American newspaperman who is just back from southern Hopei, of which Peiping is the capital. He says the Communist plan is to have Generals Liu Po-ch'eng and Chen Yi consolidate their armies this winter in the Tapieh-shan, a rugged hilly area in central China north of the Yangtze, and they are pouring in hundreds of political workers there and to the south. Then next spring they will strike at the Nanking-Shanghai area. He is concerned by a growing mental rigidity of Communist leaders in Hopei, the increasing use of terror against any form of opposition, and the extermination of large sections of the population. Oddly enough, propaganda in Hopei has largely dropped its anti-American line and is concentrating on abuse of the Generalissimo. The combined result is to create in the peasants a terror and furtiveness he has never before seen in Communist areas—and he has seen most of them.

I have heard other reports of similar changes in Communist areas in Shantung. Since Hopei and Shantung are two of the regions in which they have been established the longest, this may well suggest something of the future.

October 29 / Nanking / Now we have a storm over the outlawing of the Democratic League by the Government on charges it is too close to the Communists. If the League dissolves voluntarily—there is little else for it to do—and its members behave themselves they will be unmolested. Although this move seems a little pointless, the League seldom left much doubt as to where its major sympathies lie. This is the end of any third party or middle-of-the-road activity. Some members will join the Government, some the Communists, and the rest will simply fade away.

November 7 / Yesterday the Democratic League announced its formal dissolution. And today we will all assist in commemorating the Russian Revolution at the International Club with the foul liquor which has become customary in Nanking on all national holidays.

December 3 / The Generalissimo returned from an extensive trip to Peiping and Dr. Stuart saw him last night. He told me he thought the Generalissimo was discouraged for the first time and more tired than he had ever seen him.

December 5 / Shen, the Generalissimo's private secretary, has told me that despite press denials a shot was taken at the Generalissimo in Peiping and it was no accident. Shen adds it was a plot by the Tientsin garrison commander who was about to be arrested for corruption, and that it had come within inches of succeeding. The Generalissimo was badly shaken, not so much by the danger involved as by what it represented in terms of revolt against the Government.

December 19 / During a conversation this morning about Dairen, George Yeh, Vice Minister of Foreign Affairs, said the Soviets in recent weeks have been showing an increasing interest in playing some sort of mediatory role in China, although there have been no specific proposals. The approaches have been made to a group of high Chinese officers, mostly in Intelligence, who have had some training in the Soviet Union and speak Russian. It is not the dominant clique in the Army, but it does have influence because it includes the Generalissimo's son, Chiang Ching-kuo. The argument has been that a military solution is impossible, but that a political one is feasible and the Russians might be helpful. Although George says the effort is making some headway, I cannot help but wonder how much of the story is for our benefit.

December 22 / Dr. Stuart has had a letter from Wedemeyer crying *mea culpa* about his speech to the State Council. He complains about the slowness with which a China aid program is moving through the Congress and feels his statement has contributed to that. On balance he thinks it hurt China more than it has helped and wishes he had not made it.

Once again there have been curious suggestions about Soviet participation in China. I paid little attention to the rumors. I was wrong. I now find out that Premier Chang

Chih-chung has talked with Dr. Stuart about it. He said he and Chiang Ching-kuo had broached the subject to the Generalissimo and had suggested asking the Soviet Embassy to cooperate in seeking Communist agreement for a resumption of the peace talks. The Generalissimo was skeptical, but finally in subdued fashion authorized Chang to make a cautious approach. He said he could not do it himself since he has reason to believe the Communists might welcome such a move. He gave Chang no indication of what terms he might consider. Chang has made the approach and seems mildly encouraged.

January 16, 1948 / The mobs are running wild in Shanghai today. We have had our own fracas here, which ended with the students fighting each other. But it has been more serious in Canton, where the British Consulate and many foreign business firms have been sacked. And Communist bands are wandering about the countryside as they please. They have even raided within ten or fifteen miles of Nanking.

February 1 / Back from a brief trip to Tsingtao. It was the old pre-war German concession and a very profitable one because it could tap most of the wealthy province of Shantung. It is a strange sight for China. It was entirely built by the Germans and all the architecture is European. Now it is the major American naval base in China, and the language is English. The harbor is lovely, enormous, and surrounded by hills. Unfortunately it was cold, and the bay, which is fed by fresh streams, was frozen over, but the sun was shining and the red roof tiles glittered against a blue sky reflection. Down on the waterfront next to a large Coca Cola ad there is a larger billboard which reads "Welcome to the Red Tower Cathouse." The Navy, incidentally, has a commissary which is an exact duplicate of Piggly Wiggly. Fun for a change.

Around the hillcrest perimeter of the city, Communist guerrilla bands raid periodically. Doubtless it is more for nuisance value than anything else, since they are not yet in a position to launch a serious attack on a major American installation.

February 3 / The last ten days have been an endless series of riots in Canton and Shanghai, both bad spots for such things. There has been a lot of burning in Canton, and in Shanghai the Mayor, a very good and gutty guy, was badly beaten up while the taxi dancers tore shops and restaurants to pieces. No one incident has much meaning in itself, but the piling up does. Even the cheeriest and blindest souls now find an uneasy soughing in the wind. Not the least of the contributory factors is the vacillation and ineptitude of the Government at a time when it should be decisive and strong if it would avoid even worse trouble.

For days now reports have been pouring in from a variety of Chinese and foreign sources which seem to add up to an important change in the psychological outlook of the Government. It is impossible to put your finger on any one thing or remark which says so; rather, it is a subjective reaction to a whole picture. The change seems obviously based on the following: military developments of the past few weeks have put the Communists in a position where they have practical control over all China north of the Yangtze except for a few urban enclaves and some lines of communication; parallel economic deterioration continues despite all remedial action; paralysis within the Government prevents formulation of effective remedies, to say nothing of implementation; and, despite the presence of a number of good and able men who know what needs to be done, there is a growing conviction that any amount of American aid will be useless in turning the tide.

To all this must be added a probably insoluble conflict in Chinese thinking. Thoughtful Chinese know that if American aid is to have any effect it must be accompanied by an amount and scope of American supervision and control of Nationalist activities such as have never been attempted or even suggested, and which at this stage would amount to a virtual protectorate. To counter this intellectual knowledge, natural Chinese pride and sensibilities are so strong emotionally that they would inevitably prevent real cooperation in any such effort, and they know it.

The general impression is that high Chinese officials, the Generalissimo excepted, no longer have any faith in the possibility of winning against the Communists. The best they hope for is that events will precipitate another world war which will bail them out as the last one ended their ensnarement with Japan. Failing this, and if they cannot win on their own terms, particularly the right wing groups, they would rather go down to defeat—a primitive blind and collective sense of self-immolation, perhaps even of knowing they are doomed by any terms other than complete victory.

The Aid Program and reform

The China Aid Program of 1948 of itself turned out to be rather meaningless. It fed several millions of people who otherwise would have been hungrier than they were, and it kept a variety of industries in operation longer than would have been the case without it. In terms of its stated objectives, however, the contribution was nothing – this through no fault of the program, which was well thought out and efficiently managed. Its real significance, in retrospect, was as an indication of changing American attitudes in foreign affairs, which were gradually being reflected in new and emerging policies around the world.

As far as China was concerned, it must be remembered that even when all hope of negotiation had vanished the National Government still remained the legal government and was so recognized by all other countries, including the Soviet Union. In this situation, the United States might maintain the usual correct diplomatic relations, and be essentially detached from internal Chinese affairs, thus allowing them to be settled by the Chinese themselves. Despite later charges to the contrary, this was basically the course followed by the Soviet Union. Or the United States could give aid in varying forms and degrees to a government it recognized, with the objective of helping it in the face of internal opposition. This was the problem with which General Marshall, as Secretary of State, had to struggle.

His instinct was to follow the former course and to leave the solution of Chinese problems to the Chinese themselves, but there were strong pressures advocating a more active role. Marshall was convinced that the Nationalist military plight was in no respect being caused by any shortage of arms and equipment. He had, furthermore, learned from bitter experience that the Generalissimo paid no attention to American military advice, and would not do so in the future. Finally, he had come to the conclusion that the Nationalists could not win militarily without drastic economic and political reform which no one else could bring about for them. At this time, not even the most determined protagonists of the Kuomintang were advocating the use of American combat troops, or even of military advisors on any operational level. The Chinese had already made it abundantly clear that such action would be unacceptable; nor was there any American opinion which favored direct involvement in the civil war. There was, on the other hand, strong pressure for greatly increased economic aid. This is what the Nationalists themselves wanted, in addition to easy access to supplies of munitions, which they already had anyway;[1] the only question in their minds was how to pay for them.

Precisely here there was a frustrating paradox. Early in 1947, Chinese agricultural and industrial production was by no means discreditable. Shipping had been fully restored, although land communications were perennially disrupted by the fighting. Exports were rising. The foreign exchange position was by no means critical, due largely to lend-lease residues, surplus property transfers, large UNRRA supplies, and a substantial Canadian credit, as well as other bits and pieces. China was in a position to finance needed imports. In fact, it was in better shape in this respect than any western European country at the time. In addition, the best estimates were that private holdings of foreign exchange amounted to as much as half a billion dollars, although it could have been embarrassing for the Government to acquire this capital considering who some of the owners were.[2] And yet, in all directions there was increasing evidence of impending disaster.

A principal cause of trouble was the mounting budgetary deficit which was covered by staggering currency issues that no longer had any backing. The inflation became astronomical as prices spiralled up and currency value down. Speculators compounded matters by hoarding commodities that were in short supply. Corruption had become a way of life. The problem was not a lack of foreign help: UNRRA supplies, for example, were clogging the docks in Shanghai because they were arriving faster than the economy could absorb them. The problem was that the Government was doing none of the things it should have done to make effective use of what it had. These were the circumstances which had led the Export-Import Bank to cancel the half billion dollar earmark for China, the Department of State to take a chary view of a Chinese request for a billion and a half dollar loan, the Treasury to recommend denial of a request for a massive loan of silver to replace paper currency,[3] and, finally, Marshall to inform the Congress that during 1947 he would not request further aid for China. He did not see how further aid could be of assistance until China itself had taken certain prior measures, and able and highly placed officials had

1 *China White Paper*: see Marshall's testimony to the US House Committee on Foreign Affairs, pp. 354–57, and annex 173 on availabilities and actual deliveries.
2 *Ibid.*, p. 371.
3 *Ibid.*, p. 367–69.

repeatedly indicated that they were quite aware what these measures were. There was no strong reaction in the Congress against this view.

The Wedemeyer Mission foreshadowed an important change in this respect, especially when Wedemeyer's recommendations were kept secret, and pressures for some kind of aid were intensified. Probably the turning point came late in 1947 when it became apparent that foreign exchange and gold reserves had now diminished appreciably through squandering and mismanagement.[4] This low level of reserves was seized upon by the Nationalists and their supporters to support the argument that now they needed help to give them a breathing spell in which to institute reform. Many in Washington who had previously been disinterested or vacillating were persuaded that it was worth the chance.[5]

During the fall of 1947 the Department of State, which had been engaged in a continuing study of the economic situation, began to realize that the foreign exchange level would reach the danger point by the first of the year. In view of this reversal, Secretary Marshall on November 10 informed the Congress that he would ask it for additional aid to China. He based his decision on what now sounds like a counsel of despair, namely, that a credit of twenty-five million dollars monthly for one year would give the Nationalists yet another opportunity to implement the necessary internal reforms. This was essentially what Wedemeyer had recommended, except that he had wanted a five-year commitment, whereas Marshall was sufficiently unsure anything would make much difference that he thought it unwise to make any agreement for more than one year.

On November 17 Premier Chang Ch'un sent an urgent appeal to the Secretary for immediate help, adding quite frankly that the situation was much worse than it was when he had assumed office six months earlier. A few days later an informal aide memoire was given to the Embassy and the Department stating that although the Government deeply appreciated the program being submitted to the Congress, it could not wait for the usual legislative process; it needed help at once.[6] In commenting to the Department on November 24, Dr. Stuart said, "Even the higher officials are beginning to lose hope. The effect on military morale is disastrous. In this drift toward catastrophe they clutch at American aid as at least postponing the inevitable. This is all that such monetary aid can do unless there is also among the Kuomintang leaders a new sense of dominating purpose, of sacred mission, of national salvation, expressing itself in challenging slogans, arousing them to fresh enthusiasms, leading them to forget their personal fears, ambitions and jealousies in the larger, more absorbingly worthwhile cause. . . ."[7]

On December 22, the National Government handed Dr. Stuart a memorandum called "Some Fundamental Considerations on American Aid to China." Almost peremptory in tone, it outlined a general program for one and a half billion dollars over a four-year period. There was one ominous part to it, whose implications in no sense escaped the attention of Washington. The memorandum, in stating

4 *Ibid.*, p. 371.   5 *Ibid.*, pp. 387–90.
6 *Ibid.*, pp. 373–75.   7 *Ibid.*, p. 375.

the intention of the Government to employ qualified American personnel to help in implementing the program, added that "The Chinese Government itself will express the aforesaid intention to the American Government . . . the employment of these personnel will not, however, be made an international legal obligation of the Chinese Government in order to avert infringement on China's sovereignty and administrative integrity. . . . The American aid to China shall contain no political condition other than what may be stipulated in the aid plan for Europe. On the other hand, terms which will be stipulated in the aid plan for Europe may apply, wherever practicable, to China." It was clearly realized in Washington that this sensitivity was so deeply ingrained in Chinese thinking that when the time came for implementation of the program no effort was made for formal agreements on reform; rather, reliance was placed on informal persuasion for implementation of a sweeping reform program which Premier Chang Ch'un announced on January 28, 1948. It was a comprehensive and realistic statement of what needed to be done.[8]

The President on February 18 sent his request to the Congress asking for an appropriation of 570 million dollars for a fifteen-month period, of which 510 million would be used to finance imports of essential civilian commodities, and 60 million for a few selected industrial and transportation reconstruction projects. In his defense of the program to the Congress, Marshall said nothing to indicate any decrease in his pessimism about the prospects. The best he could see from his proposal was that it might give the Government the opportunity to do those things which only it could do. His warning was explicit: "We must be prepared to face the possibility that the present Chinese Government may not be successful in maintaining itself against the Communist forces or other opposition that may arise in China. Yet, from the foregoing, it can only be concluded that the present Government evidently cannot reduce the Chinese Communists to a completely negligible factor in China. To achieve that objective in the immediate future it would be necessary for the United States to underwrite the Chinese Government's military effort, on a wide and probably constantly increasing scale, as well as the Chinese economy. The US would have to be prepared virtually to take over the Chinese Government and administer its economic, military and governmental affairs."[9] One can deny that there is truth in the doctrine of the slavish repetitiveness of history, as well as disagree that history has no lessons, and still suggest that those who followed Marshall as a formulator of American foreign policy, with but few exceptions, either have not read their history, or have read it badly. In this same statement, Marshall made another relevant and more general comment to which I will return shortly.

The Congress, quite obviously, shared at least some of Marshall's skepticism. There is nothing to be learned from following in detail the movement of the China Aid Act through the Congress, except for those interested in the mechanics and manipulation of this cumbersome legislative process. As finally passed on

8 *Ibid.*, pp. 378–79.
9 *Ibid.*, p. 382.

April 2, the bill limited the program to twelve months. The amounts appropriated were 338 million dollars for economic rehabilitation and 125 million for special grants to be made at the discretion of the President. The legislative history of the latter item makes clear the assumption in the Congress that the Chinese Government would probably use it for acquisition of military equipment and munitions. The continuing doubts of many Congressmen were reflected in the preamble of the act which said that it "shall not be construed as an express or implied assumption by the United States of any responsibility for policies, acts, or undertaking of the Republic of China for conditions which may prevail in China at any time."[10] This would have to wait a while. It is now a matter of history that the program, which was administered as expertly and efficiently as was possible in the chaotic circumstances, failed. It might be noted, parenthetically, that when the authorized period of one year expired the Congress agreed that the President might continue to expend residual balances, largely for relief purposes, and with the proviso that nothing new be started in areas being taken over by the Communists. Hence, it might be argued that the decision was being left to the Communists as to where and when various phases of the program would be terminated. They proceeded to make those decisions as rapidly as possible.

It is distinctly relevant to recall something else Marshall said at the time. He, after all, was the principal architect of the Greek-Turkish Aid Program, the Marshall Plan, and NATO – all successful. In testifying on the China program he said, "There is another point that I wish to mention in consideration of this matter. There is a tendency to feel that wherever the Communist influence is brought to bear, we should immediately meet it, head on as it were. I think this would be a most unwise procedure for the reason that we would be, in effect, handing over the initiative to the Communists. They could, therefore, spread our influence out so thin that it could be of no particular effectiveness at any one point." Fortunate, indeed, would be the empire which recognized that it was neither omnipotent nor omniscient.[11]

10 *Ibid.*, p. 389.
11 *Ibid.*, p. 382. After the civil war was finished on the mainland the question as to the adequacy of American military and economic aid to China would figure prominently in the bitter discussion in the United States over what had happened, and few aspects of the debate would be as distorted. The hinge of the argument was the arms embargo which Marshall imposed during 1946 while he was attempting to implement the military truce as the prerequisite to reorganization of the armies. This totally disregards the overall picture, which was very different. American aid during the war had been substantial and was primarily military, plus a five hundred million dollar gold stabilization loan, which, incidentally, vanished without a trace. The aid continued after V-J Day. In the immediate postwar period the principal item was a half billion dollar contribution to the UNRRA China program and another half billion dollar grant under Lend Lease. The first half of 1947 was a period of indecision while the United States considered what it might usefully do; and China itself was uncertain as to what it wanted, although obviously cash was preferred. The Wedemeyer Mission in July 1947 crystallized the discussion. What was lost sight of in the subsequent argument was that any foreign aid and advice, no matter how generous, can be only as

As against the military and economic background, the political events during the spring of 1948 might seem farcical, as indeed they did at the time; but perspective revealed also tragedy, and some clarification of the direction in which the United States was moving. Perhaps the tone was set early in March, when Dr. Stuart made some remarks to an American newspaperman which were interpreted to mean that he favored coalition. The way in which he tried the next day to suggest that he did not really mean that at all only compounded the confusion. At his press conference on March 10, Marshall was asked whether the United States still favored coalition with the Communists. In a lengthy reply, the Secretary reviewed the course of events, beginning with the President's policy statement of December 1945. He added that this was still American policy; that when he was in China the Nationalists had followed a policy of a political settlement with the Communists instead of suppressing them by force.

When these comments were also interpreted to mean that the United States had not yet abandoned support for the idea of coalition, the Department of State on the following day issued a press release which, while reaffirming the December 1945 statement, added: "When asked specifically whether broadening the base of the Chinese Government meant we favored the inclusion of the Chinese Communist Party, he [the Secretary] replied that the Communists were now in open rebellion against the Government and that this matter (the determination of whether the Communists should be included in the Chinese Government) was for the Chinese Government to decide, not for the United States Government to dictate."[12]

On the same day, President Truman, who had seldom been known to equivocate about anything, was asked the same questions. He reaffirmed his own statement of December 1945 and said that the objective of General Marshall had been to help the Generalissimo solve the predicament in which he found himself; and then in expressing his hope that Chinese liberals would be taken into the Government added that "we did not want any Communists in the Government of China or anywhere else if we could help it."[13] And that was that. There would no longer be evasion about the matter. Unhappily, in the years of bitter argument

---

effective as the will and determination of the recipient to make it so. As Acting President Li would himself state in 1949, this will simply did not exist. The total of American aid between V-J Day and mid-1949 should be eloquent testimony of American generosity. The value of military and economic grants was slightly over two billion dollars, which did not include supplies abandoned by departing American forces for which no value was available. In addition there were surplus property sales with a procurement value of one billion dollars, but an agreed reimbursement value to the United States of $232 million. Furthermore, China received a quarter of a billion dollars in aid from other foreign sources. Hence, there was a total of more than three and a quarter billion dollars. The fact that as late as 1950 the Chinese Communists were able to fight the first half of their intervention in Korea with American materiel captured earlier from the Nationalists should also say something as to whether the Nationalists were ever short of military supplies.

12 *Ibid.*, p. 272.
13 *Ibid.*, p. 273.

on China policy which lay ahead, it would be expedient for those under acri-
monious attack for having supported or participated in the American stand during
the Marshall period to attempt to gloss over whether coalition really was
American policy. There is no longer any real point – perhaps there never was – in
the pretense. Coalition was the intent of the Marshall Mission. Most of us
involved had strong doubts that the policy would work; but we supported it and
believed that, as we saw the circumstances at the time, there was nothing to be
lost by trying and if it worked there was much to be gained. Very few believed
there was much chance that the eventual outcome would be other than it was,
regardless of what anyone outside did or did not do, because the evidence on all
sides showed the unwillingness or incapacity of the Government to undertake the
needed reforms. Nothing that has happened during the intervening two decades
has caused me to change my mind about this.

March 1 / Nanking / March decided to come in like a
lamb today and it is now sunny and only moderately chilly.
The fruit trees are beginning to blossom. For a moment they
even make it possible to forget there is a civil war going on.

I have sandwiched in a quick trip to Shanghai to speak
to the National Catholic Educational Conference about the
Fulbright Foundation which has just been established. I
accepted the invitation mainly because I thought I might
have a chance of finding out what they are doing in
their first post-war conference. (They run parochial schools
throughout China.) They outplayed me, however, and refused permission to attend any session except the one at
which I spoke, which was the public meeting.

Otherwise Shanghai was the same rat race, only more
jittery. I have never seen a place where the rumors are
quite so numerous, so fantastic, or so readily accepted by
people who should know better. Of course a cost of living
index which is now 150,000 times what it was ten years ago
is hardly calculated to be reassuring.

March 7 / Now there is and for some days has been a great
commotion over the announcement of the new American
aid program. The announcement itself was badly garbled
and then unnecessarily complicated by largely irrelevant
matters. The worst was that Dr. Stuart started talking about
things on which he should have been silent. As far as I can

figure out, the Prime Minister got permission from a reluctant Generalissimo to try once again to get negotiations
with the Communists resumed. Dr. Stuart thought he could
create a favorable climate with a statement which really
did put the stamp of American approval on such resumption, even if he claims now that all he meant was that the
American people would like to see the war ended. For four
miserable days everything he said only made matters worse.

Secretary of Commerce Henry Wallace added his mite to
the confusion with his view we should get out. And from
Washington there is a story that we have decided to start
seriously on the rebuilding of Japan, which understandably
is certain to create a new panic here. All things considered,
the Chinese must be pardoned if they wonder just what is
going on.

March 15 / As a result of a new crop of rumors, there have
been several official announcements denying the possibility
of any Soviet mediation and even denying that such has
been proposed. The fact is, however, that Roschin, the
Russian Military Attaché, did make such an offer just
before he returned to Moscow. It was certainly not accepted,
but just how wide a crack was left open is something else.
There are too many groups which have played with the
idea for it to have been a firm refusal. Furthermore, the
military and economic situations have become so hopeless
that there must be important groups which see such mediation as the only way out of complete and early Communist,
perhaps even Russian, domination. It is impossible to
estimate how strong these groups may be, but even they
must know that any form of coalition would be Communist
dominated now. For that matter there is little reason why
the Communists should accept less. Another intriguing possibility, however, may be emerging.

As the central structure crumbles, the local warlords are
increasingly looking to their own future and welfare, and a
degree of regionalism is appearing such as China has not

Even granting that all such schemes in the last two years smacked of deathbed repentance, they were not as illusory as they seemed even at the time. During the final months the Generalissimo in desperation did agree to the Joint Commission on Rural Reconstruction—Sino-American—for agrarian reform in west China. Even though by then it was too late, the JCRR was so spectacularly successful one cannot help but wonder what the outcome might have been had similar plans been genuinely implemented from 1945 on. The JCRR was subsequently transferred to Formosa, where it was equally successful.

seen since the twenties when the Generalissimo started lining up the satraps. The ones anywhere north of the Yangtze can hardly in the end be much more than puppets and of little value to anyone. This need not necessarily be true in the south, and it might be worthwhile to explore the feasibility of bolstering several local regimes to act in the first instance as border marches between north China and the rest of Asia. This might conceivably give enough respite for putting in reforms which might make south China impervious to Communist penetration and eventually set some kind of example for others. Whether Chinese Communist penetration in the south has gone too far and whether leadership capable of carrying out these reforms can be found are the imponderables. The odds seem against it.

It seems not impossible the Russians themselves may have some kind of territorial partition in mind behind their mediation offer. The Chinese Communists, after all, are still a long way from Southeast Asia, and both Communists and Kuomintang have been fighting one way or another for a generation. They might be tired of it, although the top men never seem to get tired. Left to their own devices they will probably drag this thing on to the bitter end.

March 20 / This has been a lovely day, sunny and warm enough to sit outside. The sun feels good after the gray dreariness of the winter. There will be more rain and misery, but the worst is over. The willows are coming out fast and the spring flowers are blooming with all the promise of new life. Also the magpies have returned, about twice the size of robins, black and bright blue, a quarrelsome crew, but amusing when one of them comes to the windowsill and taps on the pane.

There is a curious revival of stories about a coalition. Weird as it seems, many of them sound persuasive. Somebody is playing some kind of game, but I'll be damned if I can put my finger on it.

Same wine, same bottle

The first constitutional session of the National Assembly was scheduled for March 29 to elect a new President and Vice President, widely assumed as a routine meeting. The Generalissimo would be re-elected as President. There were no other aspirants. But it was soon apparent that the monotony ended here, and that the Generalissimo had a genuine revolt within the Kuomintang on his hands. This time it was not the right wing with which he had to contend; it was the liberal elements who were staging a desperate and final effort to make themselves heard for reform.

Initially the revolt appeared in a struggle for seats in the Assembly, but the real objective was the vice presidency. The Generalissimo had let it be known that he wanted Dr. Sun Fo, son of the founder of the Republic. There were three other candidates whom no one took seriously. The real opposition centered in General Li Tsung-jen, for many years one of the most universally respected leaders of the Kuomintang and also one of the two leaders of the Kwangsi clique.[1] The other leader of the clique was General Pai Ch'ung-hsi, who had held every high military post and was the head of the Moslem community in China. These two men were above reproach, and they had the added advantage of having had the basis of their power, since the days of the Northern Expedition, in the southern part of the country, which was now beginning to appear ominously as quite possibly the last bastion on the mainland of the Kuomintang.

At one point, when the struggle was deadlocked, the Generalissimo announced that he would not be President. He ordered the Assembly to elect Dr. Hu Shih, the distinguished scholar and former Ambassador to the United States, as President and Dr. Sun Fo as Vice President. He would be Prime Minister and from this vantage point exercise control. In a panic, the Assembly refused and demanded that he stay on as President; but even this maneuver did not get him what he wanted. To his speechless fury, the Assembly by a narrow margin elected General Li as Vice President.

The post-Assembly jubilation and expectation that at last there would be changes proved to be short-lived. General Li retired to Peiping, where he did nothing, claiming that he was immobilized because the Generalissimo still kept control of the Party machinery, the purse strings, and the Army. The Generalis-

---

1 Generals Li Tsung-jen and Pai Ch'ung-hsi, who led the Kwangsi clique, were cronies from the days of their youth. Early members of the Kuomintang and among the few who were never corrupted, they were in the top echelon of the Party long before Chiang Kai-shek. In fact, as confusion became chaos after the death of Dr. Sun Yat-sen, qualified American observers considered them the most serious contenders for the succession, giving no more than passing reference to Chiang. This misjudgment of course may indicate no more than how little even the "experts" really know about the inner workings of Chinese politics. But then even the Generalissimo imagined he could separate the two old friends. They preferred public humiliation.

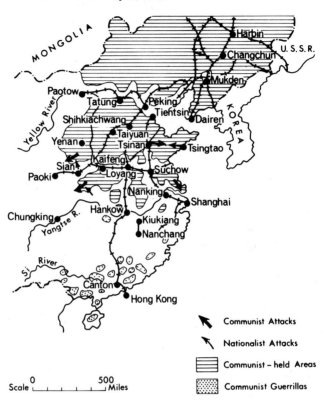

Situation as of May 6, 1948

Communist Attacks
Nationalist Attacks
Communist – held Areas
Communist Guerrillas

Scale 0 500 Miles

simo left little doubt of what he thought of opposition to himself when at the presidential inauguration he completely ignored the Vice President elect. There was little doubt that the widespread popular hopes for reform had been destroyed.

The keystone to this arch of despair was the appointment of a new Executive Yuan. Most of the old familiar names had been prominently mentioned, but a compromise in the continuing internal struggle in the Kuomintang, Dr. Wong Wen-hao, was named as Prime Minister. Dr. Wong had an international reputation as a geologist and was chairman of the National Resources Commission, as well as a man of unquestioned personal integrity; but he was a political cipher. The cabinet he was given was a masterpiece of proven incompetence.[2] The final touch was that General Pai Ch'ung-hsi was dismissed as Minister of National Defense and relegated to a command up the Yangtze without measurable authority. The Generalissimo had made it clear that he, and he alone, would make all the decisions. Even Dr. Stuart was discouraged.

2 *China White Paper*, pp. 274–76, and annex 153 (a)–(e).

Although it referred specifically to the military picture, a report to Washington on July 23 by the Economic Cooperation Mission, which administered the economic aid program, was typical of the reactions of almost all newcomers to China during the previous year. In part, the report said, "The Mission was really startled about the military facts in China and to find such an enormous gap between what they had supposed to be the case and the actual truth."[3] If the Chinese had been as efficient in China as they had been in Washington, the outcome might have been different.

In the meantime, student riots during the hot spring and summer were slowly raising the curtain on the last act.

3 *Ibid.*, p. 319.

March 29 / Nanking / The National Assembly opened this morning on schedule and with an unexpected amount of interest being shown by delegates and the public. We had all expected it to be a pro forma performance that would elect a President and Vice President, meaning the Generalissimo and his nominee for deputy, do so quietly, and go home. It is already apparent the delegates are taking seriously the usual public assurances of free speech and action, and are indulging liberally in both. Some disappointed would-be delegates are expressing their sentiments with a hunger strike in the Nanking Hotel. Most surprising is the volume and bitterness of criticism against the Generalissimo. In addition, his choice for the vice presidency, Dr. Sun Fo as the son of Dr. Sun Yat-sen, is most vociferously not the choice of an impressive number of delegates. Ch'en Li-fu this morning insisted that no matter what I hear to the contrary, General Li Tsung-jen, with formidable liberal backing and organization, definitely has his eyes on the slot. Ch'en was downright grumpy about it.

The first two sessions today have been real bedlam, with everyone saying what he pleased and all at the same time. No one paid the slightest attention to the general committee reports, which at best were uninspired. Finally this afternoon the Generalissimo could stand it no longer. He gave them the roughest tongue lashing I have heard in a long time on the responsibilities of representing the people. After that manners improved considerably.

In the light of conditions in this country, there is something unreal about the performance; it is also more than a little pathetic and even touching. It is as though the delegates were trying to prove something to the world and even more to themselves, in a frantic hope that if something good could be demonstrated then other good things would flow therefrom.

April 7 / The Generalissimo's bag of political tricks seems unlimited. After days of inconsequential bickering and in the face of increasing strident criticism, he has let it be known that he will accept no political office whatsoever. This repetition of the Retreat to Fenghua, his birthplace, which he staged years ago when faced with an earlier political revolt has again had the same consequences. Appalled by the prospect of losing the man who has single-handedly held them together over the years and in the absence of a replacement of comparable stature, the clamor now is that he must stay on—whether on his own terms is a little less certain. But it is quite an experience to talk with delegates in the lobbies and see the real consternation that possesses them.

The Generalissimo, however, while indicating that the People's will be done, has also suggested that this will can take several forms. One which he has discussed with Dr. Stuart is that he assume the prime ministership and that the august Dr. Hu Shih, a prime leader in the Chinese intellectual renaissance of the twenties and a former Ambassador to the United States, become President. Just what would be gained by changing the structure of government to the French type when the substance of power would remain in the same hands is somewhat nebulous. Equally vague is just who thought up this extravaganza in political experimentation. Maybe Dr. Hu did.

April 10 / Dr. Hu attended a Fulbright Foundation Board of Directors meeting this morning. He was obviously fascinated with the picture of himself as potentially titular chief of state. All his comments carried an aura of dress rehearsal for the part. The royal manner, in any event, is something he has never lacked. Dr. Stuart, whose own self assurance assumes rather more modest forms, was visibly amused.

April 13 / The Generalissimo has finally decided to stop playing around with ideas and to get back to business. So he will be President and Dr. Hu has reverted to the status of unofficial elder statesman. From his apologetic manner of assuring me this is all for the best, and from his conspicuous absence from the public scene, it is obvious his vanity is hurt and I could guess he will eventually take his chagrin to another climate. His parting shot was: "Anyone is a fool who tries to beat the Generalissimo at the game he invented."

Now for the vice presidency. The word has been passed around the corridors that the man is to be Dr. Sun Fo; but the assurance with which it is being done has the hackles up again.

April 15 / Six candidates were nominated for the vice presidency: Sun Fo; Li Tsung-jen; Ch'eng Ch'ien, doddering warlord of Hankow; Yu Yu-jen, a venerable of the Kuomintang and President of the Judicial Yuan; Mo Teh-hui, a Manchurian political boss; and Hsu Fu-lin, an independent, liberal newspaperman. The last three were eliminated on the first ballot and Li was first. Li still led on the second ballot, but without a majority; and the Generalissimo sat in the front row absolutely speechless and livid with rage. I would not want to be one of those hauled into the presence after adjournment this evening. The corridors were chortling, a little apprehensively perhaps, but still chortling.

April 17 / The last two days have centered on the back rooms and nothing has happened publicly. Under great pressure Ch'eng Ch'ien has withdrawn his name. Li also did when the Generalissimo made the mistake of trying to drive a wedge between Li and General Pai Ch'ung-hsi, Li's closest friend of many, many years' standing. Pai is not only a military power in his own right, but a political figure of consequence by virtue of being head of the sizable Moslem community in China. Pai balked at the pressure on him and Li of course withdrew beside his friend.

This leaves the Generalissimo, to his embarrassment, with only one candidate and a lot of fine words about democracy.

April 20 / The Generalissimo has swallowed his pride and anger. Sun Fo has also withdrawn under orders. And that leaves no one.

April 28 / Days of political juggling which not even a Chinese sorcerer could unravel finally brought all three back into the race. The voting this morning was almost deathly silent. Ch'eng Ch'ien was eliminated on the third ballot. The steam roller broke down on the fourth ballot and Li won by a narrow margin. The finale was anything but silent, except for the Generalissimo whose face for once plainly showed he knew he had taken a shellacking. So Ch'en Li-fu was right. He usually is where politics is involved.

May 1 / The exhilaration in Nanking over the Assembly continues. All agree that, on the surface anyway, the old vested interests around Sun Fo took a bad beating. Li has become the symbol of discontent, demand for reform, and a new ideal in an old party. Now it becomes a struggle between Li's fortitude and nerve on the one hand and the unquestioned political genius of the Generalissimo on the other.

Several intriguing straws in the wind come from the Kuomintang Revolutionary Committee (KMTRC), which is located in Hong Kong. The head of it is Marshal Li Chi-shen, an early and respected member of the Party, and for many years the head of its extreme right wing. He is in a sort of discreet exile, half voluntary and half suggested to him by the Generalissimo. He claims to have a timetable for getting rid of the Generalissimo, but is vague on details with us, possibly because he has heard of Philip Fugh's pipeline to the Generalissimo. Li admits the KMTRC has been in touch with him. It has also been making the coyest kind of goo-goo eyes at T. V. Soong, who is now Governor of Kwantung in his comfortable Cantonese foxhole. This could be important because, although it is far to the south and away from the central struggle, Canton is a major center of China. Traditionally, revolutions in China have come from the south.

May 21 / Leo Eloesser of the World Health Organization, who knows China in and out, has returned here from a four-month trip in southern Hopei and northern Honan observing sanitary conditions. He found the Communists preoccupied to the exclusion of everything else with the prosecution of the civil war and with land reform, the latter getting them the support of the peasants. He found the reform being pushed ruthlessly and the stories of atrocities against the landlords not exaggerated, although in the areas he visited this class had less than ten per cent of the land. Wealthy landlords are tried by the entire village for "crimes against the people" and conviction means stoning to death by the populace.

Theoretically, he said, the death penalty is reserved for murderers and rapists, but is used in other cases. One of which he knew concerned a rich farmer who put his sheep on the land of a poor farmer. The latter accidentally killed one when he drove them off his land and was unable to pay the retribution demanded. The rich farmer then made him put the dead sheep in a coffin and mourn it as his father. For this the rich farmer was killed when the Communists took over. But Eloesser says some of the brutality has been easing up in recent months.

Land distribution averages one-fourth acre per person in the family. although it can reach two acres in localities where the soil is poorer. In general the land is about the quality of that around Albuquerque, New Mexico.

He found systematic propaganda education wherever he went. In the larger centers there was a considerable anti-American content, mostly focusing on President Truman, but the farther out he got into the countryside the more the emphasis was on internal problems—not inconceivably because there they have never heard of the United States. Much of the propaganda took the form of adaptations of the Chinese classics to contemporary themes. He did not find that this improved them. One curious fact is the excessively high proportion of men to women, for which he could find no explanation.

There was an endless stream of refugees coming to Hopei and Shantung from the east, all in a more miserable condition than any he had seen anywhere in the world. During the years of Japanese occupation and even before, about a million Chinese a year had gone to Manchuria from the Shantung-Hopei area. The Japanese had encouraged this because their people did not like the severe climate, and labor was needed. Now in considerable numbers they are walking back to where they came from because of the wretched conditions and the havoc of the civil war.

May 28 / Several of us drove for the weekend to Hangchow south of Shanghai in an obstreperous station wagon appropriately named Rasputin. The occasion was an eclipse of the sun for which Georgetown University had set up an observation post on a hill outside the town. It was a rugged climb up the hill, but worth it. Despite a heavy overcast which kept us from seeing the sun, the actual moment of totality was exciting. Almost as though a switch had been thrown it became quite dark, the temperature dropped ten to twenty degrees, and a high wind suddenly sprang up. Two minutes later everything was as it had been before. I suppose my ancestral superstitions rose up; it was eerie. Father Hayden, who must understandably have been annoyed when we barged in on him at his busiest moment, was the very soul of cordiality and hospitality and when the eclipse was over produced a bottle of vintage brandy which we consumed out of charming bamboo cups he had carved himself.

The ride from Shanghai to Hangchow also had its

moments. The countryside has the broad, rolling quality of the Yangtze Valley, but the condition of the road made anything but casual observation out of the question. We cruised along in the middle of a heavy dust cloud which came at us from all directions, even through cracks in the floorboards of the car. Rasputin displayed an uncanny knack of seeking out and finding every rut in the road along the way. We also managed to run out of gasoline at an inconvenient spot. By the time we arrived in Hangchow we all looked very much alike and very disreputable. As fate would have it, when we arrived our Consul General in Shanghai and his wife, who were spending the weekend there too, were sitting on the porch of the hotel, all washed and pressed. They somehow looked as though they wished we would not speak. I could hardly blame them.

Hangchow, once we uncaked ourselves, turned out to be a lovely town. It looked like a nineteenth-century Chinese scroll built around a series of small lakes with a backdrop of low hills. It is fairly modern in a pleasant and leisurely sort of fashion.

June 7 / Shanghai / The predicted riots for today fizzled. There were just too many troops and tanks on the streets for anything to get started. The only excitement was the explosion of a chemical warehouse a couple of blocks from where I was at the time. It was spectacular and looked like a small atomic bomb. We learned later there were a hundred people in the building.

June 10 / Nanking / Dr. Stuart has called on Soviet Ambassador Roschin and said a number of things to him which would make Washington's hair curl if it knew—which it does not. Roschin was previously the Military Attaché, one of the best liked and most popular members of the diplomatic corps. He has never been known to give away anything, but Dr. Stuart, who has never even been inside the Department of State, has no conception of his relationship to it, and no amount of persuasion ever moves him from his image of himself as an independent agent whose sole purpose is the restoration of peace in China; but he can do many things no one else can do, with or without authorization from the Secretary of State.

He proposed a broad and overall rapprochement for the improvement of Soviet-American relations. He then suggested the good offices of a neutral third power to this end. As to the China situation, he was more than frank: the Generalissimo, he said, knows the facts but misses their implications; he said he continually advises the Generalissimo on what he should do; the latter says he will follow the advice and never does. Roschin, understandably in the circumstances, was most cordial and very noncommittal. After all, he now knows what he must have suspected. He can now afford to wait for the inevitable end.

Eric Chou, a knowledgeable reporter for the liberal newspaper *Ta Kung Pao*, insists that Chiang Ching-kuo is the force behind the anti-American group in the Government and continually uses pressure on his father in this direction. Madame Chiang (he is not her son) opposes his views. The Generalissimo has admitted to Dr. Stuart that he cannot allow his American ties to be too conspicuous.

June 11 / Dr. Stuart is urging the Generalissimo to make a public statement calling on China to unite for a solution of common problems and to drive out both American and Russian imperialism in order that China may emerge as a great world force for peace and the mediator in the present world struggle!

As more and more people around here are increasingly convinced all is lost, a debate grows as to what the future stance of the Communists will be and how events will develop. Most of it is pretty bitter too. Much must be largely speculative, since we really cannot be sure what Communist thinking is, beyond unanimous agreement that winning the war is the primary goal. The principal argument is the extent to which traditional institutions will modify Chinese Communist ideology once the war is won. It must be assumed that as long as the war goes on the

Communists will make any compromise necessary in order to survive and win. But it would be a mistake to assume further that compromise will be permanent once the pressure has been removed. Not since 1927 have they taken orders from anyone and they are hardly likely to do so when they are the victors. Many feel that ideology and institutions will react on each other, but no one is rash enough to pinpoint where that middle ground will be. The nature of relations between Yenan and Moscow will be a key indicator here.

Those who hold that ideology will win cite the return of Li Li-san to Manchuria as evidence. A colossal amount of nonsense has been written and spoken on this topic, but I doubt if any of us has any real idea of what it means. For all I know, it actually may be the sign of Kremlin ascendency, as this school of thought would have it; but I would be surprised if it were much more than the pill Mao must swallow as a temporary measure while he anticipates needing help from the Russians. I would be even more surprised if Mao did not in this period keep firm control over the instruments of power—Li or no Li. And, in any event, maybe the Russians are more interested in Manchuria than in anything else anyway.

The other extreme, which sees Chinese institutions, nationalism, xenophobia, and suspicion of the Russians in time banishing ideology, seems equally unlikely. Communism in one form or another has come to China for a long time to come. Western democracy, especially the American brand, is an unfamiliar idiom to the Chinese, far more alien than communism. There is a tradition of autocracy on which the West has made little dent. The American economic system is something the Chinese do not understand, have never had, and do not now want. Any group, whatever its political persuasion, always speaks of socialism as the desirable and possible form. Even the Shanghai bankers and industrialists, who come closer to us than any other group, have very close connections with the Government, draw much of their capital from it, and as often as not are officials themselves. Even those who complain the most about the abuses of this "bureaucratic capital," as it is called, do not favor a free enterprise system. The big Chinese complaint, even in Shanghai, about American economic policy in Japan is that we are not socializing industry and that we are encouraging free enterprise. They are not worried about the size of the new trusts, but that their control is in private hands.

The argument then comes to the question whether it really makes any basic difference to American interests what the outcome is. Surprisingly, American businessmen here are fairly unanimous that it matters little who is in power; they can continue to do business. Even some of the groups and individuals who are new to the Kremlin satellite theory about China and deplore the possibility as dangerous are interestingly enough not alarmed about business prospects. Many of our military people, even those with long Chinese experience, see the problem as whether China in the event of war would be a major or a minor liability on our side. The Walter Lippmann thesis, as Bullitt tells it to me, is that China is a morass, that we should pray for the collapse of the Nationalists, encourage the growth of regionalism, and then lure the Russians into the swamp to drain their strength instead of ours. There is some plausibility to the argument and some evidence for it, especially to those who remember the problems Japan had in trying to conquer China. The questionable assumption is that the Russians can be lured. They doubtless make as many mistakes as we do, but they are not stupid.

The Communists will also have to solve the basic economic problems which are destroying the Kuomintang, and they will have to mount and ride the same mammoth social revolution which is still and will be for a long time the story of Asia. Whether they can will probably not be finally answered in our lifetime, but for a while anyway they can ride the crest of popular optimism generated by their own

faith and convictions and on their promises of a change. It
would be fatal to underestimate their capabilities and popular appeal; and I am by no means sure that overt American
hostility and opposition will not strengthen, rather than
weaken, that which we deplore. All the power of the United
States will not stem the tides of Asia; but all the wisdom of
which we are capable might conceivably make those tides
a little more friendly than they are now. Anything less can
only be self-defeating, regardless of whether the Communists really are the future of China or are only another
chapter in its revolution.

June 15 / For a welcome change it is cool today. The only
trouble with it is it came in on the heels of a series of
torrential rains. When they started the Yangtze had already
flooded over four million acres. God only knows what it is
now. It is a bad time for this since it will damage the rice
crop and food is short enough already. As a result the
dollar has gone to CN 1,800,000, and the price of rice has
passed the ten million mark, or roughly ten thousand times
what it was when I arrived. Apart from the misery, inflation
has other consequences, some comical and some serious. I
recently found a good shoemaker in Shanghai who charged
me ten dollars for a pair of shoes. I could not carry the
Chinese equivalent by myself and had to hire a rickshaw
to do it. The Embassy bought a house the other day for
$60,000. The Central Bank did not have enough cash on
hand to exchange our draft and the seller had to wait two
days for more to be printed. By that time his money had
depreciated twenty-five per cent.

The anti-American campaign is building up again and
much of it is focused on our policy in Japan. The reaction
to the last announcement of new economic reconstruction
programs was incredibly violent and at the moment it is
hard to tell where it will lead. All is so fantastic and extreme
here it would not be difficult to acquire an illusion we
really can walk on water.

June 20 / The aftermath of the National Assembly has been

anything but helpful, despite the promise in the successful rebellion led by Li Tsung-jen. He is in a most depressed frame of mind, wondering what he can do since the Generalissimo controls the Army, Government finances, and a large part of the Party machinery.

The new Legislative Yuan is also in a state of rebellion. No one faction in the Party has a majority, with the result that the Generalissimo has been unable to secure approval for any strong man as Premier. The Executive Yuan is, if anything, weaker and more ineffectual than its predecessor. It is generally considered as an interim government until the factional fight within the Party has been resolved, if it ever is. The only noticeable change in the Executive is that civilian officials are weaker and the top military leaders more incompetent. The prevailing mood is despair. Even officials at the very highest levels openly say there is no hope and it is merely a matter of waiting for the final collapse.

One of the principal weaknesses continues to be the unwillingness of the Generalissimo to relinquish personal control and direction of every phase of national life or to divorce himself from his Confucian feudal outlook. Time and again he has promised changes and then done nothing. Time and again he has promised to bring in abler men and then appoints the most incompetent he can find. Time and again he has promised to break the rule of the cc clique and then continues to rely on it. More and more people are saying there will be no change until he goes, but no one has any suggestions as to who could replace him. He alone can seem to lead, but in private conversations he admits he does not know what to do.

Along with the military deterioration there is corresponding economic decline. The US dollar, which two years ago was worth two thousand Chinese dollars, is now worth nearly two million. All commodity prices have followed the same scale of inflation and in many instances have far outstripped that of the exchange rate. The cost of living index today is more than fifty thousand times what it was two

years ago. No effective measures whatsoever have been taken to check the tide. Even the passage of the American aid bill did not have the slightest effect on the inflation. There is some apathetic hope it may yet slow it down for a while, but no thought that it will alter the eventual outcome. Even those who think the program is too small and too late know that the Government is incapable of making good use of any program.

Most opinion is there are only two alternatives to complete victory by the Communists. The first one would be intervention by the United States with enough aid and sufficient control to make it work, and the simultaneous takeover of actual command and direction of the civil war. This we will not do and it is highly improbable the Chinese would let us even if we tried. The other suggested course is that the Generalissimo be replaced by some other group which would make the necessary accommodation with the Communists and establish a coalition. The growing sentiment is in favor of this course, both in the Government and in industrial circles. Even recognizing the dangers of a coalition, they still prefer that to the present situation. University and intellectual groups as well are almost unanimously in favor of coalition. It seems hardly possible any Government succeeding the Generalissimo could hope to survive unless it ended the civil war. The most important political question at the moment, therefore, is whether the Generalissimo can put down a revolt in his own Party and re-establish control, or whether the opposition can overthrow him and reach an understanding with the Communists.

The last act

To the western mind, accustomed to speed and precision in the events of men, the last act was unconscionably and even frustratingly long. The Chinese, thinking in terms of generations or centuries, found the pace frightening and stunning, productive mostly of bewilderment that it should be so.

Perhaps one activity of the Embassy during 1948 was typical of the monotonous, nightmarish atmosphere. Monthly reports were prepared summarizing developments during the previous month for certain officials in Washington, primarily the Cabinet, who were involved in Chinese affairs, but whose other activities made it impossible for them to keep up with the daily volume of reporting. These dispatches came to be known, with more accuracy than elegance, as "stink pieces." It was only late in the summer we realized that, quite without design, each one invariably began: "During the last month the military, political, and economic situation has continued to deteriorate. . . ." And that is the way it was.

The student riots in 1948 began as usual in May as the period for examinations approached. Many thought they would abate, again as usual, when the time of tension had passed; but this year it was not so. They not only continued throughout most of the summer, they grew larger and more violent. From previous experience, the students had learned that direct attack on the Government was the quickest way to provoke retaliation and suppression. This time they chose the indirect approach of demonstrating against the announced American policy of reconstruction in Japan. This was embarrassing for the Government, which shared the overt objective of the students, as did certain business groups which feared Japanese competition and were not above encouraging and directing the disorders. By mid-June the rioting had become so violent and widespread that Dr. Stuart felt compelled to take the rather unusual step for an ambassador of making a direct appeal to the students on the basis of his many years as a teacher.[1]

This proved effective with many, but did not change the leadership. Late in August the Executive Yuan was forced to pass a law forbidding all future demonstrations; and they ebbed away as the weather cooled and the students lapsed into apathy. But reports received from all sorts of contacts confirmed that the Government had only succeeded in further alienating the student and intellectual groups. From this damage there would be no turning back.

The ban on demonstrations coincided with the announcement on August 19 of drastic economic reform measures. General Chiang Ching-kuo, son of the Generalissimo, was named economic czar in Shanghai, with full powers, and initially gave every indication of carrying out his orders with complete ruthlessness. This was all well and good, and in the beginning provoked the kind of feverish hope which had characterized the early days after the rebellion in the National Assembly. The flaw was that, instead of initiating reform, the measures actually froze the business situation, not only in Shanghai, but also in all the other urban centers. Economic activity came to a virtual standstill.[2] The measures were especially hard on the small and medium businessmen, not on the large speculators against whom they should have been directed, but who instead only intensified their hoarding. When food producers refused to send their stocks into the city, an emergency food shortage resulted.

By the time Chiang Ching-kuo resigned on November 1, having found out that vested interests were stronger than he was, the whole structure had collapsed. Thenceforth, the economic life of Shanghai made the German post–World War I inflation look like a passing fancy.[3] The consequences for the country as a whole, however, were not really comparable and should not be exaggerated. They were real and disastrous enough for those dependent on urban market life, but important as this group was, it was still a small minority. Most of China was agrarian and, in any modern sense, not in the marketplace or basically affected by it. It had other problems – or had had, for now most of the territory was under Communist control, and the Communists were being very determined and effective with their agrarian reform measures.[4]

It was ironic that on November 4 the official Kuomintang newspaper, the *Chung Yang Jih Pao*, published an editorial that was highly critical of the Government and suggested that it could learn a great deal from the Communists.

As the Communist military sweep during the latter half of 1948 continued

1 *China White Paper*, p. 277.   2 *Ibid.*, p. 278.
3 *Ibid.*, pp. 399–401.   4 *Ibid.*, annex 159.

unabated, the political scene became one of frantic activity in a search for some kind of negotiated settlement which might salvage anything from the accumulating wreckage. Only the Generalissimo and Washington remained aloof from any participation, although neither really did anything to stop the effort.

Direct contacts with the Communists were renewed by all sorts of groups; and with each new contact their terms for settlement became stiffer as they scored one military victory after another. They were now in a position to dictate the terms, and they knew it. The final outrage, as far as the Generalissimo was concerned, was publication of their own war criminals list on which his was the first name. Within the Government and the Kuomintang there were groups which were sufficiently desperate in their attempts to save their own hides that they might have been persuaded to accept even this condition.

The Russians also were feeling their way around to see what they might have to contribute, but since they could hardly be expected, even if they had so wished, to do other than reinforce the Communist position, little came of it. It was only another element in the general confusion. More realistically – or at least so it seemed at the time – there were numerous efforts, based on an assumption that China north of the Yangtze was lost, to establish and consolidate some kind of base south of the river and on that line to stop the Communist advance. The Yangtze, after all, is a formidable geographical obstacle to any armed force, let alone to an army marching on foot and with neither experience in or equipment for amphibious warfare. There was reason to think the idea was not utterly fantastic, but it turned out to be the old, familiar pattern again. The various cliques within the Kuomintang could not be persuaded to lay aside their self-seeking ambitions in the interest of a common cause. Perhaps they no longer really believed there was a cause left.

All this chaos had its counterpart within the Embassy, as was reflected in its exchanges with Washington. Embassy views had gradually been changing. There had been the normal and usual turnover of personnel. This was true also for the rather sizable Military Advisory Group which the Government never did permit to perform any of the functions for which it had been sent out. There was also the large and relatively new economic aid mission. In short, by now a substantial majority of American officials in China had had no China background whatsoever, and brought with them from their most recent service in Washington or Europe the increasingly hardline attitudes of the cold war. As far as they were concerned, coalition or negotiation with the Communists was no longer even a debatable alternative. Complete defeat was preferable since, in their view, coalition only meant the same thing in the end. They also brought with them the hope that in China the same solutions would work which they justifiably foresaw for Europe; but since they were not stupid men, it took them no longer than it had taken anyone else during the preceding two years to become appalled by the situation they found, and to conclude there was nothing the United States could do about it, beyond possibly slowing down the inevitable.

In the middle of this chaos and despair stood Dr. Stuart, who was being more

Chinese than the Chinese. A decreasing number of persons supported his view that the United States should encourage, support, and help those trying for negotiations. Even when Washington told him on more than one occasion that it now opposed coalition, that it favored continued resistance to the Communists in any form but that, except for programs already in being, it would do nothing more, Dr. Stuart never relaxed his efforts for some kind of peaceful settlement.[5] The only concession he made was when a somewhat exasperated Secretary of State instructed him to inform the Generalissimo that any suggestions he made were on his own responsibility; he did so. We shall probably never know the range and extent of his activities at this time, since he carried his records in his head, nor did he tell us much. He generally kept his own counsel, the more so when he found that his staff opposed him. I am personally convinced that he never gave up until there was no longer anything to give up.

5 *Ibid.*: various exchanges between the Ambassador and the Secretary are to be found on pp. 280–86.

July 5 / Nanking / Back from two weeks in Bangkok to find that nothing startling has changed; only more of the same. While I was away the exchange rate went to five million and prices followed suit. Money is becoming meaningless and you wonder how people eat. It may be a hot summer in more ways than one.

I would give a lot to know the real reactions of the Communists to the Cominform break with the Yugoslavs. The Cominform blast contained much on land reform, the leadership of the industrial proletariat, and Kremlin infallibility that is directly contrary to local practices; and yet Yenan in its statement deadpanned it right down the Cominform line.

July 13 / Without anything too specific to go on, it now looks as though the days of the Government are numbered. Never before have I known so many in the highest ranks to be so completely frustrated and hopeless. Even General Ho Ying-chin, Minister of Defense, says all is lost. But the Generalissimo continues to talk blithely about a range of plans which have nothing to do with the facts.

Li Chi-shen still insists he can seize power and he will do it soon. Some close to him think he will try in a few days. Suddenly there is a rash of reports that Chou En-lai is

Many of the most experienced China specialists, especially those without experience in other parts of the world, admitted that the Communists were indeed Communists, but noted that they were also Chinese and hence would follow their own line of development and never be subservient to Moscow's dictates. The history of the Party since Mao Tse-tung assumed control seemed to affirm this position, and the Yugoslav break with Moscow to reaffirm it. Hence, the apparently close cooperation between Peking and

Moscow from October 1949 (foreshadowed in the July 1948 Yenan statement) until the death of Stalin was a rude shock and temporarily silenced the earlier view. What no one anticipated was that the post-Stalin rupture would find Peking championing orthodoxy against Moscow moderation and revisionism.

secretly in Peiping dickering with Fu Tso-yi, who commands in north China, and with Li Tsung-jen. It is difficult to believe this is true. It is no longer possible to judge any sources of information with any reliability. It also looks as though an economic crash in Shanghai is imminent unless quick remedial measures are taken on inflation. Some think August a likely time, but it could happen at any moment.

July 15 / Soviet Ambassador Roschin has had a long talk with the Minister of Information suggesting that the civil war be stopped in the interests of all concerned. P'eng agreed so long as there was no encroachment on Chinese sovereignty and added that China could not desert its American ally. Roschin left an impression that he was fearful the Chinese Communists would follow the example of Yugoslavia. He did not indicate whether his approach had been on his own initiative or under orders. P'eng tells us he thinks a joint US-USSR mediation would be an ideal solution. Indeed it would, indeed it would.

The KMTRC again says Li Chi-shen is making his move in a few days and that he now has an agreement with Li Tsung-jen to join him. We have recommended to Washington that someone from the Embassy talk personally with Li Chi-shen at once and urge him in his initial proclamation to make his anti-Communist position clear, although I am by no means sure he would do it. There are at least a dozen different views in the Embassy as to what we should do. One thing is sure. If Li fizzles, a lot of us are going to look mighty silly holding a bag of hot air. Lewis Clark, who succeeded Butterworth in charge of the Embassy, reports from Peiping that he can find nothing to substantiate the report Li Tsung-jen will join, although I don't know why Li should tell him.

S. Y. Liu, Director, says the Central Bank is flat broke and completely out of foreign exchange.

July 16 / Dr. Stuart gave the Generalissimo a line of malarkey this morning and urged him to call the most respected men together so they can all work together for

the good of China. The Generalissimo allowed it was a
good idea and he would think about it—he always does. Dr.
Stuart also told him all he knew about Li Chi-shen. The
Generalissimo said we overrate him. With this kind of round
robin talky-talk, it is small wonder Li Tsung-jen refused to
tell Clark anything.

Kunming students are fighting with the police again. All
building has stopped in Nanking on account of strikes.

July 19 / Washington really cropped our ears at the last
minute and ordered us to stop fomenting rebellion against
a recognized Government! It also told us to stay away from
Hong Kong. Still nothing but silence and inaction from
both Lis.

Dr. Stuart again has the Roschin-P'eng talks on his mind
and is playing with the idea of taking another personal
crack at coalition. He told us he had tried it once on his
own which we did not know—and failed, but that this
might be a good time to try again, especially since it was
still American policy. I felt I had to point out my doubt
it was still policy. It was true nothing had been said publicly
except for one confused exchange of statements, but that
I was certain Washington would be most unhappy with any
coalition. He made no comment, but I have an idea he will
pursue the matter in his own fashion. He is never terribly
concerned with what Washington thinks anyway. He feels
the continued fighting so deeply he would do anything and
pay any price to stop it. And who knows—he just might
succeed.

One difficulty in finding out how much he knows or what
he is up to is that he does not tell the same story twice, nor
will he put anything in writing. This time he considerably
watered down his version of what Roschin said, but
strengthened his own interest in talking further with P'eng
about the possibilities of a joint mediation. This time too
he intimated that P'eng said more to him than he admitted
when the subject first came up about the extent of Government interest in mediation; but he shows great disinclina-
tion to tell us any more.

Clark is really peeved. He has a notion that just because
Li Tsung-jen and T. V. Soong sneer at him about Li Chi-
shen's future there must be something to the stories of a
connection between them. Maybe there is.

I had a long talk this morning with Li Wei-kuo, secretary
to the Generalissimo. He admits there is a need for a propaganda effort to point out similarities betwen Chinese
and Yugoslav Communists and will do what he can; but
he adds there must be a great effort not to antagonize the
Russians until the United States makes an all-out commitment to the Kuomintang. On the military side he says
Government troops cannot be concentrated effectively because of local pressures and yowling in the Legislative Yuan.
I suggested using the emergency powers, but he said the
Generalissimo does not want to do that. He was also skeptical about the advisability of asking for the powers from
the Yuan, but said he would think about it.

August 4 / Most of the Embassy has come around to the
position that the United States should openly announce
its opposition to coalition or to American support for one
if it should come about; but Dr. Stuart at last flatly and
openly disagrees with this and says he favors a coalition. I
had not thought he would so categorically commit himself.
He refuses to admit there is no longer any good or feasible
political answer from our standpoint.

Meanwhile the Generalissimo is preparing for a Kuomintang conference at Kuling to reorganize the Party. One
group wants to break it up, while another wants to leave
matters as they are. The Generalissimo favors the latter. Dr.
Stuart will go with him and fish in waters which are none
of his business.

August 11 / There are signs that the first major break away
from the Kuomintang could come in the north. Fu Tso-yi
in Peiping and Wei Li-huang, who commands in Manchuria, are holding extensive conversations looking toward
cooperation between north China and Manchuria, particularly in supplies and economic matters, and are doing so
independently of the Central Government. I have become

convinced that north China is the heart of the matter and that he who holds that will soon hold the rest of the country. I am appalled at the difficulties involved in trying to establish any sort of foothold in the south China morass. One of the crucial points in any northern regional agreement would be the Manchurian leaders and their troops. Wang Hua-yi, who is a political force there in his own right, insists the Manchurians would follow any anti-Communist Government which did not include the Generalissimo, that the entire Chang family resources would back this, and that Chang Hsueh-shih would bring one hundred thousand troops over from the Communists.

[*The Changs were the ruling warlords of Manchuria in pre-Japanese days. Their distaste for the Generalissimo went back to the Sian Incident in 1936 when the Generalissimo was kidnapped and, under threat of death, agreed to stop his push against the Communists and concentrate his efforts against the Japanese. Chang Hsueh-liang, titular head of the Chang family, accompanied the Generalissimo back to Chungking under a guarantee of safety. He was immediately placed under house arrest and is still on Formosa if he is alive.*

Nothing came of these maneuvers. Hope for success was based on an assumption that the Communists had only penetrated Manchuria after the Soviet withdrawal in 1946 and that since there was more than enough good land and hence no agrarian problem, they had not had need for strictly political indoctrination. It is only now that work on the Imperial Japanese archives is bringing out evidence that Communist guerrillas and political cadres had penetrated Manchuria in the middle thirties, operated most successfully, and were a continual thorn in the Japanese side. One interesting question is whether the Russians during their period of occupation ever became aware of this. Their looting of the area would seem to suggest that they did not. In retrospect, it would also seem that the only intelligence information about Manchuria which was worth very much was that of the Communists.]

August 19 / Sweeping new economic regulations were announced today to revalue the currency, stabilize prices, ration rice, and end the black market—the millennium. Chiang Ching-kuo is economic director in Shanghai and is already making very tough noises. There are enough loopholes and exceptions in the rules that it is unlikely there will be much change beyond a temporary psychological boost. After all, the favored ones must remain favored.

August 20 / Canton / Canton is so very much like every Chinatown in the United States that it seems quite familiar.

And why not, since almost every Chinese in the States originally came from a small village on the outskirts of Canton. It is the perfect picture of what most Americans imagine China to be like, with its five and six story buildings, endless multicolored banners, and narrow crowded streets. It is the kind of backdrop favored by class B movies. This much Hollywood does authentically. Shameen Island in the Pearl River, which was the early western concession, still has much of the old flavor with its western counting houses, wide streets, and towering trees. It is an island of quiet in the bustle that is so typically Canton.

We called on T. V. Soong. He had little to offer beyond an air of self-assurance. It is apparent, however, that he is busily engaged in building himself a stronghold in Kwantung province against the eventuality there might be nothing else left in China, in which case he could be boss man. I guess he might as well occupy his time with this fantasy as with anything else. This could very well be the last ditch on the mainland. It would be ironic for the Kuomintang Revolution to end its days here where it began more than a generation ago. Otherwise the picture is much the same as it is anywhere else.

August 23 / Hainan / Hainan is really the jumping off point to another world. The northern half of the island is flat, uninteresting, and covered with scrub brush. Everything is in an advanced stage of disrepair and neglect. Even the automobiles at our disposal are a vintage I can hardly remember. The southern half of the island is something else. It has mountains, tropical vegetation, and one of the most magnificent harbors in the world, filled with cobalt water. The neglect is the same except that it seems less distressing since the tropics are more adept at covering their scars. The Japanese used the harbor as the staging point for their southern adventures and really developed it; but there came a day when a series of American carrier strikes reduced it to rubble. The wreckage still lies around, and the valuable iron mines back up in the hills have more administrative personnel than miners.

One thing shocks me. Here is the only Chinese food I have ever found which is uninspiring. Each dish is built around coconuts or bananas. It is fine for an occasional dish, but monotonous as a steady diet.

A missionary here showed me two fascinating documents which a former Italian Consul had given him. They are the history of the early Communist cell on the island— allegedly the first one in China—and an account of military operations against them in the twenties which never succeeded in completely breaking up their military units. It is extraordinary how many names of prominent Communists today show up in the rosters of the guerrilla units of that time. If the documents are authentic, and they seem to be, they are historically valuable finds.

August 25 / Hong Kong / Hong Kong is always a pleasant change in a synthetic sort of way. I am sure life would be enjoyable, but when I'm here I miss China. Set in a stunning stage of mountains, islands, and water, it is still a piece of England and English ways dressed up for an oriental costume ball—that is, except for the Chinese slum areas which are unobtrusive and of course not mentioned in polite society. It is fun for a vacation, but not quite real.

Through carelessness I missed a chance for a visa to Macao which I wanted to see for sentimental reasons and to find out how much of my childhood Brazilian Portuguese would be usable. It seems the Portuguese have improved on the British weekend by working only when and if you can catch them in a coffee shop. So it is back to Shanghai and Nanking.

September 12 / Nanking / The other day a group of refugee students here did a comprehensive job of wrecking a theatre to which they had been refused free admission. The Chief of Police later admitted he had not interfered because he did not want to risk another incident.

Until fairly early this year the population trend, especially among students, was away from Kuomintang China and to Communist areas. The movement has now largely stopped and in its place there has been a flood of students out of Communist areas. There are between twenty and thirty thousand of them in Peiping, twenty thousand in Nanking, and ten thousand in Hankow. These figures do not include those who have already been resettled elsewhere. Middle school students make up a large proportion. Those in Peiping come from Manchuria, where conditions are bad for all civilians. Those in Nanking and Hankow are from Honan and Shantung, two provinces in which what is left of the organized Kuomintang Army is making what is probably its last large-scale stand against the Communist armies in China proper. When this fails and Mukden falls there will be nothing left with which to make any effective resistance.

Since the students arrive destitute, the problem is what to do with them. Schools they want to enter cannot take care of them, and they resist any other plans. Efforts to enlist them in the Army have met with a reluctance from them equalled only by that of the Army to have them. Experience with student divisions has not generated much confidence in them as soldiers. Their attitude: "What! Join the Army with a war going on?" Meanwhile they have nothing to do, only the barest subsistence living, and unlimited time in which to vent their dissatisfaction in rowdy activities. The Kuomintang, instead of making capital of this migration, which must indicate disenchantment with what they actually found, is trying to keep it quiet, presumably to cover up its inadequacies in meeting the problem.

September 19 / Hsuchow / This is a pleasant town on the Yangtze halfway to Shanghai—not to be confused with another town in North Kiangsu which is the field headquarters for Nationalist Armies between Nanking and Peiping. It has rained all the time and so there has been no temptation to do anything besides sit back and relax. It is old and quiet and clean, and famous for its gardens since it was the place to which all the Imperial mandarins retired. The idea seems to have been that it would not do to have retired high officials grow restless in their original homes. They might get ideas. So they were sent to Hsuchow where an eye could be kept on them as a group. They amused themselves by cultivating their gardens and playing with their favorite concubines. The result is that Hsuchow is also famous for its beautiful women. And it is true that the standard of looks of the average person on the streets is far above that anywhere else in China. A wholly admirable system—if you were a mandarin.

September 23 / Mukden / On the way up we spent some time loafing in the air over Tsinan in Shantung. It was a spectacular vantage point from which to watch the Government lines crumble and the Communist forces occupy the city. It all moved so rapidly it was as though some giant fingers were manipulating pawns. This is the last holdout spot in Shantung. North along the corridor to Manchuria the Communist artillery was systematically making rubble out of the airfield at Chinchow.

Mukden is grim, desolate, and hungry. The marks of starvation on the people are becoming dreadful. No one walks fast or smiles, all have that yellow hunger look. It is terrible to see a great city die and it cannot conceivably be much longer before it falls. That will be the end of Manchuria. It has rained the whole time and we all have colds. The only note of relief is the Military Attaché, who is short and a paratrooper, wandering around in full battle regalia and carrying a box of Kleenex.

October 2 / Peiping / It is fall here, sunny, the persimmons turning red-golden on leafless trees, and on the surface the world is very far removed. So I have tried to stay on the surface and doze; but death is showing here too, and considering the accelerated crumbling of Government positions during the past ten days Peiping too may go very fast. It is depressing to see the hordes of refugee students camped out in the Temple of Heaven where they befoul and litter up the place and build fires on the dazzling white marble. They seem fairly well disciplined now, although they are

idle, on a subsistence diet, and with no idea of what the
future holds. Peiping is uneasily aware of their presence,
fearful of trouble, and there is little sympathy for them on
grounds they had no business coming here at this time.

But there will always be a Peiping. This afternoon Peggy
Durdin and I were riding in rickshaws. The coolies were
chattering as gaily as ever. As we passed along a gray stone
wall, a fragrance came over it. One coolie said to the other,
"Do you smell that? What it it?"

"It's a late flowering tree."

"Ah, yes. Isn't it pleasant to pull a rickshaw in Peiping in the fall, and smell the trees!"

October 18 /Taipei, Formosa / Ten days here have been a wonderful change. I lie in the sun up in the mountains, eat fish, and have almost gotten over the Mukden cold. This must be one of the most beautiful spots in the world. The only trouble is that mainland economic troubles are beginning to be felt here and the food situation is becoming critical.

Formosa pays little attention to the mainland and still broods over the wounds of the rebellion. Enough reform has been introduced to blunt the edge of discontent. The rest is held down by the repressive hand of the secret police and the evasive and sullen soldiery. No one says anything except banalities.

October 22 / Nanking / This is one of those days with a heavy overcast and a bit of fog that always makes the city quiet. For some reason the people in the street stop their endless noise and yelling on a dull day. Even the rice queues are quiet and orderly. This is a growingly depressing sight which has previously been rare. In six weeks food prices have gone up five hundred per cent and today they are changing hourly. Since the August economic decrees rice has been disappearing and now there is almost none to be seen or bought in the towns. People stand in endless lines day after day, usually fighting, squabbling, tangling with the police, and now and then wrecking a rice shop. That does no good because there isn't anything to loot. There is a passive strike against the Government by rice producers and merchants.

The curtain falls

On November 1 the Communists captured Mukden and any remaining Government forces in Manchuria were scattered and vanished. On December 1 they captured Hsuchow in Kiangsu, thus ending the only large conventional battle of the civil war and destroying the only remaining Kuomintang armies still in being north

Situation as of November 5, 1948

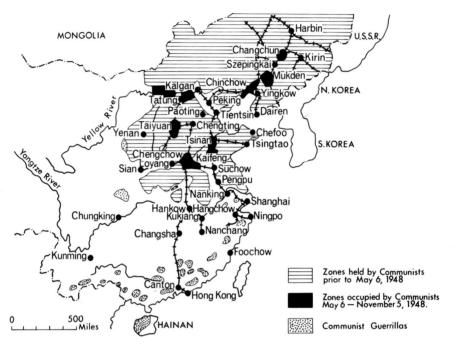

of the river. Only occupation of the Peiping-Tientsin enclave and scattered mopping up operations remained to complete the conquest north of the Yangtze. Occupation of the south now depended for the most part on how long it took the Communists to walk their armies to the borders of southeast Asia and to the foothills of the Himalayas in the face of disorganized and demoralized resistance.

For the United States only one problem was left. It was already understood that aid and advisory programs would be discontinued step by step as the Communists pushed their conquest ahead. The question was what to do about the thousands of American citizens, mostly businessmen and missionaries, who were about to find themselves in territory under Communist control, which was not likely to allow them much scope for the various activities in which they were engaged.

The problem was more difficult than it may sound. It was simple as far as military personnel was concerned. They were under strict orders from the Pentagon not to be in territory occupied by the Communists and not to become involved in any operational activities. In mid-November they were ordered to leave and they did – literally overnight in order to avoid any possibility of an attack by advance Communist units which had already reached the north bank of the river. The same applied to civilian Government personnel, except that the problem of timing was more complicated.

The real difficulty concerned private American civilians who were scattered all over the country and much more dependent on their own resources for moving. Even more serious was whether they wanted to go. The American Government had no way of making them leave, but it did have an obligation to issue evacuation warnings when it deemed the time had come. The decision was left to the Embassy and it was not an easy one. On the one hand, there were nightmare memories of what had frequently happened to foreigners in periods of upheaval during the half century since the Boxer Uprising, and these counseled earlier rather than later departure. It is true that the Communist record in this respect had been impeccable, but there were bound to be transitional periods as someone else retreated, and the mobs might take over until the Communists could arrive. On the other hand, there was a reluctance to disrupt lives any sooner than necessary, with the added nagging thought that somehow in the end it might not be necessary after all. In addition, the Nationalist Government was using great pressure to delay the warnings as long as possible, with the plea that they would only add to the difficulties of the Government. When it became obvious that the doom of Hsuchow was sealed, the Embassy decided that the time had come.

This did not end the matter. A surprising number of businessmen were convinced they could continue to operate, as they had during previous upheavals since the collapse of the Manchu Dynasty. But the most troublesome were the missionaries, partly because they were more scattered and isolated in rural areas; even more because to them departure meant the end of a whole way of life, an uncertain future and, most difficult of all, the admission that a whole lifetime of work and dedication had failed. This is not easy for anyone. Most did leave, but enough remained to be a source of serious friction once the Communists made it clear they were no longer wanted.

As for the Embassy itself, all dependents and all except essential staff were evacuated early in December. Dr. Stuart and a few officers stayed on in Nanking, which was soon to be occupied by the Communists. They were placed under house arrest, but not otherwise molested, and eventually they were repatriated. Since the bulk of the Government was rapidly moving to Canton, most of the Embassy followed it there, and then by the end of 1949 to Formosa.

October 25 / There is a curious and surprising amount of agreement here that the military and economic picture is so bad now that the Government has no choice except to enter a Communist dominated coalition. Dr. Stuart goes even farther and wants to work actively for it and is unhappy because some of his colleagues are somewhat less enthusiastic than he is.

By devious channels we learn Dr. Stuart has sent word to Li Chi-shen he wants Philip Fugh to go to Hong Kong to see him. It is not clear just what he has in mind, but it is undoubtedly connected with his coalition fixation.

Evacuation warnings for Americans in north China were to be sent out tomorrow noon, but late last night a frantic plea from the Generalissimo in Peiping asked us not to jog his elbow; all will be under control in a few days. One of these days a lot of Americans are going to find themselves occupied by the Communists and there will be hell to pay somewhere.

October 28 / We are still wavering on the evacuation notice. I suspect that decision will be forced on us by the Generalissimo's order to Wei Li-lhuang not to fight his way out of Manchuria down the land corridor to north China, but to get out by sea through the port of Yinkow, a move sure to fail because the Communists will catch him snarled up with inadequate shipping and cut him to pieces. This will eliminate the largest remaining organized force in north China. The troops east of Mukden are also taking a real beating.

Meanwhile the State Department tells Dr. Stuart to inform the Generalissimo any advice he is giving is personal and without the approval of the United States Government. Increasingly the evidence is that he is up to his ears dickering in internal Chinese politics. I am morally certain he is actively working day and night on a coalition. Philip let it be known that the Generalissimo knows this when he said he was going to Hong Kong to see Li Chi-shen as soon as the Generalissimo approves. I would not be surprised if Marshall knows this too, but he takes a hands-off-China attitude, knowing full well Dr. Stuart will do as he pleases and perhaps being just as glad he is willing to do it on his own. I don't suppose there is anything to be lost by any maneuver. Philip is also going to Canton, which brings Soong into the picture and adds weight to his recent statement that there will be big changes soon.

October 31 / This is the first nice day of a normally nice month; it is Sunday, and the flap is on in Mukden. This

morning all communications with Manchuria were cut. And
tomorrow we finally issue emergency evacuation warnings
for north China and that will cause another flap.

On a sudden impulse Dave Barrett (our Assistant Military Attaché whose knowledge of Chinese ways is legendary) and I decided to fly as far north as we could to have
a look for ourselves. But planes were not taking off. The
reason soon became apparent, as Chinese Air Force planes
began to shuttle in from the north. Dave impassively
watched several of them disgorge their contents, and then
somewhat pompously announced: "John, I have seen all
I need to see. When the generals begin to evacuate their
gold bars and concubines, the end is at hand."

Nanking and Shanghai are tense to the point of panic,
and there is still no food. Never have I seen anything like
the emptiness of the stores and the lines of people hoping
something, anything, will come in. In China now, where
events usually move slowly, everything is moving at a
fearful rate. All the Chinese I know have either left, are on

their way out, or are busily engaged in hedging against
what may come. So there is not much of anyone left to
talk with. And among the foreigners I am the last survivor
from Chungking. It was three years ago today I arrived
there.

November 2 / Mukden surrendered yesterday and that, I
guess, is that. All that is needed now is a few mopping up
operations and the sweep to the Yangtze will be complete.
Nothing can save Peiping, Tientsin, and other less known
enclaves because there is nothing left with which to defend
them. I assume we will evacuate our naval base at Tsingtao
as well.

November 14 / Until the last few days there have been very
few actual military activities in Nanking itself, which made
it something of a quiet island, especially since it has not
been densely populated since the Tai-p'ing Rebellion in the
nineteenth century. Now it is swarming with the military
and with refugees. The first large-scale evacuation of
foreigners is taking place today and I have been riding the
convoy trucks all morning. More and more troops keep
pouring into the city and all are milling around without
doing much of anything constructive. The incongruous part
of the whole thing is that the press keeps on talking of great
Government victories. But only this morning there was a
major Communist breakthrough on the west flank of
Hsuchow. It came a few days earlier than I had thought it
would, so perhaps it is all closer to Nanking than we had
guessed.

The hardest sight is the refugees. No matter who they
are, or where or when, all refugees look alike—cold, hungry,
unshaven, forlorn, and lost. They don't know where they
came from or where they are going. They are just wherever
they are and don't know what to do about it. This is not only
true of the Chinese; it is almost as true of the foreigners,
who have a pretty good idea they will get out of the country, although they know some of them may not. Even the
missionaries who have been in China for decades are just

as helpless, and who can blame them. They have only our word that they should move on—somewhere, anywhere, but move, and so they move. When I think how many lives are being uprooted today and all the days around it and all that it means, it is hard to sleep. And still they pour through by the thousands, on and on.

November 17 / Today there is a small lull in the evacuation. There is also much mad scrambling in circles; but just to add a comic touch the Government is loudly proclaiming great victories and the Chinese have suddenly started a wild celebration—over nothing. The letdown will be that much worse. The last two days have brought the worst melange of crazy and conflicting rumors I have ever heard. Bill Bullitt said yesterday it made him think of France in May 1940.

The personnel of our Military Advisory Group were shipped out last night. All eight hundred men, their dependents, and their accumulated impedimenta vanished between sundown and sunup. This morning all compounds and apartment buildings were deserted, doors and gates swinging forlornly. I went over to the compound where the stockpiled supplies had been abandoned. There was enough stuff there for a group army, hundreds of uncrated refrigerators, thousands of books, a huge record collection, two hundred football helmets, and on and on. The first Chinese were just beginning to prowl around. By nightfall not an object was left.

November 25 / The suicide of Chen Pu-lei is one of the most talked-of recent events in Nanking. Chen was one of the elders of the Kuomintang and perhaps the closest advisor to the Generalissimo for many years, as well as his confidential secretary. Before dying he wrote letters to the Generalissimo, to Yu Yu-jen, President of the Control Yuan and himself an elder, to Wu Chih-huei, oldest living member of the Kuomintang, and to his wife and sons. He deplored the condition of China, reproached himself bitterly for his own failures, and concluded that the situation left him no choice. Chen apparently took the action after an oral appeal to the Generalissimo for reform which was rebuffed. If the Generalissimo was impressed by the final action, he has given no signs of it; but some of his colleagues, perhaps more mindful of the great traditions, are badly shaken men.

December 1 / Hsuchow fell today at the end of the biggest pitched battle of the war. Now only Fu Tso-yi holds out between Siberia and the Yangtze, and if he holds out or even puts up a fight instead of arranging a deal it will only prove there is something new under the sun. Nanking begins to look like a city that was, and night after night the trucks rumble down to the barges on the river as the Government continues its move to the south. It is done at night to avoid any possibility of a Communist attack by day on the shipping going downstream.

December 14 / Yesterday I flew to Peiping for one last look at the dream city of the world. The ravages and aftermath of Hsuchow were plainly visible on the way up. All throughout the Peiping-Tientsin area the air was filled with the blue haze of burning villages and the flashes of sporadic fighting as the armies close in for the final kill. The roads were clogged with motion.

The gods at the Temple of Heaven must have known it was a last visit because Peiping staged a perfect day such as only Peiping can. It was warm and clear, with the sun shining on the persimmons. There is something eternal about the peace and sophistication of Peiping which I doubt anything can ever ruffle.

During lunch with Dave Barrett, our Assistant Military Attaché, there was an ominous and insistent rumble of artillery in the distance. Word soon came that the Communists had taken the Western Hills and were shelling the airport. If we wanted to get out we had better do so in a hurry.

Nanking is only a shadow. Practically all foreigners have left. We have only a skeleton staff of whom part will follow the Government to Canton and a few will stay behind to be occupied by the Communists, including Dr. Stuart. Among the Chinese only a few officials are left, plus of course the bulk of the people who always have to remain where they are no matter what happens. They stay off the streets, keep quiet, and like all peoples from time immemorial just watch and wait to see what happens next. They have waited before, they can wait again.

Tomorrow I leave.

December 15 / *Shanghai* / The genius of Shanghai must be chaos. This place is as much confusion as Nanking is stillness. Any semblance of order and organization has disappeared and it is every man to salvage what he can for himself.

There is much brave talk about the defense of the

Yangtze and of making it the line beyond which *no passaran!* The Government has built a wooden picket fence around the city to demonstrate its intentions.

At dawn I leave for Hong Kong, Manila, Washington. . . .

January 15, 1949 / The Communists occupied Tientsin.

January 21 / The Generalissimo retired from office and returned to his birthplace at Fenghua; General Li Tsung-jen became Acting President. For the next several months, the Generalissimo continued to meddle informally in everything, while Li frantically tried everything he could think of to get a settlement with the Communists, but their terms in effect amounted to unconditional surrender. One of these attempts was a tentative agreement between Li and the

Soviet Embassy for a new Sino-Soviet understanding to neutralize China in any future international conflict, and to eliminate American influence from China. When General Li asked for a public statement of American support for his efforts, Washington instructed Dr. Stuart to inform him that it considered it "incredible that Li Tsung-jen should seek a United States statement indicating support for the purpose of strengthening his position while at the same time arranging a tentative agreement with the Russians calling for elimination of American influence from China."

January 31 / General Fu Tso-yi surrendered Peiping.

April 20 / The Communists crossed the Yangtze at night without opposition.

April 23 / The National Government officially moved to Canton, as the Communists occupied Nanking.

May 16 / Hankow fell.

May 25 / Shanghai was occupied.

June 12 / The Generalissimo, who had never really stopped meddling, became head of the Central Policy Committee and hence resumed effective control.

October 1 / Mao Tse-tung proclaimed in Peking (so renamed as it again became the capital) the formal establishment of the People's Republic of China.

October 15 / The Communists captured Canton, as what was left of the Government moved back to Chungking.

November 25 / The Government moved west to Chengtu.

November 30 / Chungking surrendered.

December 5 / Acting President Li left for the United States for medical treatment. He would remain there for more than fifteen years and then, perhaps tired of the exile life, make his peace with the Communists and return to Peking.

December 9 / The Government moved to Formosa.

December 27 / As Chengtu surrendered, the year ended with all mainland China under Communist control.

Only Tibet and the islands of Hainan and Formosa remained. Tibet and Hainan were conquered with little difficulty. Subsequent developments made Formosa a very different matter.

On May 5, 1949, Acting President Li Tsung-jen had himself written the requiem to President Truman:

Throughout our war of resistance against Japanese aggression, the United States of America continuously extended to us her moral and material assistance, which enabled our country to carry on an arduous struggle of eight long years until final victory was achieved. The sincere friendship thus demonstrated by the United States has contributed not only to strengthen further the traditional ties between our two countries but to win the deep gratitude and unbounded goodwill of the people of China.

This policy of friendly assistance was continued when some years ago General George C. Marshall, under instructions from your good self, took up the difficult task of mediation in our conflict with the Chinese Communists, to which he devoted painstaking effort. All this work was unfortunately rendered fruitless by the lack of sincerity on the part of both the then Government and the Chinese Communists.

In spite of this, your country continued to extend its aid to our Government. It is regrettable that, owing to the failure of our then Government to make judicious use of this aid and to bring about appropriate political, economic and military reforms, your assistance has not produced the desired effect. To this failure is attributable the present predicament in which this country finds itself.

Epilogue

As long as Americans have any interest at all in China, it is probable that the argument as to what happened and why will continue to be acrid and partisan. It was a traumatic experience for the United States, partly because public opinion was quite unprepared for it and the speed with which it happened, partly because of the sudden stunning realization that one quarter of the human race, with whom many Americans felt they had a special relationship, had virtually overnight joined the enemy. The reasons why the American consensus is so rigidly and even pathologically opposed to communism is another whole study in itself; suffice it for our purposes here that it is a fact.

This combination of circumstances made the Communist victory in China a natural target in domestic politics, especially since one of the major parties had not won a presidential election in twenty years and desperately feared that if it lost the next one it would go out of existence. The question of what had happened in China became so much a part of the American political folklore that, like Mother and the daily bath, it was no longer a rationally arguable topic. The harsher edges of McCarthyism have become blunted a bit in recent years; but there is no evidence that the basic damage done to American society, of which he was only the ugliest symbol, has been repaired, or will be for some time to come.

Much of the incomprehensibility of what had happened could easily arise from a look at the inventory of assets and liabilities in 1945. Superficially at least, there was nothing to suggest that the Sino-Soviet Treaty of August 1945 was not an accurate reflection of the realities of the situation. All the parties to the Treaty and to the earlier Yalta Agreements obviously thought it was. Even the Chinese Communists, whatever their private thoughts, raised no objections. Their evident willingness until the summer of 1946 to participate in a coalition with the Kuomintang, as long as it did not threaten their existence, can only suggest their awareness of their seeming relative weakness in terms of ability to seize national power. And yet, within four years they were the masters of all China, with the exception of the small island of Formosa to which the bedraggled remnants of the Kuomintang had been able to flee largely through the invincible determination and self-assurance of Generalissimo Chiang Kai-shek. Whether he could have continued to maintain himself on that island without the subsequent interposition of American military power after the outbreak of the Korean War is of course another question.

It may seem that there are about as many explanations for the Communist success as there are people who try to find them. On the extreme right, it was said to have resulted from the treason of a small, dishonorable group. On the extreme left, it was dismissed as the foreordained and inevitable course of history. Both views are equally nonsense and, apart from the basically mischievous character of simplistic or devil theories of history, can most charitably be attributed only to moral and intellectual laziness, if not downright torpidity.

Most explanations, depending on the points of view of those advancing them, have been somewhere between the two extremes. It should be enough to cite only a few to illustrate their range: the debilitating effects of the war against Japan, although the Communists had been at war just as long; corruption in the Kuomintang, which was admitted by all; the inability of the Generalissimo and those closest to him to break out of their Confucian feudal mentality; the political ineptitude and lack of military power of liberal groups in the Kuomintang; the eight-month arms embargo which Marshall imposed; the alleged insufficiency of American aid, military and economic; Russian help for the Communists. In varying degrees, there was some truth in each explanation, and each one was a factor.[1]

There is another explanation which seems to underlie the rationalization of many people, although it is never stated explicitly. This is a kind of fascination with communism as an ideology, endowing it with a mystique, evil no doubt, but possessing a satanic inevitability which can be overcome only by the supreme efforts of virtue. Certainly no greater compliment has ever been paid to Marxism; nor could it have come from anything other than a deep, if unconscious, doubt as to the virtue of one's own position and views.

The performance of the Red Army should not be overlooked as a contributing factor. General L. M. Chassin in his superb and definitive book, *The Communist Conquest of China*,[2] has attributed the victory largely to superior morale, echoing the dictum of Mao Tse-tung that the best equipment in the world is no better than the calibre of the men who use it. Mao and his commanding officers had proven General Stilwell right: treat the Chinese peasant like a human being and if you can give him something to believe in, he will be as good a soldier as any on earth. This really was something new in China, where the soldier, including the troops of the Generalissimo, had been treated as the scum of society, and then not unpredictably proceeded to behave that way. It was easy for the Communist troops, with their unshakable discipline and correct behavior, to become quickly identified in the peasant mind as the protectors of the people, not as their oppressors and butchers. Ideology meant nothing to the peasant; being treated decently meant a great deal.

To this must be added the calibre of the Communist high command. General Marshall once told me he believed that they would have been an ornament on any general staff in the history of warfare and, furthermore, that Mao Tse-tung

1 In general, the explanations can be divided into two main categories. The first includes the varying degrees of opinion within the vague outlines of the China Lobby which basically blamed the United States for the debacle and were convinced the outcome would have been different if only the United States had done something else. The other category did not see that anything else the Americans could or might have done would have changed what happened, and saw the causes in the failures and limitations of the Kuomintang itself. It is impossible to separate people out by such obvious groupings as businessmen, intellectuals, missionaries, etc. Individuals from all groups were found on either side, with many on both. If there was any division—and even here there were many exceptions too—it was that those who knew China best saw the fault in the Kuomintang, and those who knew it least blamed the United States.
2 Lionel Max Chassin, *The Communist Conquest of China* (Cambridge: Harvard University Press, 1965).

was one of the great guerrilla strategists of all time. There were other military men at the time who had reservations about this on grounds that the Communists had won against an army which, despite its superior equipment, was incompetent in every known respect and in which the few officers who did know their business were perennially hamstrung by the interference of the Generalissimo and his medieval ideas of warfare. In all too short a time, the Korean War dispelled these doubts; no one who fought in it or knows anything about it will ever again question that the Red Army is a formidable adversary. Major General David Barr, one of the American commanders in Korea who had also been the last and most frustrated Chief of the Joint United States Military Advisory Group in China, said later that if the Chinese had intervened in Korea only twenty-four hours earlier than they did he would not have brought out a single man from that disaster.

Professor T'ang Tsou in his brilliant study, *America's Failure in China*,[3] advances the rather plausible thesis that from the days of the Open Door Notes the United States has set certain objectives and then been unwilling to commit sufficient resources to secure those objectives; but at the same time has also been unwilling to revise its objectives to conform to resources it was willing to use. Professor T'ang wrote this before the massive American involvement in the much smaller problem of Vietnam. Unless one accepts the neanderthal morality of General Curtis LeMay, who has pointed out that nuclear bombing could in two hours put North Vietnam back into the stone age, it is hard to envisage just how the American commitment of resources in that war could be much larger than it is. This commitment quite clearly has not secured the stated objectives, and in my opinion has no slightest chance of doing so. There seems to be a limit to the uses and applicability of even unlimited power. Vietnam is not the only current example of this.

Taking all the foregoing into account, there has to be a broader explanation of what happened in China and why. It is important to try to understand it for its own sake, because what happened in China is one of the most important developments of the twentieth century. It is important to understand it because it was the first major American involvement outside its own boundaries after the end of World War II. It is important to understand it because that involvement has been followed, albeit reluctantly, by other involvements which have injected the American presence into every nook and cranny of the non-Communist world – and it is beginning even in Communist areas – and because with obvious variations the pattern of involvement has been repeated over and over. With the exception of the spectacularly successful Marshall Plan in Europe, there have been few

3 T'ang Tsou, *America's Failure in China* (Chicago: University of Chicago Press, 1963).

ventures which have not been limited in their accomplishments, or even, as often as not, outright failures. Increasingly, thoughtful and well-intentioned Americans are troubled by this and are asking whether there is a fatal flaw in the American approach and, if there is, what is it. The macrocosm that is China should be helpful in this respect.

I believe that General Chassin was at least pointing in the right direction when, in writing only about the military picture, he identified the key factor as morale. But one must ask why the Communists had high morale and the Kuomintang did not. I believe the answer is simple, even if the remedy sometimes must be infinitely complicated, and I believe it is generally applicable. The Communists won in China because they correctly analyzed and understood what it was that the mass of the people wanted, and they then proceeded to satisfy those wishes – or at least persuade the people that they were satisfying them or would do so in the future. This answer, of course, implies a particular interpretation of history and of the mainsprings of human behavior.

There are tides in history, either general or applicable only to certain groups or times. These tides, or drives, cannot really in the end be denied – although they can be modified, speeded up or slowed down, veered slightly in direction – except when one collective desire comes in direct conflict with another one of sufficient force to wear down or destroy it, either by attrition or catastrophically. This does not mean, as some people would have it, that the unconscious desires of the people and their instincts are always right, although I suspect they are more often right than wrong. One need only cite the consensus of Nazi Germany, which fulfilled deep, if terrible, needs in the German unconscious, to know what evil can result. In our times, one cannot rule out the possibility that one of these aberrations could destroy man on this earth, but I do not believe it will happen that way.

Where, then, does the leader fit in, the Carlylean hero, the charismatic figure? In my view, the leader does not make history. He may, and often does, influence it. He changes its course somewhat; he gives it one kind of style or another. He can decide whether more or fewer people live or die now or later. He is the technician who gives the collective unconscious desire form and substance – or he fails to do so. The true leader, the charismatic personality, knows intuitively or understands the desires of those whom he would lead, and has the skill to implement them. When he forgets or loses his skill, he also loses what the Chinese call the Mandate of Heaven. Those would-be leaders who have never understood, or who had the understanding but lacked the skill, are consigned to the footnotes of history.

It seems to me that China is a case in point. The Kuomintang came to power because the Chinese people wanted to be rid of the Manchu Dynasty and the later warlords, and free from foreign encroachment. It achieved the first objective, and was making progress on the second. Chiang Kai-shek could reach the heights he did because he could become, albeit sometimes reluctantly, the symbol of resistance to Japanese aggression. Having accomplished that, he did not know where to go. But the Chinese people did – and so did the Communists. In some oversimplification, the Kuomintang can be divided into two main groups. There was, first, the Generalissimo himself and those closest to him, the warlords and militarists, the Confucian feudalists of the Ch'en Li-fu variety, the landlords and the opportunists who saw something for themselves. Nothing is more revealing of this mentality than the original version of the Generalissimo's book, *China's Destiny*, which clearly shows that he has never understood the twentieth century, is indeed quite uncomfortable in it. But China is living in the twentieth century; the people of China wanted a better life than they had, and the Generalissimo and those around him either did not realize this, or in some cases did not even care.

The other part of the Kuomintang was composed of the Political Science Group and the other like-minded cliques which could also count on the support of the Democratic League and independent liberals. For the most part, these men had been educated in the West, were at home in the modern world, understood the enormous problems confronting China, and knew what needed to be done to satisfy the legitimate aspirations of the people of their country. But they had two staggering liabilities. In the first place, they never controlled any military power or any of the Party and Government apparatus. They could speak, but they could not enforce. The second liability may have been even more damaging, if more subtle. Having been western educated, they had lost touch with their own people. They could know what had to be done and still feel more at home in the Faculty Club at Harvard or the International Club in Shanghai than they could in the villages where the work of China is done. There is no society which would not have welcomed them – except their own.

This is a problem which is plaguing all the newly emerged and still developing countries. The Nehrus, the Nkrumahs, the U Nus, the Sukarnos were charismatic leaders in the struggles for independence. Some of them even knew what had to be done afterwards, but they somehow failed to persuade their people they knew how to do it. Nehru once said he sometimes did not know whether he was Indian or English. These men are disappearing one by one. It will be interesting to watch the course taken by the new leaders, whoever they may be, with measurably fewer of the benefits and handicaps resulting from long, direct exposure to the

West. The new African countries are a fascinating example, where more and more of the young leaders are rejecting American, European, or Russian guidance, and are trying to find their own ideology and solutions in terms of their own peoples, their own experience, their own circumstances.

As for the Communists in China, the leadership largely came from agrarian backgrounds; with but few exceptions their education was Chinese. After 1927 massive Kuomintang pressure denied them access to the more seductive pleasures of Shanghai, and they never lost the peasant touch. Mao Tse-tung and his followers staked their careers and their lives in defying Stalin and asserting that a communist revolution could come to China on an agrarian base. Mao believed that in the end the people are the only real power. The people of China are peasants. The peasants will give allegiance to the Emperor most likely to satisfy their wishes.

Mao understood these wishes to be land reform, reasonably honest and efficient government, moderate taxation, minimum interference in the private lives of people, and freedom from being despoiled by marauding armies. Until 1949 the Communists gave them just this. They won with an obviously impressive consensus. Whether Mao still remembers his own lessons or retains his skill at interpretation and implementation is now obviously very much an open question. Whether he has lost or can retain the Mandate he so clearly inherited will depend, finally, on how much he remembers and still understands of Chinese history, which is much like the history of all men.

Long before the final Communist victory, it should have been clear – and it was to a few people, most of them not in positions of much influence – that despite the impressive physical inventory the Kuomintang simply did not have the essential qualities for retaining power, and that the Communists did, abundantly. Everyone has his own date at which he believes the point of no return was passed. The Generalissimo, who can be very stubborn, seemingly believes it has not yet come.

The lesson for the United States should be that it wanted certain things for China and for itself which the Chinese people, rightly or wrongly, did not want; furthermore, that it chose to seek them through a legal instrumentality, the Kuomintang, which the Chinese people also rejected. Not all the military and economic power which was brought to bear against the Communists could deny the people what they wanted – or at least thought they wanted. This question of what people think they want, or should want, is crucial in assessing whether the United States has or has not learned anything out of the China debacle.

Even taking into account what the United States hopes to achieve from its foreign policy – and some of its hopes seem rather greedy for a country which has so much when so many others have so little – it would be rather hard to find fault with the general desire for a better life for everyone. Americans are genuinely aggrieved when others seem not to share their aspirations. What we fail to understand is that not all peoples want the same things; or if they want the same things they want them in their own fashion. It is quite possible to want the American "things" without wanting the American "way." If the choice has to be made, it is quite possible to prefer your own way to the foreign things. It also happens that people can be in a situation where they quite literally do not know enough to want anything else. Probably nothing has been more frustrating to the community project workers in India than to see new methods brought in and demonstrated successfully, and then, the minute the technicians leave, to see the villagers revert to the old ways. So limited were the people's outlooks, or so bound were they by old superstitions, or from their own experience so unbelieving that life could be better, that nothing made an impression sufficient to create lasting changes. If people get what they want, by the same token they do not get what they do not want.

How can a system and a way which have worked so magnificently for Americans be anything but good for others? In a perverse sort of way, this blind spot is almost endearing, if somewhat naive. We might have taken the attitude, as others have done, that we have done so well because we are more intelligent, and others do badly because they are stupid. On the contrary, there has been an egalitarian notion that since we have done it, so can others – but it helps of course if you do it our way. Only, it does not necessarily work that way.

The Marshall Plan worked magnificently because it was what we and the Europeans wanted desperately. The American plan in China did not work because just as desperately the Chinese people did not want it. Some aid programs in India are not yet successful because so many peasants do not know enough to want them. The accomplishments of the Alliance for Progress are still of dubious value, some because they are blocked by elite groups who do not want them, some because they are not responsive to what the people themselves need and want. There are other examples. Certainly the most scandalous now is Vietnam. I have little or no idea what the people of Vietnam, north and south, really want. I think the evidence rather good that they do not want what the United States and a ridiculous government in Saigon have thus far unsuccessfully been trying to force on them – for their own good, of course.

If, then, there is a broader lesson for the United States in what happened in China, it is the futility of trying to do to, with or for other people, what they do not want. If that lesson is not yet sufficiently learned, then there is a continuing

Achilles heel in American policy. Assume even that what we want for other people is right – not even Americans are always wrong – it is futile to try to impose it on them unless they can be persuaded to want it themselves and to agree on the means of obtaining it. Quite possibly the most revolutionary idea ever to come out of China is the right and legitimacy of revolution itself, the tradition that when the people decide the Emperor, as wielder of the Mandate of Heaven, no longer performs satisfactorily, he is finished. The Emperor is dead; long live the Emperor – as long as he performs.

The pictures

Photographs are reproduced by permission of
Henri Cartier-Bresson
Captions are adapted from M. Cartier-Bresson's book
From One China to the Other
(New York, Universe Books, © 1956 by Robert Delpire),
in which the photographs were first collected

Page 16 / A street trader is delighted to meet a friend who has just bought a length of cotton material. Respect, benevolence, and calm, virtues which the Chinese are unwilling to lose in any circumstances, are practiced on the eve of one of the greatest changes in China's long history.

Page 31 / As the first soldiers of the People's Army arrive they are cheered, but at the same time regarded with a good deal of anxious curiosity. In China, a soldier had always been considered a looter, living off the country, for which reason the military profession was greatly despised.

Page 43 / A hawker selling peanuts and Chinese cigarettes – more or less successful fakes of foreign brands. Behind him is a bookshop in the window of which are portraits of Chiang Kai-shek and Sun Yat-sen, together with a phrase from the latter's writings: "The revolution is not over, my companions will have to continue it." In front of the portrait, four marriage certificate rolls.

Page 56 / Pushing handcarts over the hump-backed bridges of Shanghai.

Page 72 / Reading the newspaper.

Page 120 / A blind man, led by a child whom he keeps on a leash. The old Imperial paving is longer lived than the concrete sidewalks laid by the municipality under the Kuomintang.

Page 123 / Shanghai. The banks of the Hwang-pu. Until 1937 the park was "forbidden to Chinese and dogs." When the city fell to the Japanese in 1937, any white man passing this point was forced to bow his head. Chinese junks have remained unchanged for many centuries. The warship is American. From the mid-nineteenth century on, the British admiral's flagship was traditionally anchored on this spot.

Page 124 / "The little teachers" are taught to read a few of the commoner characters, which they undertake to teach, in their turn, to other children and adults. Eighty-five per cent of the Chinese population were illiterate. Primary schools teach 1,000 characters. A newspaper uses 2,500. A well-educated man knows at least 10,000.

Page 149 / In the Forbidden City. A solitary pedestrian, perhaps an ex-official, thinking of the events which everyone is expecting.

Page 201 / Under the Pai-lo arches in one of Peiping's principal streets. People stop to eat hot soup sold by open-air cooks.

Page 224 / Ten thousand recruits, mobilized principally from the ranks of small traders, line up at eight o'clock in the morning to form a new Nationalist regiment.

Page 241 / The banner bears the inscription "Let us work for the people's happiness." The "Pointed Nose" represents, in China, the white man. He is followed by his servants, in dog and falcon masks.

Page 270 / A cyclist has to carry an enormous parcel of paper money in order to buy a few small things.

Page 279 / At every street corner speculators buy and sell silver dollars for paper money.

Page 284 / Children waiting for a distribution of rice. They are gentle and polite, but their faces reflect the sadness of centuries of suffering.

Page 289 / The endless flow of retreating soldiers across Nanking. They are making south, every man for himself.

Page 291 / The last rickshaw trip – to the ship which is to take off foreigners.

Page 294 / Shanghai, December 1948. The gold rush. The Kuomintang had decided to distribute some of the reserve at the rate of 1½ ounces per head. Enormous lines formed outside the banks and overflowed into neighboring streets, dislocating all traffic. Some people waited more than twenty-four hours, trying to get rid of paper money. About ten people were crushed or trampled to death.

Index of names and places

Names of the principals in this narrative (e.g. General Marshall, Chiang Kai-shek) and the cities of Chungking and Nanking have not been indexed, since they figure prominently throughout the period covered.